Migration Law in Croatia

Migration Law in Croatia

Goranka Lalić Novak

This book was originally published as a monograph in the International Encyclopaedia of Laws/Migration Law.

Founding Editor: Roger Blanpain
General Editor: Frank Hendrickx
Volume Editor: Helen Oosterom-Staples

Wolters Kluwer

Published by:
Kluwer Law International B.V.
PO Box 316
2400 AH Alphen aan den Rijn
The Netherlands
E-mail: lrs-sales@wolterskluwer.com
Website: www.wolterskluwer.com/en/solutions/kluwerlawinternational

Sold and distributed by:
Wolters Kluwer Legal & Regulatory U.S.
7201 McKinney Circle
Frederick, MD 21704
United States of America
Email: customer.service@wolterskluwer.com

ISBN 978-94-035-4810-4

e-Book: ISBN 978-94-035-4820-3
web-PDF: ISBN 978-94-035-4830-2

The Author

Goranka Lalić Novak is an associate professor at the Department for Administrative Science at the Faculty of Law, University of Zagreb, Croatia. Prior to joining Faculty of Law, she was Director of the Programme for Migrations and Asylum at the Croatian Law Centre (2005–2008) and Director and Project Manager at Croatian Helsinki Committee for Human Rights (2001–2005). She holds a PhD in Law from the Faculty of Law in Zagreb, an MSc in Political Science from the Faculty of Political Science in Zagreb and an LLM from Faculty of Law in Zagreb. She is an author of several books and many articles in the field of public administration and governance of migration, asylum and integration. Her most recent book is *Legal and Institutional aspect of Asylum* (Faculty of Law in Zagreb, 2016) (in Croatian). As an expert, she participated in projects aimed at improving the legal status of asylum seekers and refugees in Croatia (2008–2019), the integration of migrants at the local level (2017–2018), and in the MIPEX assessment of Croatia (2015). She is the president of the Croatian Law Centre, one of the most prominent civil society organisations in Croatia. She is a member of the Scientific Council for State Administration, Justice and Rule of Law of the Croatian Academy of Sciences and Arts, as well as a member of the Croatian Academy of Legal Sciences and Institute for Public Administration.

The Author

Table of Contents

List of Abbreviations

CoE	Council of Europe
EEA	European Economic Area
EU	European Union
MFEA	Ministry of Foreign and European Affairs
MoI	Ministry of Interior
NGO	Non-Governmental Organisation
OG	Official Gazette of Republic of Croatia
RoC	Republic of Croatia
TCN	Third-Country National
UN	United Nations
UNHCR	United Nations High Commissioner for Refugees
VIS	Visa Information System

List of Abbreviations

Foreword

Contemporary migrations in Croatia include both emigration and immigration, mostly from the countries in the Balkan region. However, in comparison to Western Europe, Croatia is still not perceived as a preferred destination for migrants, but more as a non-immigration country, although it has faced mass displacements of the population as a result of the wars and conflicts during the 1990s. After the dissolution of former Yugoslavia, the autochthone population sought protection within groups of the same ethnic origin, or in the newly established countries perceived as their national or ethnic homeland, therefore a dominant form of migration was a co-ethnic one. In terms of immigration flows, Croatia was not perceived as one of the preferred destinations for migrants and refugees from outside Europe. Asylum and migration-related issues were not perceived as important issues in the public or political discourse, as the number of migrants and refugees was very low when compared with Western countries. At the same time, under the EU accession requirements, Croatia had to quickly develop migration and asylum policies and align its legislation with *acquis communautaire* on migration, border security and asylum. After Croatia joined the EU on 1 July 2013, the transposition of EU regulations continued at a fast pace. Consequently, migration and asylum legislation are among the fastest-changing legal fields in Croatia.

Today Croatia is faced with different challenges related to migration flows. There is still a constant and massive emigration, especially highly educated young professionals. Due to the ageing of the population and emigration, it can be expected that Croatia will have to invest resources in attracting migrants and develop inclusive migration and integration policies. At the same time, Croatia is expected to curb irregular migrations, protect the external border of the EU and establish asylum policies which will prevent secondary movements of asylum seekers. During mass migration in 2015–2016, Croatia experienced extensive flows throughout its territory, with more than 650,000 people who have passed through the Balkan route of migrations. In 2018, there is an increase in the number of migrants and refugees who are trying to enter Croatia on their way to western European countries. The growing number of irregular migrants, although relatively low when compared to the other EU Member States, has created public anxiety and as a result, public and political debate on refugees and migrants has hardened.

In light of the global challenges connected with migration and asylum issues, it is yet to be seen how the legal framework will respond to those challenges, both at the EU and national levels. It can be expected that Croatian legislation will follow changes in the EU *acquis communautaire* and EU policies. The additional challenge is administrative capacities for the implementation of the legislation, considering that the administrative system has its logic of development. In any case, it will be interesting to follow those developments in the coming period.

This monograph represents the attempt of addressing the area of migration and asylum law in Croatia in an informative, comprehensive and systematic way. The presentation of legislation takes into account the period until 1 January 2019, and all translation is provided by the author. Special thanks are given to Ms Anamarija Kovač, LLM, for her valuable help in cross-checking all references in the text.

Zagreb, March 2019
Goranka Lalić Novak

General Introduction

§1. Immigration History and Statistical Information

1. Croatia is located in Central and Southeast Europe, bordering Slovenia to the northwest, Hungary to the northeast, Serbia to the east, Bosnia and Herzegovina and Montenegro to the southeast, and the Adriatic Sea to the southwest. Its territory covers 56,594 square kilometres. Due to its geostrategic position between Central Europe, the Mediterranean and the Balkans, the territory of modern Croatia was exposed to migrations for centuries that over time generated and changed the ethnic composition of the population. Throughout its history, Croatia has been an emigration country, but also the immigration destination for different types of migrants. Croatian emigration from the fifteenth century onward can be divided into an 'old' and a 'new' stage, with World War I as the historical landmark of the divide.[1]

2. During the Middle Ages, the cities in Croatian territories hosted many German and Italian artisans and merchants who were granted the right to reside and settle, to own administration, to reduce customs duties, and protect against violence. The rulers bestowed the land around the cities to domestic people, but also to aliens, which influenced the strengthening and enrichment of the nobility of the foreign origin, from the sixteenth to the nineteenth centuries in Slovenia and Croatia, and in the eighteenth century in the Slavonia and Vojvodina. Foreign artisans brought more advanced tools, better working techniques and work practices in some crafts, thus supporting the economic development of the cities.[2]

3. Development of the institution of asylum on the Croatian territories can be traced back to the Middle Ages, in the form of a church asylum governed by the laws of canon law. Also, the asylum law can be found in statutes of several coastal towns, such as the Dubrovnik Statute (1272), where granting asylum was considered a part of Dubrovnik's sovereignty. The asylum was provided to distinguished citizens from Western Europe who for political reasons left their states as well as to refugees from the Ottoman Empire. However, the most significant group of refugees in Dubrovnik were Jews who escaped from the Iberian Peninsula. The Republic was also guided by its interests and refused to provide a sanctuary due to political

1. Snježana Gregurović & Dubravka Mlinarić, Challenges of Migration Policies in Croatia: Migration History, Trends and Prospects. AEMI Journal, 10, 99 (2015).
2. Jelena Zlatković Winter, Imigracije u Hrvatskoj: skica povijesnog toka (*Immigration in Croatia – An Outline of Historical Development*), 9 Migracijske teme 3–4, 303 (1993).

and economic circumstances. In receiving fugitives and providing sanctuary, Dubrovnik Republic conditioned refugees with the restraining of any action against foreign states and governments from the Dubrovnik territory, otherwise losing the right to asylum. In the middle of the eighteenth century, due to the influx of a large number of refugees, the Senate of Dubrovnik set up an Office for Aliens, which was obliged to submit monthly reports on the number of refugees and their status, number of persons who were provided with asylum and those expelled. Since the fourteenth century, refugees were able to acquire citizenship provided that they lived in Dubrovnik with their family for a longer period and had a financial guarantee or acquired real estate in the Republic. From the eighteenth century, citizenship could be rewarded after ten years of continuous residency in the Republic.[3]

4. In the area of continental Croatia, asylum becomes the institution of secular law by the decision of Queen Maria Theresa (1776), and ever since the decision to grant asylum depends only on the ruler's decision.[4] The Queen's decision is considered a compromise between the Church's asylum and the need of the state to apply its laws throughout its territory. The decision contained a list of criminal offences whose offenders were excluded from the asylum and reduced the number of places where the asylum could be claimed. The monasteries were excluded as places of asylum, which was of particular importance since in practice many persons were seeking asylum in monasteries. The extradition to the state authority was carried out without approval and even without the knowledge of the bishop, and the state authority assessed whether the offence committed by the fugitive made him excluded from the asylum.[5] Therefore, it can be concluded that with the Queen's decision of 1176 the church's right to asylum was abolished because the Church lost its ability to exercise its privilege to grant asylum.[6]

5. Until the mid-sixteenth century, most of the South Slavic countries came under the rule of the Ottoman Empire, which influenced the mass migration of the population on the Balkan peninsula – as the Turks arrived and moved on from the south to the north, the movements of the peoples went along this direction. With the Turkish incursion into Europe, Croatia gradually lost parts of its territory. After the Battle of Mohacs (1526) between the Kingdom of Hungary and the Ottoman Empire which led to the partition of Hungary for several centuries between the Ottoman Empire, the Habsburg Monarchy, and the Principality of Transylvania, and the

3. Goranka Lalić & Mirela Krešić, Zaštita azilanata na hrvatskom području: od crkvenog azila do suvremenih tendencija (*Protection of the Asylum Seekers in Croatia: From Church Asylum to Contemporary Tendencies*), In: Zdravka Leutar (ed.), Zbornik radova Međunarodne znanstvene konferencije Socijalni rad i borba protiv siromaštva i socijalne isključenosti – profesionalna usmjerenost zaštiti i promicanju ljudskih prava (Zaklada 'Marija De Mattias', 2011).
4. Goranka Lalić Novak, Azil: pravni i institucionalni aspekti (*Legal and Institutional Aspect of Asylum*) (Pravni fakultet Sveučilišta u Zagrebu, 2016), p. 164.
5. Goranka Lalić & Mirela Krešić, *supra*.
6. Vladimir Bayer, Prestanak prava azila u Hrvatskoj (*Termination of Asylum Law in Croatia*) (Biblioteka Instituta za historiju države i prava na Pravnom fakultetu u Zagrebu, 1957).

dynastic struggles in Hungary, the Habsburgs powers were extended to the remaining parts of the Croatian territory. The Ottoman Empire further expanded in the sixteenth century to include most of Slavonia, western Bosnia (then called Turkish Croatia) and Lika. Moving the Ottoman border to the west and the Adriatic coast led the population to move in the same direction. However, even before the establishment of Ottoman rule in parts of Croatia, the first groups of Orthodox Serb and Vlach population from the parts southern of Sava and Danube migrated to Croatia, particularly in its eastern areas. Every conflict between the Habsburg Monarchy and the Venetian Republic on one side with the Ottoman Empire on the other, during the eighteenth century, influenced significant migrations along with territorial changes.[7] With the gradual expansion of the Ottoman Empire to the Croatian territories, the most numerous migrations were of so-called Vlachs or Morlachs, the descendants of the Paleobalkan population from the area of the triple frontier between Herzegovina, Serbia and Montenegro, who were systematically populated by the Habsburg rulers at the border areas, forming the Croatia Military Frontier – Habsburg Empire-controlled part of Croatia, which was administered directly from Vienna's military headquarters. Serbs, Croats, Germans, Austrians and others did also settle in this border area. As a result of their compulsory military service to the Habsburg Empire, the population in the Military Frontier was free of serfdom and enjoyed broader political autonomy, unlike the population living in the other parts of today's Croatia. As a counter-initiative, on the other side of the border, the Ottoman Empire inhabited a population of South Slavic origin but already converted to Islam.[8] Habsburg-Ottoman wars also initiated emigration waves which were the origins of the present-day Croatian ethnic minorities in Italia, Hungary, Austria, Romania, Slovakia and the Czech Republic.[9]

6. With the end of the Habsburg-Ottoman wars, the liberation of Slavonia and the Karlowitz Peace (1699) began a period of political, economic and social developments which influenced the immigration of different groups from the other parts of the Monarchy – Germans in two colonisation waves during the eighteenth century, and Slovaks, Hungarians, Jews and Czechs during the nineteenth century. During the first wave (1768–1771) 4,978 German families (16,989 people) immigrated to Croatian territory and during the second (1784–1789) about 7,600 families (38,000 people), who formed German communities in several parts of Croatia.[10] Czech immigrants played a significant role in Croatian economic life as they influenced agricultural and crafts developments, and textile, leather and food industries. They preserved their language and customs until 1918, and afterwards were more or less assimilated by the Croat majority, most often due to marriage connections. Polish immigrants were in majority intellectuals, workers and farmers, who were

---

7. Mario Bara & Ivan Lajić, Prisilne, iznuđene i organizirane migracije u etnodemografskom oblikovanju Hrvatske: primjer Slavonije (*Forced, Impelled and Organised Migration in the Ethno-Demographic Shaping of Croatia: The Example of Slavonia*), 25 Migracijske i etničke teme 4, 337 (2009), p. 341.
8. Jelena Zlatković Winter, *supra*, pp. 309–310.
9. Drago Roksandić, Vojna Hrvatska – La Croatie Militaire (Školska knjiga, 1988).
10. Emil Heršak, Panoptikum migracija – Hrvati, hrvatski prostor i Evropa (*A Panopticum of Migration: Croats, the Croatian Area, Europe*), 9 Migracijske teme 3–4, 227 (1993), p. 259.

assimilated into society in the same manner as Czechs.[11] This planned colonisation was carried out by the Austrian authorities, led by economic and religious but also national interests, and lasted until the end of the nineteenth century.[12] To a large extent, the immigrants influenced the modernisation of Croatia by establishing manufactures by their capital, by introducing new work methods and resources, and by applying new knowledge and skills by employing foreign workers and experts.[13] According to the 1857 census, of 865,009 inhabitants of Croatia and Slavonia, 33,145 residents were aliens. Of these, 17,873 originated from the other parts of the Monarchy.[14] Between 1900 and 1910, 43,000 aliens arrived in Croatia territories. According to the 1905 statistical information, from 1880 to 1905 there were some aliens from Austro-Hungary and other countries who were naturalised in Croatia, mostly Czechs and Italians who acquired citizenship in 1885, and others from Austria, Moravia and Germany. There were also individual arrivals from Romania, Bulgaria, Russia, Turkey, one Swiss, three French and two from the US.[15]

7. During the Austro-Hungarian period, in Croatian territories, the asylum was related mainly to extradition. As a rule, from the extradition to another state were exempted nationals but also aliens who were charged with committing a political offence. Extradition of foreign nationals was regulated by criminal legislation, bilateral extradition treaties and a series of subordinate regulations.

8. The second part of the nineteenth century and the beginning of the twentieth century was marked with the emigration from the Croatian territories, which during the 1880s reached massive proportions. The majority of emigrants were from rural areas (86%) and emigrated mainly due to economic reasons (crisis in farming, indebtedness of farmers, over-population of rural areas, etc.).[16] Generally, the unskilled population migrated to overseas countries, usually men from 15 to 40 years of age, while later, workers were seeking employment in the countries of Central and Western Europe (Germany, France and Belgium).[17] It is estimated that from the mid-nineteenth century until World War I around 350,000 Croatian inhabitants emigrated to overseas countries, which amounts to 11% of the total population. From the mid-nineteenth century until World War II, approximately 25,000 persons emigrated from Croatian territories to the European countries.[18] Emigration from Croatia after World War I and political changes that followed consisted mainly of administrative servants, experts and businessmen (around 100,000 persons) who

11. Jelena Zlatković Winter, *supra*, pp. 311–312.
12. Mario Bara & Ivan Lajić, *supra*, p. 342.
13. Jelena Zlatković Winter, *supra*, p. 314.
14. *Ibid.*, p. 319.
15. *Ibid.*, p. 320.
16. Ivica Nejašmić, Depopulacija u Hrvatskoj: Korijeni, stanje, izgledi (*Depopulation in Croatia: Roots, Condition, Prospects*) (Globus, 1991), p. 91.
17. Emil Heršak, *supra*, p. 268.
18. Ivica Nejašmić, 1991, *supra*, pp. 98 and 105.

previously immigrated with their families to Croatia from other parts of the Austro-Hungarian Monarchy, and after a dissolution of Monarchy returned to their countries.[19]

9. With the dissolution of the Austro-Hungarian Monarchy in 1918, Croatian lands entered the new union of the Kingdom of Serbs, Croats and Slovenes (1918–1929),[20] which was in 1929 renamed to Kingdom of Yugoslavia (1929–1941). The period from 1918 to 1941 was marked by a significant increase of immigrants from Bosnia and Herzegovina as the less economically developed region, to agricultural areas in Croatia, especially those populated with a higher number of minorities.[21] Following World War I, the Government introduced the agrarian reform and colonisation of the population from the overpopulated and/or less developed parts to eastern Croatia. Between 1919 and 1941, about 150,000 people moved to Slavonia, Posavina, Moslavina and Bjelovar-Križevci and established 105 agrarian colonies.[22] Military volunteers in the Serb and Montenegrin army from the wars of 1875 to 1918 were privileged in land acquisition and colonisation. There were some 8,000 volunteers, colonists with general conditions, optants and refugees that moved with their families into the north-eastern part of Croatia, which, according to estimates, resulted in 30,000 new inhabitants in that area. They were mostly settled in about one hundred land settlements.[23] Although colonisation mainly involved internal movements of people, between 1918 and 1938, as a part of colonisation, about 6,400 Czechs, Slovaks and other aliens, mostly farmer families, moved to eastern Croatia.[24] However, that period was marked by the emigration of aliens from Slavonia, mainly those who settled there in previous periods as officials in the administrative-administrative apparatus or as businessmen and experts. Some left for socio-cultural reasons, partly hoping for better economic and living conditions in newly-established national states. The majority, however, emigrated because in the changed socio-political circumstances they remained without the possibility to support themselves, and some were forced to emigrate. One of the measures which encouraged emigration was a very long period of deciding on the application for citizenship, especially of those who settled in Slavonia after 1910.[25] In the same period, in the capital city of Zagreb in 1931, there were 13,961 registered aliens, of which most Austrians (3,347), Czechoslovakian (2,527), Hungarians (2,408), Italians (2,408) and Russians (1,307).[26]

---

19. *Ibid.*, pp. 107–108.
20. It comprised the former kingdoms of Serbia and Montenegro (including Macedonia), Croatia, Bosnia and Herzegovina, Austrian territory in Dalmatia and Slovenia, and Hungarian land north of the Danube River.
21. Snježana Gregurović & Dubravka Mlinarić, *supra*, p. 100.
22. Ivica Nejašmić, Osnovne značajke unutarnje migracije stanovništva Hrvatske 1880–1981 (*Basic Characteristics of Internal Population Migration in Croatia 1880–1981*), 8 Migracijske teme, 2, 141 (1992), p. 146.
23. Josip Vrbošić, Kategorije i brojčano stanje kolonista u Slavoniji i Baranji između dva svjetska rata (*Categories and Numbers of Colonists in Slavonia and Baranja Between Two World Wars*), 6 Društvena istraživanja, 2–3, 311(1997).
24. Ivica Nejašmić, 1991, *supra*, p. 109.
25. Mario Bara & Ivan Lajić, supra, p. 343.
26. Emil Heršak, *supra*, p. 268.

10. After the collapse of the Russian Empire and the October Revolution, thousands of Russian exiles, mainly former Russian Imperial Army officers and the intelligentsia, had fled Russia. According to some data, between 50,000 and 70,000 Russian (and Ukrainian) refugees (so-called white émigrés) arrived in the Kingdom of the Serbs, Croats and Slovenes in the period from 1918 to 1923. Some of them continued their journey to Western Europe and the United States, and those who remained settled mainly in the areas of the Kingdom where the Orthodox population lived (Serbia and Montenegro), while fewer of them had settled in today's Croatia. Major Russian communities were established in Croatian cities Dubrovnik, Split, Crikvenica, Zagreb, and some other towns in the early 1920s.[27] King Alexander Karađorđević who considered himself as a patron and sponsor of Russian, allowed the establishment of Russian schools, gymnasiums and theatres.[28] Hence, numerous Russian clubs, associations, and cultural, educational, political and professional institutions were founded in Zagreb. Many Russian students have received state scholarships while some refugees (those less adroit) were entitled to social assistance. However, most Russians were highly educated and had a significant impact on the cultural and public life of the local communities in which they settled.[29] For example, in the academic year 1922–1923, the University of Zagreb enrolled 232 students from Russia (10.1% of all those enrolled). The local population occasionally showed hostility towards Russian refugees, usually due to the view that Russians were taking away jobs, but also since the part of the society who considered themselves as political left tended to see all Russian emigrants as 'counter-revolutionists'.[30] In addition to the refugees, in the Kingdom area, many Russian soldiers were former Austro-Hungarian war prisoners. After World War I, they were no longer considered prisoners, and they were allowed to leave. However, for political reasons, many Russians refused to return to the Soviet Union, and the Kingdom recognised them as political refugees. Apart from Russian refugees, many Jews arrived in Yugoslavia between the two wars. The emergence of Nazism and the spread of the Third Reich forced the emigration of members of the Jewish community firstly from Germany, then from Austria and Czechoslovakia. The Jewish Community of Zagreb provided a refuge for Jewish refugees since 1933 and established the Emigrant Assistance Committee, which operated until 1941. The support of Jewish refugees became more difficult due to the rise of anti-Semitism and approaching the Third Reich when the Yugoslav government began expelling them.[31]

11. After the invasion of the Kingdom of Yugoslavia by the Axis powers in April 1941, the new state has been established in Croatian territory – the Independent

27. Filip Škiljan, Rusi u Hrvatskoj (*Russians in Croatia*) (Savez Rusa u Republici Hrvatskoj, 2014), p. 10.
28. Goranka Lalić & Mirela Krešić, *supra*.
29. Irena Lukšić (ed.) Ruski emigranti u Hrvatskoj između dva rata – rubovi, memorija (*Russian Emigrants in Croatia Between Two World Wars*) (Hrvatsko filološko društvo, 2006).
30. Filip Škiljan, *supra*, p. 20.
31. Goranka Lalić & Mirela Krešić, *supra*.

State of Croatia (NDH, 1941–1945).[32] NDH's authorities encouraged colonisation from other parts of the state to the Slavonia region, mostly led by the criteria of ethnic belonging. In order to ethnically homogenise the state, the agricultural population (mostly of Croat origin) from Bosnia and Herzegovina were settled in Croatia.[33] Besides, some Slovenian refugees arrived in NDH, who were forcibly expelled from Slovenia as part of the German plan of annexing parts of the Slovenian territories, and some were deported from Serbia. Also, there were persons, mainly Croats and Muslims, who were deported to Croatia from Serbia and Macedonia.[34]

12. At the end of World War II, there was a massive external migration of different categories of population: those who remained abroad as prisoners of war or forced labourers, refugees, members of defeated forces and those who collaborated with them, optants (those who opted to move to Italy from the parts of Croatia that were affiliated to Italy in the past), member of minority groups (Germans, Hungarians, Poles, Czechs, etc.), and political opponents to the newly established socialist regime. It is estimated that around 250,000 persons emigrated during and in the first years after World War II.[35]

13. In the first two decades after World War II, the highest emigration waves from socialist Yugoslavia occurred between 1955 and 1958, with the annual emigration between 40,000 and 57,000 persons. Net migration in the inter-census period 1948–1961 amounted to about 500,000.[36] Among those, according to some estimations, the share of emigrants from Croatia amounted to 56% of total emigrants from former Yugoslavia until 1961.[37] Until the beginning of 1960, the Yugoslav Government considered external migration to be illegal, and only a few had an opportunity to travel abroad with the passport. However, in 1962 all citizens who illegally emigrated from Yugoslavia were granted amnesty and could legally return to the country. In the coming years, the Government concluded several bilateral agreements on the work of Yugoslav citizens abroad (1965 with Austria and France, and 1969 with Germany, Netherlands, Luxemburg and Australia).[38] Denominated as 'workers on temporary work abroad', these persons were not officially considered 'emigrants', since they were expected to return to Yugoslavia. Economic problems, the growing rate of unemployment in Yugoslavia and, in some cases, disagreement with the communist political regime, together with a high demand for workers in

32. Its territory consisted of most of contemporary Croatia and Bosnia and Herzegovina, as well as some smaller parts of Serbia and Slovenia, but excluded some areas which today are part of Croatia (in Dalmatia, Istria, and Međimurje regions).
33. Dubravka Mlinarić, Mario Bara, Snježana Gregurović, Drago Župarić-Iljić & Simona Kuti, Croatian Migration History and the Challenges of Migrations Today, AEMI, January 2015, https://aemi.eu/croatian-migration-history-and-the-challenges-of-migrations-today/ (accessed 16 Sep. 2018).
34. Emil Heršak, *supra*, p. 275.
35. Ivica Nejašmić, 1991, *supra*, pp. 107–108.
36. Snježana Gregurović & Dubravka Mlinarić, *supra*, p. 101.
37. Baučić 1973 in Emil Heršak, *supra*, p. 281.
38. Emil Heršak, *supra*, p. 281.

the Western European countries, opened a space for rather massive external migration.[39] The main destination for economic emigration from former Yugoslavia was West Germany, which in the period 1965–1968 issued a total of 168,312 work permits to Yugoslav citizens, of which 136,312 in Zagreb and 31,415 in Belgrade. As in the previous period, the number of emigrants from Croatia was the highest in total emigration from Yugoslavia (42.4% in 1969). The external emigration reached its peak in 1973, when, according to estimations, around 830,000 Yugoslav nationals were employed in the Western European countries, the majority of them in Western Germany (514,000 migrant workers).[40] After the oil and economic crises in 1973–1974, the Western European countries started to implement immigration and recruitment restrictions, and the external migration from former Yugoslavia started to decrease to around 15,000 emigrants per year. From 1974, the number of returnees from abroad surpassed the number of emigrants from former Yugoslavia.[41] At the same time, the emigration of family members of the migrant workers increased by 172% in the period 1971–1981.[42]

14. Socialist Yugoslavia was predominantly an emigration country whose citizens were emigrating both for political and economic reasons, but it was also a country which, over the years, provided asylum for different groups of political refugees. Although it was a socialist/communist country, former Yugoslavia broke away from the Soviet sphere of influence in 1948, became a founding member of the Non-Aligned Movement in 1961, and adopted a less repressive form of the system as compared to other East European communist states. Development of the modern asylum law began after World War II, and the right to asylum was guaranteed by the former Yugoslav federal or republican constitutions. The first refugees and asylum seekers arrived during the Greek Civil War (1946–1949), and by 1952, there were over 25,000 refugees in Yugoslavia.[43] After the outbreak of the revolution in Hungary against the Soviet authorities in 1956 and the collapse of the government of Imre Nagy, more than 200,000 Hungarians sought asylum in Yugoslavia.[44] Some of them were returned to Hungary, some went to the west, and fewer remained in Yugoslavia. Also, political refugees came to Yugoslavia from Czechoslovakia, where the attempt to liberalise the communist system and the establishment of the so-called socialism with the human face of Aleksandar Dubček caused the intervention of Warsaw Pact in 1968. Former Yugoslavia also provided protection to Chilean refugees after the assassination of President Allende by the Armed Forces and the establishment of the ruling of the military junta, to Romanians who escaped the

39. Snježana Gregurović & Dubravka Mlinarić, *supra*, p. 101.
40. Emil Heršak, *supra*, pp. 282–283.
41. *Ibid.*
42. Silva Mežnarić, Osvajanje prostora – prekrivanje vremena: migracije umjesto razvoja (Discovering Space, Overlapping Times: Migration instead of Development) (Sociološko društvo Hrvatske, 1991), p. 68.
43. Vojin Dimitrijević, Pravo utočišta na teritoriji strane države (teritorijalni azil) (*Right of Refuge in the Territory of a Foreign Country – Territorial Asylum*). PhD dissertation (Pravni fakultet u Beogradu, 1965).
44. Peter I. Hidas, Our Beloved Hungarians – Hungarian Refugees in Yugoslavia in Transit to Canada, 2001, http://www3.sympatico.ca/thidas/Hungarian-history/Yugoslavia.html (accessed 20 Sep. 2018).

regime of Nicolae Ceauşescu, Albanians and refugees from the war-related areas of Iraq, Iran and Lebanon.[45] According to United Nations High Commissioner for Refugees (UNHCR), in 1987, there were 3,100 asylum seekers in Yugoslavia, mostly from Romania (1,724) and Czechoslovakia (1,653), but also from Iran (80) and Iraq (37).[46] However, although former Yugoslavia was open to providing protection to refugees, there were cases in which the protection needs were diminished by the maintenance of good inter-state relations with the countries of origin of refugees.[47]

15. In addition to the political refugees, during the twentieth century, Croatia also experienced immigration from the other republics of former Yugoslavia and the Southeast European countries, mainly for economic and educational reasons. In the period 1971–1981, around 121,000 citizens immigrated to Croatia from other Yugoslav republics, while around 73,000 persons emigrated from Croatia to other republics.[48] According to some estimations, during the twentieth century, around 519,915 people moved to Croatia.[49] One of the characteristics of the inter-republic migrations was that the migrants often chose the 'mother' republic of their nation as a destination.[50]

16. Croatia declared formal independence from former Yugoslavia in 1991. The Croatian War of Independence (1991–1995) that followed resulted in hundreds of thousands of people being displaced from and within Croatia. At the same time, Croatia was faced with an influx of (predominately) Croat refugees fleeing war events and human rights violations in Bosnia and Herzegovina (1992–1995). It is estimated that the Balkan crisis caused the displacement of approximately two and a half million people, which represented more than 10% of the population of former Yugoslavia.[51] In 1991 and 1992, Croatia registered more than 550,000 displaced Croatian citizens and around 400,000 refugees from Bosnia and Herzegovina. After the recapture of the Croatian territories (which were temporarily occupied by the Serbs) by the military operations of the Croatian Armed Forces in 1995, around 250,000 ethnic Serbs fled from Croatia mostly to Serbia and Bosnia and Herzegovina.[52] With the political stabilisation, the return to Croatia started at a slow pace. Although the majority of persons from Croatia displaced by the conflict in the 1990s had either returned to their country of origin or acquired the nationality of their country of asylum, as of the end of 2016, 25,548 refugees from Croatia remained

45. Goranka Lalić & Mirela Krešić, *supra.*
46. Svjetlan Berković, Azil u međunarodnom pravu (*Asylum in International Law*). PhD dissertation (Pravni fakultet u Zagrebu, 1989).
47. Goranka Lalić & Mirela Krešić, *supra.*
48. Silva Mežnarić, supra, p. 67.
49. Jakov Gelo, Anđelko Akrap & Ivan Čipin, Temeljne značajke demografskog razvoja Hrvatske (Basic Features of Demographic Development of Croatia) (Ministarstvo obitelji, branitelja i međugeneracijske solidarnosti, 2005), p. 80.
50. Emil Heršak, *supra*, p. 280.
51. Silva Mežnarić, Expediency of statistics: War and Post-War Casualties in Croatia and Bosnia (1991–1999), 31 Revija za sociologiju, 3–4, 211 (2000), p. 214.
52. UNHCR, Minority Return to Croatia – Study of an Open Process, 2011, ISBN: 978-953-95763-3-0, https://www.refworld.org/docid/553a08424.html (accessed 26 Sep. 2018).

registered in the region, of which majority in Serbia.[53] Concerning immigration to Croatia, it is estimated that 120,000 Bosnia and Herzegovina refugees of Croat ethnicity have acquired Croatian citizenship.[54]

17. The contemporary migration in Croatia includes both immigration and emigration. In the last years, especially after the accession to the European Union (EU) in 2013 and the opening of the labour market, there is a rather massive emigration trend of Croatian citizens. The factors which induce emigration include low economic growth, measured by GDP, a drop in general employment, high unemployment and long-term unemployment rates, a decreasing standard of living for many citizens, difficulties in finding a job that matches their level of education, long periods of unemployment, poor wages given their background and a bad business environment.[55]

18. According to the statistics of the Ministry of Interior (MoI), at the end of 2017, there were over 35,000 aliens with registered permanent or temporary residence in Croatia. In total, 7,550 third-country nationals (TCNs) with *permanent* residence were registered in Croatia, 85% of whom were citizens of the countries of the former Yugoslavia – Bosnia and Herzegovina (4,711), Serbia (766), Kosovo (657) and Macedonia (495). The permanent residence permit has been issued to the nationals of China (437), Russia (187), the US (124), Ukraine (60), and others. There were also 5,106 permanent residents of the European Economic Area (EEA), mostly from Germany (1,394), Slovenia (1,314), Italy (540), Austria (346) and the UK (229). A total of 10,736 TCNs and 11,628 EEA nationals with *temporary* residence were registered in Croatia. Again, a majority originate from the countries of former Yugoslavia – Bosnia and Herzegovina (6,112), Slovenia (2,650), Serbia (1,020), Kosovo (421) and Macedonia (340).[56]

19. Regarding forced migration flows, Croatia is a relatively new destination for refugees and asylum seekers from countries outside the region. During the migrant-refugee crisis (September 2015–March 2016) around 650,000 refugees and migrants passed through Croatia, but only twenty-two of them applied for asylum. Recently, there is increased pressure of refugees and migrants from Asia at the Croatian borders with Bosnia and Herzegovina. Although these numbers are rather small compared to 2015–2016, there is fear that a route might be used as the main route for irregular migrations towards the western EU countries. In the period 2006–2018,

53. UNHCR, Fourth Progress Report on the Implementation of the Durable Solutions Process (Sarajevo Process) for Refugees from Croatia Displaced by the 91–95 conflict, including cessation of refugee status, June 2017, https://www.refworld.org/docid/5964cf5f4.html (accessed 22 Sep. 2018).
54. UNHCR, Submission by the United Nations High Commissioner for Refugees for the Office of the High Commissioner for Human Rights' Compilation Report – Universal Periodic Review: The Republic of Croatia, April 2010, https://www.refworld.org/docid/4bcd79502.html (accessed 22 Sep. 2018).
55. Drago Župarić-Iljić, *Emigration from the Republic of Croatia after the Accession to the European Union* (Friedrich Ebert Stiftung, 2016), www.fes-croatia.org/fileadmin/user_upload/FES_ Iseljavan je_web.pdf (accessed 28 Sep. 2018).
56. Ministry of Interior, https://mup.hr/ministarstvo/dokumenti/statistika (accessed 28 Sep. 2018).

international protection was granted to a total of 750 persons. In 2017, the rate of recognition, i.e., the share of positive decisions on asylum applications in the total number of decisions, was 31% for first-instance decisions and 20% for final decisions on appeal. Three main citizenships granted protection status in 2017 include Syrians (62%), Iraqis (17%) and Eritreans (7%).[57] The number of asylum seekers is on the rise (in 2017 – 1,887; in 2016 – 2,234), but most of them left the Croatian territory before the end of the status determination process. First-time asylum applicants by country of citizenship in 2017 include Afghanistan (180), Syria (140) and Pakistan (115).[58]

20. Croatia takes part in the European Programme for relocation and resettlement of TCNs or persons without nationality who meet the requirements for approval of international protection according to the Decision of the Government of the Republic of Croatia (RoC) on relocating and resettlement of TCNs or persons without nationality who meet the requirements for international protection. Based on the responsibilities of Croatia resulting from its participation in the Programme, in July 2015[59] and October 2017,[60] the Croatian Government adopted several decisions regarding the number of refugees that will be relocated and resettled to Croatia. According to the first decision, the Croatian Government committed accepted up to 550 persons (150 persons based on resettlement and 400 based on relocation), but later it was decided to accept a further 568 persons through a second relocation scheme. In 2018, according to the second decision, Croatia committed to taking 100 persons on the grounds of resettlement. By the end of 2017, 81 persons were relocated to Croatia, and 40 were resettled. A total of 17 Eritrean and 4 Yemeni nationals were relocated from Italy, and 60 Syrian nationals from Greece. All of them were granted international protection. In 2017, 40 Syrian nationals were resettled from Turkey, and in 2018, 88 Syrians.[61]

---

57. Eurostat, EU Member States Granted Protection to More Than Half a Million Asylum Seekers in 2017, 67/2018 – 19 April 2018, https://ec.europa.eu/eurostat/documents/2995521/8817675/3-19042018-AP-EN.pdf/748e8fae-2cfb-4e75-a388-f06f6ce8ff58 (accessed 28 Sep. 2018).
58. Eurostat, Asylum in the EU Member States: 650,000 First-Time Asylum Seekers Registered in 2017, 47/2018 – 20 March 2018, https://ec.europa.eu/eurostat/documents/2995521/8754388/3-20032018-AP-EN.pdf/50c2b5a5-3e6a-4732-82d0-1caf244549e3 (accessed 28 Sep. 2018).
59. Decision of the Government of the Republic of Croatia on relocating and resettlement of third-country nationals or persons without nationality who meet the requirements for international protection from 16 July 2015 (*Odluka Vlade Republike Hrvatske o premještanju i preseljenju državljana trećih zemalja ili osoba bez državljanstva koji ispunjavaju uvjete za odobrenje međunarodne zaštite*), OG 78/2015.
60. Decision on resettlement of third-country nationals or persons without nationality who meet the requirements for international protection (*Odluka o preseljenju državljana trećih zemalja ili osoba bez državljanstva koje ispunjavaju uvjete za odobrenje međunarodne zaštite*), OG 99/2017.
61. Ministry of Interior, U Hrvatsku preseljena peta skupina sirijskih izbjeglica iz Turske, 12 Oct. 2018, https://mup.hr/novosti/6166/u-hrvatsku-preseljena-peta-skupina-sirijskih-izbjeglica-iz-turske (accessed 28 Nov. 2018).

§2. Overview of National Legal Instruments

I. Historical Overview

21. After the independence in 1991, Croatia has adopted important laws concerning the area of migration that regulated the issues of acquiring Croatian citizenship,[62] aliens[63] and protection of borders.[64] Due to war events at the beginning of the 1990s and gradual developments of democratic institutions in the second part of the 1990s,[65] the migration legislation was not developing comprehensively until the beginning of the 2000s. Given that the accession to the EU becomes the most important strategic objective of the RoC since the beginning of 2000, it can be concluded that the migration and asylum system started to develop alongside the EU accession process.[66]

22. The government adopted the first official policy document in the field of migration, the *Migration Policy of the Republic of Croatia 2007–2008* in 2007.[67] The main objective was to establish a systematic and comprehensive approach to migration issues through a transparent and effective system of administration of regular migration, a fair and contemporary system of compensation claims which derive from forced migration, and a clear, transparent and effective system of control and prevention of illegal migration. The aims and goals were set very generally, and only seventeen measures and activities were envisaged, relating predominantly to the adoption of the legislation. The second strategic document, *Migration Policy of the Republic of Croatia for the Period 2013–2015*[68] has been adopted by the Croatian Parliament in February 2013, only a few months before Croatia joined the EU. The document focuses on securing that the migration trends will have a positive impact on the country's overall development, especially in the field of economy. The Migration policy establishes measures to be implemented in the following areas: visa policy, the status of foreign nationals, the acquisition of Croatian citizenship, asylum, integration policy, irregular migration and Croatian diaspora.

23. In 2003, the Aliens Act was adopted and came into force at the beginning of 2004.[69] Together with the accompanying implementing regulations (the Ordinance on the status of aliens, the Ordinance on travel documents for aliens, visas, border passes and rules for treatment of aliens and the Ordinance on issuing travel documents, visas and special identity cards to aliens), the Act regulated the conditions

---

62. Croatian Citizenship Act (*Zakon o hrvatskom državljanstvu*), OG 53/1991.
63. Act on Movement and Stay of Aliens (*Zakon o kretanju i boravku stranaca*), OG 53/1991 and subsequent amendments (OG 22/1992, 26/1993, 29/1994).
64. State Border Protection Act (*Zakon o nadzoru državne granice*), OG 9/1992.
65. The status of the refugee groups (temporary protection) from within the region were regulated by Directives, internal instructions and regulations and not based on any specific law.
66. Goranka Lalić Novak, 2016, *supra*.
67. Migration policy of the Republic of Croatia 2007–2008 (*Migracijska politika Republike Hrvatske za 2007./2008. godinu*), OG 83/2007.
68. Migration Policy of the Republic of Croatia for the Period 2013–2015 (*Migracijska politika Republike Hrvatske za razdoblje 2013. – 2015. godine*), OG 27/2013.
69. Aliens Act (*Zakon o strancima*), OG 109/2003, 182/2004, 115/2005, 79/2007.

and manner of entering, the movements and sojourn, and the employment of aliens in Croatia. The new Aliens Act,[70] adopted in 2011, revised the provisions on regulating the residence and work of aliens, by following the EU acquis.

24. The Act on Amendments to the Croatian Citizenship Act[71] amended the conditions for the regular acquisition of Croatian citizenship by naturalisation; it prolonged the necessary duration of the alien's stay in the RoC from five to eight years. The Act introduced the definition of a member of the Croat nation, and for expatriates, it introduced a generation limit by prescribing the third degree of kinship with the original Croatian immigrant. It also laid down the requirement for verification of the knowledge of the Croatian language and script, culture and social order. The acquisition of Croatian citizenship has been facilitated for persons who held residence in the RoC on 8 October 1991 and have a permanent residence permit, and who have thus not acquired Croatian citizenship.

25. In the development of the Croatian asylum system, it is possible to identify three phases marked by the specifics of legislation and practice.[72] The first, *early phase* covers the period 1997–2004, in which asylum is just beginning to develop in practice. Refugee status issues were resolved under the provisions of the Act on Movement and Stay of Aliens. This Act did not contain a *non-refoulement* principle and ban of punishment of refugees for illegal entry or residence, guaranteed by the UN Convention Relating to the Status of Refugees (1951 Refugee Convention) and the 1967 Protocol Relating to the Status of Refugees. It also did not regulate the rights and obligations of asylum seekers within the framework of reception nor did it contain procedural safeguards for the procedure of determining refugee status. In practice, the asylum legislation and practice have not been in line with international and European standards regarding access to the asylum system and the procedure for determining the status of refugees. The second, *transformational phase* covers the period of 2004–2008 during which the asylum system is emerging and evolving. As part of the obligations that Croatia had made from the Stabilization and Association Agreement, in June 2003 the first Asylum Act[73] had been adopted. The Act prescribed the principles, conditions and procedure for granting of asylum and the temporary protection, the status, rights and obligations of asylum seekers, asylees and aliens who have been granted temporary protection, as well as the conditions and procedure for abolishing the asylum status and for termination of temporary protection of aliens. Although it approximated the legal framework with the EU acquis and the 1951 Refugee Convention, the substantive and procedural provisions of the Asylum Act contained serious shortcomings and, consequently, were inconsistent with relevant international and European standards. Third, the *stabilisation phase* covers the period from 2008 to the present, and it is marked with the

70. *Ibid.*, OG 130/2011.
71. Act on Amendments to the Croatian Citizenship Act (*Zakon o hrvatskom državljanstvu*), OG 53/1991, 70/1991, 28/1992, 113/1993, 4/1994, 130/2011, 110/2015.
72. Goranka Lalić Novak, 2016, *supra*.
73. Asylum Act *(Zakon o azilu)*, OG 103/2003.

stability of the legal and organisational framework. The second Asylum Act has been adopted in 2007 and has been in force from 1 January 2008 until July 2015.[74]

26. *The Migration Policy of the Republic of Croatia for the Period 2013–2015* acknowledged the importance of the integration of aliens into Croatian society. According to the Migration Policy, it is 'very important to continuously implement the measure which secures, with the aim of preventing discriminatory practices and attitudes towards immigrants in the economic, social and cultural life, the right to equal status to Croatian citizens, with a focus towards acquiring citizenship'. Within this aim, the importance of a partnership with civil society and the private sector was recognised.[75] Based on the Migration Policy, the first strategic document in the field of integration of aliens, the *Action Plan for removing barriers to the realisation of individual rights in the field of integration of foreigners for the period from 2013 to 2015*, had been adopted in 2012.[76] The envisaged measures for the integration of migrants were aimed at ensuring their equal status in the economic, social, and cultural life vis-à-vis Croatian citizens. Particular emphasis was placed on the area of education, employment, housing, and the prevention of discriminatory procedures and behaviour towards foreigners.[77]

II. Applicable Legislation and Strategic Documents

27. Today, most of the Croatian legislation concerning migration and asylum has been developed following the EU *acquis communautaire*. Legislation regulating asylum and migration is based on the Constitution of the RoC.[78] According to Article 26, aliens are equal to Croatian citizens before the courts, governmental agencies and other bodies vested with public authority.

---

74. *Ibid.*, OG 79/2007, 88/2010, 143/2013.
75. Teo Giljević & Goranka Lalić Novak, *Coordination Instruments in Croatian Integration Policy: Classification, Evaluation, and Proposals for Improvements*, 18 Hrvatska i komparativna javna uprava, 3, 373 (2018).
76. Action Plan for removing barriers to the realisation of individual rights in the field of integration of foreigners for the period from 2013 to 2015 (*Akcijski plan za uklanjanje prepreka u ostvarivanju pojedinih prava u području integracije stranaca za razdoblje od 2013. do 2015. godine*), https://pravamanjina.gov.hr/UserDocsImages/arhiva/30092013/Akcijski%20plan%20za%20uklanjanje%20prepreka%20u%20ostvarivanju%20pojedinih%20prava%20u%20podru%C4%8Dju%20integracije%20stranaca%20za%20razdoblje%20od%202013%20do%202015%20godine.pdf (accessed 5 Oct. 2018).
77. More about the integration of aliens and refugees in Croatia *see* in: Goranka Lalić Novak & Teo Giljević, Integration of 'New' Refugees in the Non-immigrant Countries along the Balkan Route of Migration – Overview of Legal Framework and Practices. In: Dalibor Jílek & Pavel Pořízek (eds), Ročenka uprchlického a cizineckého práva 2017 (Kancelář veřejného ochránce práv, 2018), pp. 53–470; Goranka Lalić Novak & Tijana Vukojičić Tomić, Integracija stranaca i manjina u lokalnu zajednicu kao zadatak lokalne samouprave (*Integration of Aliens and Minorities in Local Communities as the Role of the Local Self-Government*). In Ivan Koprić, Anamarija Musa & Teo Giljević (eds) Građani, javna uprava, lokalna samouprava: jesu li mogući povjerenje, suradnja i potpora (Institut za javnu upravu, 2017), pp. 273–294.
78. Constitution of the Republic of Croatia (*Ustav Republike Hrvatske*), OG 56/1990, 135/1997, 113/2000, 28/2001, 85/2010– consolidated text, 5/2014.

28. The right to asylum is guaranteed by Article 33 of the Constitution according to which 'an alien and stateless person may be granted asylum in Croatia unless they are being prosecuted for non-political crimes and activities contrary to the fundamental principles of international law. No alien legally in the territory of the Republic of Croatia shall be banished or extradited to another state, except in cases of enforcement of decisions made in compliance with an international treaty or law'. The central legislation regulating asylum is the Act on International and Temporary Protection[79] which prescribes the principles, conditions and the procedure for international protection and temporary protection, the status, rights and obligations of asylum seekers, asylees, foreigners under subsidiary protection, foreigners under temporary protection, as well as the conditions and procedures for the revocation and cessation of asylee status and subsidiary and temporary protection. The Act is aligned with the EU *acquis communautaire*.[80]

29. The central legislation in the field of migration is the Aliens Act of 2011, which was subsequently amended in 2013, 2017 and 2018,[81] in the process of alignment with the EU *acquis communautaire*. The Act regulates the entry, movement and the work of aliens and the conditions of work, and the rights of posted workers in Croatia, stipulating the conditions for approval or refusal of entry and departure, issuing of visas, the conditions for stay in the country (temporary and permanent residence permits) and registration, the conditions to leave the country and return measures, the movement of aliens in uniform, the rules on the processing and storing of personal data of aliens, the issuing of identity cards for aliens, and the conditions for issuing passports and other documents to aliens. It also regulates the conditions for entry, stay and work of nationals of the EEA Member States and their family members, stay and work of TCNs having approved permanent stay in another EEA Member States and of their family members, and stay and work of highly skilled TCNs. Certain provisions in the Act are further elaborated in various implementing acts (decrees, ordinances, rules and decisions).

30. The State Border Protection Act[82] regulates state border control, border police operations within the state, international border police cooperation and cooperation of border services at borders.

31. All procedures relating to the status and rights of aliens, asylum seekers and refugees are administrative procedures by nature. The provisions of these special administrative procedures are defined in the specific legislation, the Aliens Act and Act on International and Temporary Protection, which are *leges speciales* to general

79. Act on International and Temporary Protection *(Zakon o međunarodnoj i privremenoj zaštiti)*, OG 70/2015, 127/2017.
80. About the influence of the Europeanisation on the development of asylum system, *see*: Goranka Lalić Novak, Europeizacija hrvatskoga sustava azila: mehanizmi i instrumenti utjecaja Europske unije na javne politike i institucije (*Europeanization of the Croatian Asylum System: Mechanisms and Instruments of European Union Influence on Public Policies and Institutions*), 22 Društvena istraživanja 2, 237, 2013.
81. Aliens Act (*Zakon o strancima)*, OG 130/2011, 74/2013, 69/2017, 46/2018.
82. State Border Protection Act *(Zakon o nadzoru državne granice)*, OG 83/2013, 27/2016.

administrative procedures. For cases which are not defined by *lex specialis*, the subsidiary use of the General Administrative Procedure Act[83] is mandatory. This Act regulates the provisions enabling the state administration bodies and other state bodies, bodies of local and regional self-government units, legal entities vested with public powers, within the scope determined by law, to act and adjudicate in administrative matters.

32. Judicial control of administrative decisions rendered under the Aliens Act and the Act on International and Temporary Protection is regulated by the Administrative Disputes Act.[84] This Act regulates the competence, composition of the court and procedural rules under which administrative courts issue decisions on the lawfulness of decisions and actions of public authorities and the rights, obligations and legal interests of natural and legal persons and other parties.

33. Concerning integration of migrants and refugees into Croatian society, the current strategic document is the *Action Plan for the Integration of Persons who have been granted International Protection for the period from 2017 to 2019*[85] which was adopted by the Government in November 2017 as a national framework for integration. The new Action plan covers the following areas of integration: social and healthcare, accommodation and housing, language skills and education, employment, international cooperation, inter-agency cooperation, raising awareness about the issues that persons who have been granted international protection are faced with.

III. Administrative and Judicial Authorities

34. The leading authority for the overall implementation of migration and asylum policies is the Ministry of the Interior (*Ministarstvo unutarnjih poslova*). It consists of the headquarters (the central level administration), the police administration (the regional level) and the police station (the local level). It is, however, a unified hierarchical organisation with a high subordination of lower organisational units towards the higher organisational units, and with the centralised organisation. The territorial organisation of the Ministry of the Interior (MoI) is based on the model of the so-called divergent organisational structure, in which organisational units cover a particular territory, and altogether the entire territory of Croatia.[86]

83. General Administrative Procedure Act (*Zakon o općem upravnom postupku)*, OG 47/2009.
84. Administrative Disputes Act *(Zakon o upravnim sporovima)*, OG 20/2010, 143/2012, 152/2014, 94/2016, 29/2017.
85. Action Plan for the Integration of Persons who have been granted International Protection for the period from 2017 to 2019 (*Akcijski plan za integraciju osoba kojima je odobrena međunarodna zaštita za razdoblje 2017. do 2019. godine*), https://ljudskaprava.gov.hr/UserDocsImages//dokumenti//AKCIJSKI%20PLAN%20ZA%20INTEGRACIJU%202017-2019.pdf (accessed 5 Oct. 2018).
86. Pušeljić, M. i Jelenski, M., Policijski sustavi – realizacija policijske funkcije kroz ustroj, 16 Policija i sigurnost, 1–2 (2007), p. 4.

35. The competent body for control of the State borders is the Border Police of the MoI. Against the decisions of the police in the field of border control, an appeal can be filed which is dealt with by the Commission of the MoI. Visas are issued by the diplomatic mission or consular office of the RoC and may also be issued by a diplomatic mission or consular office of another country with which the RoC concluded an agreement on representation in the issuing of visas. In some cases, the visa can be issued by the MoI. Against a decision on annulment or revocation of a visa, an alien can file an appeal with the Ministry of Foreign and European Affairs (*Ministarstvo vanjskih i europskih poslova* – MFEA). The main body for deciding on temporary and permanent residence applications is the MoI, through the police administration or police station based on the place of temporary residence or intended stay of an alien. An alien can appeal against the decision to the MoI's Commission. The competent body for deciding on applications for asylum is the Department for Asylum of MoI's Directorate for Administrative and Inspection Affairs.

36. All decisions of the MoI can be the subject of judicial review by one of the administrative courts (*Upravni sud*), established in 2012 in Zagreb, Split, Rijeka and Osijek. The High Administrative Court of the RoC (*Visoki upravni sud Republike Hrvatske*) rules on the following cases: on appeals against judgments of the administrative courts and appealable decisions, on the legality of general acts, on conflicts of jurisdiction between administrative courts, and in other cases prescribed by law. If the procedure violates the Constitutional rights of the individual, a Constitutional complaint can be filed with the Constitutional Court (*Ustavni sud*).

§3. Overview of International Legal Instruments

37. Croatia is a signatory to most of the United Nations (UN) and Council of Europe (CoE) conventions relevant for the status and protection of fundamental rights of migrants. Former Yugoslavia already ratified many of them, and Croatia acceded to them by succession.[87] According to Article 141 of the Constitution 'International agreements concluded and ratified in accordance with the Constitution and made public shall be part of the Republic's internal legal order and shall in terms of legal effect be above the law. Their provisions may be changed or repealed only under the conditions and means specified within them, or in accordance with the general rules of international law.'

38. Until the end of 2017, Croatia failed to ratify two international human rights conventions signed by the Government, i.e., the International Convention for the Protection of All Persons from Enforced Disappearance and the European Social Charter (revised). Croatia has not yet officially accepted Article 14 of the International Convention on the Elimination of All Forms of Racial Discrimination, which

87. Decision on the publication of multilateral international agreements to which the Republic of Croatia is a party on the basis of the notification on succession (*Odluka o objavljivanju mnogostranih međunarodnih ugovora kojih je Republika Hrvatska stranka na temelju notifikacija o sukcesiji*), OG 12/1993.

prevents Croatian citizens from lodging complaints to the UN Committee on the Elimination of Racial Discrimination. Even though it supported the draft proposal of the Optional Protocol to the International Covenant on Economic, Social and Cultural Rights, Croatia failed to initiate the procedure for signing the Protocol. Croatia did not sign the International Convention on the Protection of the Rights of All Migrant Workers and Members of Their Families.[88]

88. Human Rights House Zagreb, Human Rights In Croatia: Overview of 2017, Zagreb, March 2018, http://www.kucaljudskihprava.hr/wp-content/uploads/2018/04/KLJP_PregledStanja_ENGWeb.pdf (accessed 18 Oct. 2018).

Part I. Border Control and Entrance

Chapter 1. Organisation of Border Control

39. The RoC is situated at the crossroads of the countries of western, central and eastern Europe and the Mediterranean countries. The total length of the state border of the RoC is 3,332 km, of which 2,370.5 km is a land border (including river borders). It borders Bosnia and Herzegovina (1,011 km), Slovenia (668 km), Hungary (355 km), Serbia (318 km), Montenegro (23 km) and Italy (sea border).[89] The outside border of the EU is estimated at 2,260 km.

40. The competent body for control of the State borders is the Border Police of the MoI. Exceptionally, the Armed Forces of the RoC may provide support for the protection of the state border when the MoI or the Croatian Prime Minister considers this necessary for security and or humanitarian reasons. In this situation, the members of the Armed Forces should act according to the instructions of the police.[90]

41. At the national level, control of the state borders is coordinated by the Border Management Unit, the organisational unit of the Police Directorate within the MoI. The Unit consists of several departments: Department for State Border Protection and Compensation Measures, Department for Neighbouring Countries, the Illegal Migration Department, the Maritime and Aerodrome Police Department, Reception Centre for Foreigners, Mobile Unit for Implementation of State Border Control and Department for the National Coordination Centre and Risk Analysis.[91] The state border control at the regional level is conducted by twenty police administrations, of which two (PU Bjelovarsko-Bilogorska and Požeško-Slavonska) carry out only activities related to irregular migration and aliens' stay. In the police administrations, depending on their category, the Sector for Borders, Border Services and the Illegal Migration Service will be established.

42. The control of the state borders includes protection of the state border and control of crossing the state border (border controls), with the aim to:

89. Croatian Bureau of Statistics, 2017 Statistical Yearbook of the Republic of Croatia, Zagreb, December 2017.
90. Article 5, State Border Protection Act.
91. Regulation on Internal Organization of the Ministry of the Interior (*Uredba o unutarnjem ustrojstvu Ministarstva unutarnjih poslova*), OG 70/2012, 140/2013, 50/2014, 32/2015, 11/2017, 129/2017, 5/2018, 66/2018, 109/2018.

- securing the inviolability of the state border and the state territory;
- protection of human life and health;
- prevention and detection of crimes and offences and the perpetrators;
- prevention of illegal migration;
- prevention and detection of other dangers to public security, legal order and national security.[92]

The border police perform the tasks of supervising the state border, preventing and detecting illegal entry and stay and the suppression of cross-border crime in the depth of the state territory, and international border police cooperation.[93]

92. Article 3, para. 1, State Border Protection Act.
93. Article 1 and 4, State Border Protection Act.

Chapter 2. Right to Enter the Country

§1. Conditions for the Right to Enter

I. Third-Country Nationals

43. Conditions for entry into and exit from Croatia are regulated by Schengen Borders Code[94] which stipulates that:

- a TCN has to possess a valid travel document, a valid visa or a residence permit;
- a TCN has to justify the purpose and conditions of the intended stay and has sufficient means of subsistence, both for the duration of the intended stay and for the return to their country of origin or transit to a third country, or can acquire such means lawfully;
- a TCN is not a person for whom an alert has been issued in the SIS to refuse entry;
- a TCN is not considered to be a threat to public policy, internal security, public health or international relations.[95]

44. It is considered that an alien does not possess a valid travel document if:

- the document does not include all the foreseen data;
- the period of its validity expired, except for cases defined in international treaties;
- documents are damaged, or forged;
- it is not recognized for crossing the state border;
- if he or she attempts to use the document of another person;
- if he or she is not a national of the country that issued a travel document which does not indicate whether he has the right to return to that country;
- there is no space for stamping the input stamp.[96]

45. The Government may decide that the nationals of certain states may enter and leave Croatia if they hold:

- a valid travel document which includes a valid stay permit issued by a signatory of the Schengen Implementation Agreement;
- a valid travel document which includes a valid type D visa issued by a signatory of the Schengen Implementation Agreement;

94. Article 35, Aliens Act.
95. Article 6, Regulation (EU) 2016/399 of the European Parliament and of the Council of 9 Mar. 2016 on a Union Code on the rules governing the movement of persons across borders (Schengen Borders Code), OJ L 77, 23 Mar. 2016, pp. 1–52.
96. Article 4, Ordinance on Treatment of Third-Country Nationals (*Pravilnik o postupanju prema državljanima trećih zemalja*), OG 68/2018.

- a valid travel document which includes a valid stay permit issued by an EEA Member State which does not yet fully implement the Schengen *acquis communautaire*;
- a valid travel document which includes a national visa issued by an EEA Member State which does not yet fully implement the Schengen *acquis communautaire*, provided that they meet the entry conditions.[97]

46. A TCN who does not meet the criteria may be granted entry at a specific border crossing, on a serious humanitarian basis, national interests or international obligations of Croatia.[98] Humanitarian reasons include: emergency medical assistance, giving human organs, natural and other disasters, and unforeseen events to close family members (severe illness, death, etc.).[99] Entry into Croatia should also be allowed for persons who intend to apply for asylum, based on the Act on International and Temporary Protection.

47. Besides the valid travel document, a visa or a residence permit is required for entry and short-term stay for citizens of some countries (*see* more in Part II).[100]

48. An alien will be considered to have entered Croatia illegally if he or she:

- crosses the state border outside the place or time designated for crossing the state border;
- avoids border control;
- enters Croatia during the prohibition of entry and stay in Croatia or EEA;
- enters on the basis of another person's or forged travel document or other documents necessary for crossing the state border, such as visa or approval of stay.[101]

49. TCNs who are long-term residents in another EEA Member State may enter Croatia with a valid passport and a residence permit issued in that other Member State, and do not require a visa. They may remain in Croatia for a maximum of three months or until their visa or residence permit issued by that Member State expires, provided that the term of validity is shorter than three months. If TCN intends to stay in Croatia for over three months, he or she has to apply for the approval of temporary stay to Croatian police authorities.[102]

97. Article 37, para. 2, Aliens Act.
98. Article 36, para. 1, Aliens Act.
99. Article 11, para. 2, Ordinance on Treatment of Third-Country Nationals.
100. According to the judicial practice, a request for entry into the Republic of Croatia can be denied to a person who used a forged document. 'It is undisputed from the established factual situation that the border control the plaintiff presented a travel document of Afghanistan, with a Greek residence permit for which it was subsequently verified that the blank stamp of the residence permit was stolen in Greece. According to the plaintiff's statement of 29 January 2015, the plaintiff was aware of this, and stated that her fiancé had obtained the said residence permit and various stamps in the travel document for an unknown amount of money.' The High Administrative Court, Usž-1767/15, a decision of 14 Oct. 2015.
101. Article 39, Aliens Act.
102. Article 184, Aliens Act.

50. TCNs can freely leave Croatia, except if: at the time of leaving, a TCN does not possess a valid travel document or other document used to cross the state border (unless it is admitted to the neighbouring state) or uses another person's or forged travel document or other document used to cross the state border; or there is a justifiable reason to believe that a TCN intends to avoid prosecution for a criminal offence or a misdemeanour, detention, arrest, bringing in or enforcement of the sentence of imprisonment, or it is required by a court.[103]

II. EEA Citizens and Their Family Members

51. Conditions for entry and residence for EEA citizens and their family members are more lenient than those for TCNs. An EEA citizen needs a valid identity document or a valid travel document to enter Croatia, provided that he or she is not barred by the prohibition of entry and stay, and does not pose a threat to public policy, national security or public health. They can enter Croatia without a visa or approval of stay, and stay in Croatia for up to three months. EEA citizens with documents can freely leave Croatia in order to travel to another Member State.[104]

52. It is considered that the EEA citizen does not possess a valid travel document or identity document used to cross the state border if:

- not all envisaged data have been entered;
- the period of its validity expired unless otherwise stipulated in the international agreement;
- it is damaged;
- it is not recognised for crossing the state border;
- has a travel document issued by a foreign country, but is not a citizen of that State and travel document does not indicate whether he has the right to return to the State which issued him a travel document or approved entry into a third country;
- attempts to use a document of another person;
- it is established that the document is forged.[105]

53. The Aliens Act stipulates that a family members of an EEA citizen include: spouse; an extramarital partner and persons in a permanent relationship if it lasts three years, or less, if other circumstances can establish the persistence of a lasting relationship; adopted children, step-children and relatives of an EEA citizen (and of his spouse or extramarital partner) by blood in the vertical line downwards, all of up to 21 years of age; adopted children, step-children and relatives older than 21

103. Article 40, Aliens Act.
104. Articles 154 and 155, Aliens Act.
105. Article 3, para. 1, Rulebook on determining the conditions for entry and residence in the Republic of Croatia of citizens of the Member States of the European Economic Area and members of their families and members of the family of Croatian citizens (*Pravilnik o načinu utvrđivanja uvjeta za ulazak i boravak u Republici Hrvatskoj državljana država članica Europskog ekonomskog prostora i članova njihovih obitelji te članova obitelji hrvatskih državljana*), OG 126/2012, 81/2013, 38/2015, 85/2015, 132/2017.

years of age, and who must be and are actually supported by an EEA citizen, his spouse or extramarital partner; relatives by blood in the vertical line upwards, who must be and are actually supported by an EEA citizen, his spouse or extramarital partner; other members of the family for whom an individual assessment showed that in view of their material and social position in the country from which they arrived are dependent on an EEA citizen in terms of providing their basic needs, or are members of their household who are dependent on their personal care because of serious health reasons.[106]

54. In regard to the family member, it will be considered that he or she does not possess a valid travel document or identity document, in addition to reasons stipulated for an EEA citizen, if: there is no room in the document for stamping the input stamp, if a special rule specifies the stamping of the input stamp, or, if required, no visa has been entered in the travel document, or with the passport there is no residence card unless otherwise stipulated in the international treaty.[107]

55. A family member who is not an EEA citizen may enter Croatia for family reunification with an EEA citizen, if he or she holds a valid travel document which includes a visa, if a visa is required, or a valid passport and temporary residence card unless an international treaty provides otherwise. In addition to a travel document and visa, a family member will be granted entry provided that he or she is not barred by the prohibition of entry and stay and does not pose a threat to public policy, national security or public health. In the case that the family member does not hold a valid travel document or visa for entry, he or she will be given a chance to obtain such documents or to prove that he or she enjoys the right of freedom of movement and stay as a family member of EEA citizen in some other way. The family member who does not have a visa can be provided with a visa at the border crossing, provided that he or she is not considered a threat to public policy, national security or public health. In such cases, visas are issued free of charge, in a summary procedure.[108]

56. An EEA citizen who does not have a valid travel document or identity document can prove that he or she is an EEA citizen by submitting a public document from which it is possible to ascertain his identity and EEA citizenship. A family member who has no valid travel document or visa can prove to enjoy the right to freedom of movement and residence as a member of the family of EEA citizen by submitting a public document which is possible to ascertain his identity and the status of a member of the family of an EEA citizen. Also, another document may be accepted as proof if the circumstances undoubtedly indicate that the person enjoys

106. Article 162, Aliens Act.
107. Article 3, para. 2, Rulebook on determining the conditions for entry and residence in the Republic of Croatia of citizens of Member States of the European Economic Area and members of their families and members of the family of Croatian citizens.
108. Articles 166 and 167, Aliens Act.

the freedom of movement right, and refusal to enter Croatia would cause significant difficulties to that person, the person travelling with him or the other persons.[109]

57. An EEA citizen and a member of his family may be restricted the right to entry and residence if they pose a threat to public order, national security or public health. This restriction should not be based on economic grounds. When considering whether the conduct of a person can be assessed as a threat, the proportionality test should be conducted: if the threat should be a real, immediate and severe threat to the fundamental interests of society. A previous conviction for a criminal offence should not be considered a reason for this restriction.[110]

§2. Administrative Procedures and Documents

58. Persons who intend to cross or have already crossed the border need to present their valid travel documents, submit themselves to border control, and may not leave the border-crossing area until the border control has been completed. They have to inform the police officer of all circumstances relevant to the crossing of the border. They have to follow instructions or orders of the border police officer.[111]

59. Border control includes control of passengers, vehicles and objects possessed by the persons crossing the border, in the border-crossing area, outside the border-crossing area, in trains, aircraft and vessels. It can be carried out in the territory of another State, in accordance with international instruments.[112]

60. According to the Schengen Borders Code, all persons have to undergo a minimum check in order to establish their identities on the basis of the production or presentation of their travel documents. These minimum checks will be always applied for persons enjoying the right of free movement under EU law. However, police officers on some occasions may consult national and European databases in order to ensure that such persons do not represent a genuine, present and sufficiently serious threat to the internal security, public order, international relations of the Member States or a threat to the public health. In regards to the entry of TCNs, more thorough checks will be applied:

– verification of the conditions for entry and, where applicable, of documents authorising residence and the pursuit of professional activity;
– if the TCN holds a visa, verification of the identity of the holder of the visa and the authenticity of the visa, by consulting the Visa Information System (VIS).[113]

109. Article 3a, Rulebook on determining the conditions for entry and residence in the Republic of Croatia of citizens of the Member States of the European Economic Area and members of their families and members of the family of Croatian citizens.
110. Article 179a, Aliens Act.
111. Article 26, State Border Protection Act.
112. Articles 25 and 27, State Border Protection Act.
113. Article 8, Schengen Borders Code.

61. The police officer may also order the person to show the items in his or her possession and carry out their examination if there is a suspicion that a person has forbidden items or objects, or to establish the person's identity. The control of a vehicle includes a visual examination of the exterior and the interior of the vehicle and its entry into the data collections.[114] According to the judicial practice, 'such a legal solution is understandable given that persons crossing the borderline between the two countries agree to enforce enhanced control of border police officers, thus their privacy, due to the legitimate public interest of border control, is maintained in a reduced extent'.[115]

62. The border police are authorised to use technical means and official dogs to perform border control activities and to set up obstacles preventing the unlawful crossing of the border.[116] Technical means are aimed at prevention and detection of illegal crossing of the border, illegal migration and other illegal activities, and the protection of the inviolability of the border.[117] The border police may carry out recording, photographing, taking fingerprints, palm prints and other biometric data using the appropriate technical equipment when performing their duties. If personal data is recorded using a recording device, these records must be destroyed within one year unless they are required to prosecute offenders or offences.[118]

63. A TCN who intends to cross or has already crossed the border can be arrested, apprehended and detained for up to twenty-four hours, and for additional forty-eight hours (in total seventy-two hours), if it is necessary to issue a decision on refusal of entry, expulsion decision or forced return, and if there is a danger of escape. Upon arrest, a TCN should be immediately notified of the reasons for arrest, in order to appoint a proxy representative who will inform the member of the family or another person, and who can request that diplomatic mission or consular post of the state of the citizenship be notified of the arrest unless specified otherwise by the international agreement. In case of a minor, the competent body of social welfare and the diplomatic mission or consular post of the state of citizenship should immediately be notified of the arrangement of an unaccompanied minor who is an alien. A TCN should be released as soon as the grounds for arrest and detention cease to exist, and at the latest by the end of the time limit of seventy-two hours, except where actions are being taken to enforce removal (forced return) or leaving the border crossing to the third country or if the decision on accommodation in the reception centre for aliens was issued.[119]

---

114. Article 27, paras 3–4, State Border Protection Act.
115. Supreme Court of the Republic of Croatia, I Kž 968/2011-4 of 15 Dec. 2011. Cited in Frane Staničić, Police Administrative Law (Policijsko upravno pravo) (Zagreb: Narodne novine, 2015), p. 137.
116. Article 7, State Border Protection Act.
117. Article 19, Ordinance on Performing State Border Control (*Pravilnik o obavljanju poslova nadzora državne granice*), OG 30/2014, 43/2014, 72/2017.
118. Article 39, paras 1 and 3, State Border Protection Act.
119. Article 130, Aliens Act.

64. Border control of aliens is also carried out when aliens leave the country. According to the Schengen Borders Code, TCNs will be subject to thorough checks that comprise of:

- verification that the TCN has a document valid for crossing the border;
- verification of the travel document for signs of falsification or counterfeiting;
- whenever possible, verification that the TCN is not considered to be a threat to public policy, internal security or the international relations of any of the Member States.

Also, thorough checks on exit may also comprise of:

- verification that the person has a valid visa, if required;
- verification that the person did not exceed the maximum duration of authorised stay in the territory of the Member States;
- checking the alerts on persons and objects included in the SIS and reports in national data files.[120]

120. Article 8, Schengen Borders Code.

Chapter 3. Refusal of Entry

65. If aliens have a valid travel document, a visa (if needed) or a residence permit, it does not automatically mean that he or she will be allowed to enter Croatia. According to the Schengen Borders Code, even if an alien fulfils these conditions, the entry to Croatia will be refused if he or she is a person for whom an alert has been issued in the SIS for the purposes of refusing entry, or he or she is considered to be a threat to public policy, internal security, public health or the international relations.[121] The entry can also be refused if an alien cannot justify the purpose and conditions of the intended stay and does not have sufficient means of subsistence. If the alien manages to enter the country against these conditions, his or her entry will be considered unlawful.

66. The reasons for refusal of entry to Croatia are further elaborated in the Aliens Act and implementing legislation. It is considered that the alien has not justified the purpose and the conditions of intended entry and stay if:

- from the invitation letter, it is not possible to establish the identity of the alien or a person who invited him or her;
- facts are indicating the unreliability of the person who invited the alien or the issuer of the guarantee letter;
- during border control the alien does not want to explain the reasons for his arrival, or change his or her statements;
- the alien has no justified reason for entry;
- it is not possible to check data;
- the alien failed to pay a fine, a tax or other financial obligation towards Croatia; the alien did not execute an individual decision of the state body, at the request of the state body;
- he or she is in transit and does not have a travel ticket to the destination country or does not have a differently organised transport, visa or residence permit in the country to which he or she travels.[122]

The alien can prove that he or she has the means to support and return if they have convertible cash, non-cash payment instruments (travel checks, cheque books, credit cards, etc.), voucher or certificate of paid tourist arrangement, other funds from which funds can be secured (immovable property in Croatia, funds from foreign direct investment), travel health insurance, possession of a means of transport, or return travelling ticket. However, aliens who have valid approval for temporary or permanent residence in Croatia, asylees and aliens granted temporary or subsidiary protection in Croatia, do not have to prove possession of means to support and return.[123]

An alien is considered to be a threat to public order if an arrest warrant has been issued for him or her; has violated the legislation, or stems from his statement or

121. Article 6, Schengen Borders Code.
122. Article 6, Ordinance on Treatment of Third-Country Nationals.
123. Article 8, Ordinance on Treatment of Third-Country Nationals.

conduct or there are information that he or she may violate the regulation; has a ban on entry and stay, or is covered by international measures of entry restrictions that are binding on Croatia. However, aliens who have valid approval for temporary or permanent residence in Croatia cannot be refused entry for those reasons.[124]

The danger to public health is any contagious disease with epidemic potential which, following the Croatian legislation and relevant World Health Organization documents, requires the taking of specific anti-epidemic measures and activities to prevent and combat it among the population.[125]

67. An alien who does not meet the entry requirements will be refused to entry Croatia and the border police officer will issue a decision on refusal of entry. Refusal of entry will be entered in the alien's travel document, and visa, if entered in the travel document, will be revoked.[126] A decision stating the reasons for the ban on entry will be issued in a standardised form. The decision is made without the hearing of a TCN unless he or she is an unaccompanied minor. If the departure of an alien from the border crossing to a third country is not possible even after eight days from the day of arrival to the border crossing, he or she can be detained in the centre for aliens.[127]

68. The legality of procedure on deciding about the entry to Croatia without hearing the alien is questionable, especially in terms of the Act on General Administrative Procedure. If an alien has filed an appeal to the decision on refusal of entry and even initiated an administrative dispute, he or she will not be given the opportunity to explain the reasons for refusing his entry into Croatia, because there is no possibility to approach the hearing. This practice prevents the alien from adequately protecting his rights, which is contrary to the Croatian Constitution.[128]

69. According to the MoI, in 2017, the entry to Croatia has been refused in 10,602 cases: 4,328 at the border with Bosnia; 2,698 at the border with Serbia; 1,862 at the border with Monte Negro; 1,159 at the border with Slovenia; and 21 at the border with Hungary. In terms of the citizenship of aliens, a majority were citizens of the countries in the region: 3,390 Bosnians; 2,155 Albanians; 1,035 Serbs and 497 Kosovars.[129]

124. Article 10, Ordinance on Treatment of Third-Country Nationals.
125. Article 2, para. 1, Aliens Act.
126. Article 12, Ordinance on Treatment of Third-Country Nationals.
127. Article 38, Aliens Act.
128. Frane Staničić, *supra*, p. 158.
129. Ministry of Interior, Survey of basic safety indicators for year 2017, January 2018. Available at: https://mup.hr/public/documents/Statistika/Statisti%C4%8Dki%20pregled%20temeljnih%20sigurnosnih%20pokazatelja%20i%20rezultata%20rada%20u%202017.%20godini.pdf (accessed 15 Feb. 2018).

Part II. Right of Residence: General Provisions

Chapter 1. Short Stay

70. Short stay is considered to be a stay for a maximum of three months in any 180-day period. The conditions for a short stay depend on whether an alien is an EEA citizen or a TCN, and whether the TCN needs a visa for entry and stay in Croatia. The alien who has entered Croatia legally, and who meets the general preconditions for entry and short term residence, may freely stay in the country following the declared purposes of stay.

§1. Conditions for Short Stay

I. Short Stay of EEA Citizens and Their Family Members

71. EEA citizens have the right to reside in Croatia up to three months from the date of entry if they hold a valid travel document or identity card,[130] so it means without a residence permit. If the EEA citizen intends to stay for more than three months, he or she must, within eight days of the expiration of three months of his or her stay, apply for a temporary stay.[131] A family member who is not an EEA citizen is entitled to stay in Croatia for a period of up to three months from the date of entry, provided that he or she holds a valid travel document.[132]

II. Short Stay of TCNs with a Permanent Residence Permit in Another EEA Member State and Their Family Members

72. A TCN with approved permanent residence in another EEA Member State can stay in Croatia for a period of up to three months of the date of entry or until the expiration of the term of validity of the visa or residence card which was issued by such other EEA Member State, provided that the term of validity of the visa or residence card is shorter than three months. If a TCN intends to stay in Croatia for

130. Article 155, Aliens Act.
131. Article 157, Aliens Act.
132. Article 168, Aliens Act.

a period longer than three months, he or she has to submit an application for the approval of temporary residence, before the expiration of the term of validity of the visa or residence card which was issued by another Member State. A TCN can stay in Croatia based on a certificate of the submission of an application for temporary residence until the decision on his application becomes enforceable.[133]

III. Short Stay of TCNs and Visas

73. According to the Aliens Act, a short stay is the stay of a TCN as defined in Article 6 of the Schengen Borders Code, which stipulates the entry conditions for TCNs for intended stays on the territory of the Member State.[134]

74. A legal or natural person who provides accommodation to a TCN on short-term stay has to register TCN's stay within one day from the arrival of a TCN on accommodation. If the service provider at the time of arrival of an alien for accommodation is not in Croatia or if the registration of accommodation cannot be performed for any other reason, a TCN has to register his or her accommodation within two days from entry into Croatia or change of accommodation.[135]

75. Besides the valid travel document, a visa is required for entry or short-term stay for nationals of the country included in the list of countries whose nationals require a visa for entry. Short-term visas can also be issued to seasonal workers who are required to have a visa to enter Croatia.[136] The list of countries whose nationals need a visa to enter Croatia is defined by the Government's regulation, in accordance with EU acquis.[137] Visa can be issued for the stay in Croatia for three months, for transit through the Croatian territory or for transit through the international transit area of an airport.[138] It has to be acquired before entering the country. There are two types of visas: airport transit visa (Visa A) and short-term visa (Visa C). Aliens with a visa can still be refused entry permission if any of the reasons for refusal to grant entry permission exist.

76. Generally, TCNs who make a short stop at an airport in Croatia and do not leave the airport premises or even the plane, do not need visa A. However, the Government of the RoC may prescribe that the nationals of certain states and the holders of travel documents issued by such states do require an airport transit visa. In that case, the airport transit visa will be issued for one, two or multiple passes through the international transit area of an airport. A multiple airport transit visa is issued for a period of up to six months.[139]

---

133. Article 184, Aliens Act.
134. Article 6, Schengen Borders Code.
135. Article 147, Aliens Act.
136. Article 75a, para. 2, Aliens Act.
137. Regulation on the Visa Regime (*Uredba o viznom sustavu*), OG 55/2015.
138. Article 11, Aliens Act.
139. Article 13, Aliens Act.

77. Short-term visas are issued for transit through or for the stay in Croatia for three months, with a period of validity for up to five years. In the case of transit, the length of authorised stay has to correspond to the time necessary for the transit. Short-term visas can be issued for one, two or multiple entries. In addition, short-term visas for multiple entries can be issued with a period of validity between six months and five years, if the alien proves the need or justifies the intention to travel frequently and/or regularly, in particular as the result of business or family reasons, and his integrity and reliability (such as the lawful use of previous visas, his economic situation in the country of origin and a genuine intention to leave Croatia before the expiration of the visa). For both types of visas, the term of validity will include an additional fifteen days, except if there are reasons of public order which prevents it.[140] It means that a TCN will not be considered to reside in Croatia illegally within fifteen days after the expiration of the visa.

78. In order to be issued a short-term visa for multiple entries with a validity period between six months to one year, a TCN has to prove a lawful use of at least two visas issued by Croatian diplomatic mission or consular office or by the Schengen Member State in the last twenty-four months before the application for a visa. Under similar conditions, short-term visas for multiple entries valid for a period of up to two years can be issued, provided that the previous visas had a validity period of one year, and for a period of three to five years, if the previous visas were issued with a validity of two years.[141]

79. A TCN applying for a short-term visa has to fulfil the following criteria: the justified purpose of stay in Croatia, a secured accommodation, a means of subsistence, valid health insurance, and a means of travel and the intention of return to the country from which he or she comes or into a third country. Documentation (not older than six months) which proves those conditions has to be attached to the application for a short-stay visa.[142] In the case that the alien is a well-known and respected person, or has been proven as a credible person who acts in good faith, some of the documents can be omitted.

80. The person who invites a TCN to a personal or a business visit (the guarantor) has to provide the TCN with the guarantee letter, which proves that the guarantor can provide the TCN with accommodation, or means of subsistence for the stay in Croatia and for the return to the home country or for travel to another country, or accommodation and means of subsistence. The guarantee can be natural (a Croatian citizen or an alien who has been granted temporary or permanent residence in Croatia and who has income or funds in Croatia) or a legal person registered in Croatia. The guarantor must officially certify the letter of guarantee.[143] The invitation letter has to be submitted with the visa application of the TCN who is coming to Croatia at the invitation of the Croatian state body, or to participate in an

140. Article 14, Aliens Act.
141. Article 28b, Ordinance on Visas (*Pravilnik o vizama*), OG 7/2013, 5/2018.
142. Articles 15 and 20, Ordinance on Visas.
143. Appendix 5, Ordinance on Visas.

international conference of public interest, or to participate in a manifestation held under the patronage of the Croatian Parliament, the President or the Government of the RoC.[144]

81. A TCN can prove that he or she has secured accommodation by the following documentation: a guarantee or invitation letter; booking a hotel or similar accommodation; a reservation or confirmation of reservation of accommodation at the private landlord with a copy of the decision of the competent office on the approval for the provision of accommodation services; a proof of lease or ownership of real estate in Croatia; a proof of ownership or chartering of a boat, yacht, or confirmation of a paid charter, etc.; with confirmation of booking or paid anchorage.[145]

82. The means of subsistence can be proved by the following documentation: a statement of the alien's regular income or of the person who is legally required to support him or her; a certified statement by which some legal or natural person (sponsor) undertakes to take over subsistence costs, with appropriate proof of solvency; a guarantee letter, with the proof of the solvency of the guarantor; cash in domestic or foreign convertible currency, means of non-cash payment (travel checks, credit cards, etc.), provided that it is not short-term payments of more substantial amounts of money with a view to false presentation of the actual financial condition (credibility).[146] According to the Government's Regulation, the amount of subsistence per day is equivalent to EUR 70. If a TCN has a guarantee letter, proof of a paid tourist arrangement or similar document, he or she must present proof of possession of the funds in the equivalent of EUR 30 per day of residence in Croatia. The TCN can be exempted from the obligation to prove the means of subsistence if the guarantor fully assumes all costs relating to his or her stay and departure from Croatia.[147]

83. A travel medical insurance has to cover any expenses which might arise during TCN's stay in Croatia, such as urgent medical attention and/or emergency hospital treatment, repatriation for medical reasons, or transport in case of death, for the full duration of the visa's validity.[148] The minimum contracted amount to be secured must be the equivalent of EUR 30,000. The insurance is to be taken out by the alien in the country of the alien's residence. If this is not possible, it is to be taken out in any other country where this is possible. Additionally, travel health insurance can be provided by a guarantor on behalf of the TCN.[149] Travel medical insurance is not needed for the holders of diplomatic passports, seafarers and other professional groups, who are already covered by travel medical insurance as a result of their professional activities.[150]

144. Article 18, Ordinance on Visas.
145. Appendix 3, Ordinance on Visas.
146. *Ibid.*
147. Article 8, Regulation on the Visa Regime.
148. Article 19, para. 1, Aliens Act.
149. Article 19, Ordinance on Visas.
150. Article 19, para. 3, Aliens Act.

§2. Administrative Procedures and Documents for Short Stay

I. Issuing of a Visa

A. Application for a Visa and Decisions-Making

84. Visas are issued by the diplomatic mission or consular office of the RoC and may also be issued by a diplomatic mission or consular office of another country with which Croatia concluded an agreement on representation in the issuing of visas. In some cases, the visa can be issued by the MoI. Before a visa is issued, the diplomatic mission or consular post in a majority of cases should request prior approval of the MFEA. Prior to approving, the MFEA has to, in the cases provided for by the implementing regulations, request the opinions of the MoI and the Security and Intelligence Agency. The opinions are binding.[151] The main criteria for deciding on a visa application are security aspects, migration policy and the prevention of illegal migration.[152] When deciding about the visa application, the diplomatic mission or consular office verifies whether the conditions for entry to Croatia are met, at the time of application for a visa.

85. Short-term visas can be issued at a border crossing in several cases: for the stay of up to fifteen days, for the transit, and to a seafarer for the transit. The visa will be issued only if a TCN was not in the position to apply for the issuing of a visa in a diplomatic mission or consular post, and if he or she enclosed, where necessary, documents proving unforeseen and unpostponable reasons for entry. A TCN can be issued a visa at the border under the following conditions: he or she holds a valid travel document or another document authorising the crossing of the state border; can justify the purpose and has sufficient resources to maintain himself during his stay in Croatia and for returning to the country from which he or she came or for travelling to a third country; can safely return to the country of origin or temporary residence or transit; prohibition of entry and stay was not issued, and international measures for restricted entry do not cover he or she; does not pose a threat to public order, national security or public health.[153]

86. A TCN has to apply for a visa at the diplomatic mission or consular office of the RoC in the country of nationality or habitual residence (except in those cases when a short-term visa can be issued at the border). In case there is no Croatian diplomatic mission or consular office in that country, the TCN can apply for a visa in the diplomatic mission or consular office in the nearest country or at the diplomatic mission or consular office of another country with which Croatia concluded an agreement on representation in the issuing of visas. In some specific situations, TCN

151. Article 16, Aliens Act.
152. Article 27, Ordinance on Visas.
153. Articles 25–27, Aliens Act.

can apply for a visa in the diplomatic mission or consular office in another country in which he or she is currently located, for example, for humanitarian reasons or force majeure.[154]

87. A TCN has to submit a visa application personally. In case justified reasons exist, the TCN does not have to apply for a visa personally, but must personally come to the diplomatic mission or consular office when requested. In the case that there are large distances and/or inadequate traffic connections in specific regions or geographical areas that could cause TCN unnecessary efforts, he or she can personally come to the consular office headed by the Honorary Consul, for the identity verification by inspecting the public documents.[155]

88. When applying for a visa, in an application a TCN needs to state the reasons for staying in the country, submit a valid passport to which the visa can be attached, pay the administrative fee and enclose documentation proving the purpose and conditions of the visit. The conditions that have to be fulfilled in order to submit the request for a visa are the following:

- it has to be submitted less than three months before the intended trip;
- it has to be submitted on the special form regulated by the Aliens Act;
- it has to include a valid travel document;
- it has to include a photograph;
- biometric identifiers have to be collected;
- paid administrative fee.[156]

89. When the TCN applies for a short-term visa for the first time, he or she has to come in person to the diplomatic mission or consular office, so that the biometric identifiers can be collected. The biometric identifiers include a photograph, scanned or taken at the time of application and fingerprints of all fingers, and those are entered in the Croatian VIS. Exempted from giving fingerprints are children under the age of 12; persons for whom fingerprinting is physically impossible; heads of state and members of a national government with accompanying spouses, and the members of their official delegation when they are invited by the Government of the RoC or by international organisations for an official purpose; rulers and other high-ranking members of the royal family if the Government or an international organisation invited them for an official visit.[157]

90. The travel document in which the visa will be affixed must be valid for at least three months after the intended date of departure from Croatia or, in case of multiple visits, after the last intended date of departure, must include at least two empty pages, and must be issued in the preceding ten years. However, in a justified

154. Articles 2, 4 and 5, Ordinance on Visas.
155. Article 7, Ordinance on Visas.
156. Article 22, Aliens Act.
157. Article 21, Aliens Act.

situation that requires urgency, a visa can be affixed in a travel document for the period of validity which is shorter than three months.[158]

91. The deadline for a decision about visa application is fifteen days from the date of the submission of the application. That deadline may be extended up to thirty days if the application needs to be further examined or up to sixty days if additional documentation is required. The visa is entered in a valid travel document in the form of a sticker. The information contained in a visa are: the type of visa, the period of its validity, the number of entries as allowed by the visa, the duration of stay, the number of the travel document, the date and place of issuing the visa, the purpose of the visit, and the personal data and a photo of a person who has been issued a visa.[159]

92. The visa can be extended due to force majeure or humanitarian reasons (such as the sudden serious illness, unforeseen event for family members living in Croatia, and organ donation) or serious personal reasons (if a family member who has undergone surgery is not allowed to leave the hospital, or if a TCN came for business negotiations with the Croatian company),[160] which prevent a TCN to leave Croatia before the expiration of the visa validity period or the duration of stay approved by the visa. Extended visas will be issued by the police administration or police station, with the prior approval of the MoI who has to receive the binding opinions of the MFEA and the SIA. Until the decision is made, the TCN can stay in the RoC. In the case of a negative decision about the visa extension, a TCN is entitled to appeal, but an appeal will not postpone enforcement of the negative decision.[161] The total length of stay for a visa extension cannot exceed 90 days in a period of 180 days.[162]

B. Refusal of a Visa Application

93. The visa will be refused to a TCN who:

- presents a false or counterfeit travel document, or documents belonging to another person;
- does not provide justification for the purpose and conditions of the intended stay;
- does not have sufficient means of subsistence, both for the duration of the intended stay and for the return to his country of origin or stay, or for the transit to a third country into which he is certain to be admitted, or is not in a position to acquire such means lawfully;
- has already stayed for three months during the current six-month period in Croatia on the basis of an issued visa;

158. Article 24, Aliens Act.
159. Appendix 7, Ordinance on Visas.
160. Article 35, Ordinance on Visas.
161. Article 30, Aliens Act.
162. Reasons according to Art. 35 of Ordinance on Visas.

– was issued the prohibition of entry and stay or is covered by international measures for restricted entry;
– poses a threat to public order, national security or public health;
– does not provide proof of holding adequate and valid travel medical insurance, where applicable;
– if there are reasonable doubts as to the authenticity of the supporting documents or the veracity of their contents, the reliability of the statements made by the TCN or his intention to leave Croatia before the expiry of the visa.[163]

C. *Annulment and Revocation of a Visa*

94. A visa will be annulled when it becomes evident that the conditions for issuing it were not met at the time when it was issued or if there are serious grounds for believing that the visa was fraudulently obtained. A diplomatic mission or consular office will annul it or, if a TCN is already in Croatia, a police administration or police station. A visa can be revoked by a diplomatic mission or consular office or by a police administration or police station, where it becomes evident that the conditions for issuing it are no longer met. A TCN to whom a visa is issued can also request the revocation of a visa.[164]

§3. Legal Position in the Event of Short Stay

95. The Aliens Act does not explicitly regulate legal position, and the rights and obligations of TCNs granted the short-term stay in Croatia. TCNs have to respect the purpose for which a visa has been issued, which means that the visa does not give the TCN the right to work and be employed in Croatia. Since a visa is not a residence permit, it means that the period of short-time stay is not in the period of legal residence required for obtaining a permanent residence permit or citizenship. The TCN with a valid visa has the right to move freely in Croatia for the time of the validity of the visa. If the TCN does not need a visa for entry and residence in Croatia, he or she can move freely and freely choose his or her place of residence for up to ninety days. During this time, they are also protected from expulsion as they are considered to be legally present in the country.

96. EEA citizens and members of their families may work and provide services in Croatia without a residence and work permit or a work registration certificate.[165]

97. According to the Croatian Constitution, all persons in the RoC, including aliens, enjoy rights and freedoms, regardless of race, colour, gender, language, religion, political or other conviction, national or social origin, property, birth, education, social status or other characteristics. All persons shall be equal before the

163. Article 31, Aliens Act.
164. Article 33, Aliens Act.
165. Article 153, para 2, Aliens Act.

law.[166] There are, however, certain exceptions as to the reach of human rights protection, such as the right to vote, or to participate in the conduct of public affairs and to have access to public services, which are reserved only for Croatian citizens.

§4. Position of Family Members

98. The right to entry is granted to a family member of an EEA under the same conditions as the right to entry enjoyed by an EEA citizen in general. Family members of EEA citizens have the right to reside in Croatia up to three months from the date of entry if they hold a valid travel document or identity card.[167] A family member who is not an EEA citizen is entitled to stay in Croatia for a period of up to three months of the date of entry, provided that he or she holds a valid travel document.[168]

99. Family members of TCN with approved permanent stay in another EEA Member State can stay in Croatia for a period of up to three months of the date of entry or until the expiration of the term of validity of the visa or residence card which was issued by other EEA Member State, provided that the term of validity of the visa or residence card is shorter than three months.[169]

100. The reasons to refuse entry permission to a family member of an EEA citizen are the same as the reasons to refuse entry to EEA citizens (lack of valid travel document, visa or residence permit, a prohibition of entry, if he or she is considered to be a threat to public order, internal security, public health or the international relations, or cannot justify the purpose and conditions of the intended stay and does not has sufficient means of subsistence).

§5. Cancellation of Short-Term Stay

101. Short-term stay will be cancelled if an alien:

- does not hold a valid travel document or another document used for crossing the state border;
- does not justify the purpose and conditions for entry and stay;
- does not have funds to support himself or herself during a stay in Croatia and for returning to the state from which he came or for travelling to a third country, and for the mentioned expenditures he also has no guarantees stipulated by the Aliens Act;
- does not settle mature financial obligations in Croatia;

166. Article 14, Constitution of the RoC.
167. Article 155, Aliens Act.
168. Article 168, Aliens Act.
169. Article 184, Aliens Act.

– there is a well-founded reason to believe that his or her stay was not used for the intended purpose.

A decision on the cancellation of short-term stay will be issued by the MoI, throughout the relevant police station or police administration. The decision will contain a prohibition of entry and stay in Croatia for the duration of one to three months. Against the decision, an alien can initiate an administrative dispute.[170]

170. Article 46, Aliens Act.

Chapter 2. Temporary Residence

§1. Conditions for Temporary Residence

I. General Conditions

102. According to the Aliens Act, a temporary residence is the stay of a TCN which is granted for a particular purpose and for a specified period, which is up to one year. The purposes for which temporary residence can be granted are family reunification and life partnership, exchange of students (secondary education), study, scientific research, humanitarian grounds, work, other justified reasons and autonomous residence. In this chapter, we will focus on the temporary stay of TCNs in general, while arrangements for some specific categories of aliens (such as students, researchers, asylum seekers, economic and humanitarian migrants, and EEA citizens) will be analysed in the next part of the book.

103. In order to be granted a temporary residence, TCNs have to meet different conditions. *First,* a TCN has to prove the purpose of temporary stay. The conditions that have to be met concerning each purpose of the temporary residence will be discussed in the next chapter. *Second,* TCNs have to provide a valid travel document, with validity at least three months longer than the period for which the temporary residence permit is issued. However, if a TCN who does not have a valid travel document submits an application for temporary residence in Croatia, the permit will be granted.[171] *Third,* a TCN has to have sufficient means of subsistence for the duration of his or her residence in the country, or his or her subsistence has to be provided in some other way. According to the Government's Regulation, a TCN must have a monthly means of subsistence which is calculated on the basis of a guaranteed minimum allowance amount under the social security legislation. The basis for calculation of the guaranteed minimum allowance amount currently is set up at HRK 800 (app. EUR 109). A TCN who is single has to prove that he or she has a monthly means of subsistence in the amount of three bases for calculation of the guaranteed minimum allowance, or HRK 2,400 (app. EUR 320). In the case of the families, the basis for calculation of the guaranteed minimum allowance will be increased – for families of two for 1.25 basis, and for each additional family member, the amount will be increased for an additional one basis.[172] *Fourth,* a TCN has to have health insurance. If a TCN is a citizen of the State which has concluded a bilateral agreement on social security with Croatia or has health insurance in an EEA Member State, the proof of health insurance can be the confirmation of the health insurance provider. If a TCN is a citizen of the State which has not yet concluded a bilateral agreement on social security, he or she has to enclose proof of private health insurance or travel insurance to the application for temporary residence,

---

171. Article 52, paras 2 and 3, Aliens Act.

172. Article 2, Regulation on the manner of calculating and the amount of funds to support third-country nationals in the Republic of Croatia (*Uredba o načinu izračuna i visini sredstava za uzdržavanje državljanina treće zemlje u Republici Hrvatskoj*), OG 35/2018.

and after arrival to Croatia has to take out health insurance in Croatia.[173] A TCN who has applied for a temporary residence permit for work under a concluded employment contract with the employer in Croatia is not obliged to submit proof of health insurance.[174] *Fifth* condition is that a TCN is not prohibited entry and stay in Croatia, and *sixth* that he or she is not considered to be a threat to public order, national security or public health.

II. Specific Conditions

104. Apart from family reunification and life partnership, studying, research, work and humanitarian grounds, a TCN can be also granted temporary residence for other purposes.[175] A temporary residence permit may also be issued to persons granted international protection, TCNs who have long-term resident status in another EEA Member State and their family members, and the TCN's children born in the RoC. In addition to general conditions, the applicant for temporary residence also needs to meet conditions which depend on the declared purpose of temporary residence. A TCN can only reside in Croatia in accordance with the purpose the permit has been issued for.

105. A TCN can be granted a temporary residence for *family reunification* if he or she is a member of the immediate family of a Croatian national, the TCN with approved permanent or temporary residence or the TCN granted international protection. A temporary residence will be granted to a member of the immediate family of a TCN with a valid stay and work permit approved for a year based on the annual quota for the employment of aliens, only if that a TCN had temporary stay in Croatia granted for at least two years.[176] The same conditions apply to the temporary residence for the life partnership to a TCN who is in a life partnership or informal partnership with a Croatian national, a TCN who has been granted permanent or temporary residence or international or temporary protection.[177] Temporary residence permits for family reunification are issued for a period of up to one year or until the expiration of the temporary residence permit of the TCN with whom family reunification is sought. If a family member had an uninterrupted temporary residence permit for the purpose of family reunification in the duration of at least two years, he or she can be granted a temporary stay for the same purpose with the term of validity of up to two years or until the expiration of the validity of the temporary stay permit of the TCN with whom family reunification is sought.[178] More information will be provided in this chapter, §4 Position of Family Members.

---

173. Article 5, Ordinance on the Status and Work of Third Countries Nationals in the Republic of Croatia (*Pravilnik o statusu i radu stranaca u Republici Hrvatskoj*), OG 52/2012, 81/2013, 38/2015, 100/2017, 61/2018, 116/2018.
174. Article 54, para. 2, Aliens Act.
175. Article 47, paras 1 and 4, Aliens Act.
176. Article 55, Aliens Act.
177. Article 56b, Aliens Act.
178. Article 59, Aliens Act.

106. Temporary residence for the *study* will be granted to a TCN who studies at a Croatian higher education institution.[179] The TCN can be granted temporary residence for the *secondary education* provided that he or she:

- is not over 18 years of age if he or she is enrolling in the last year of education;
- is enrolled in a secondary school;
- participates in a recognised, national or regional pupil exchange programme approved by the Ministry for Education and Science or in an educational project run by an educational institution;
- encloses the consent of his parent or legal guardian for his planned stay for the secondary education in Croatia;
- encloses proof that the organisation carrying out the pupil exchange programme is to be responsible for him during his stay in Croatia, especially in terms of funds for education;
- during stay, he or she will be accommodated in the family, in an accommodation space within the educational establishment or in another selected area which is in accordance with the rules of the pupil exchange programme or educational project in which he or she participates.[180]

107. Temporary residence for the *scientific research* will be granted to a TCN who concluded a hosting contract.[181] Temporary stay can be granted to a researcher and a TCN with higher education for the employment or founding of a company or registration of trades, if he or she can provide proof of completion of research activities in Croatia, or on the acquired qualification.[182]

108. Several categories of TCNs can be granted temporary residence under *humanitarian grounds*: victims of trafficking who participate in an assistance and protection programme, abandoned minors or minors who are a victim of organised crime or who remained without parental protection, guardianship or escort for some other reasons, a TCN who had the status of refugee for at least ten years or who was included in a reconstruction, return or housing care programme for refugees from Croatia, or TCNs who cooperate with the competent bodies and their participation is crucial in the criminal proceedings conducted against the employer who employed them illegally. A humanitarian temporary residence can also be granted for other serious justified humanitarian grounds.[183] In the case of regulating temporary residence under humanitarian grounds more lenient general conditions will be applied.

109. The temporary residence can be granted for the purpose of working in Croatia, either within the annual quota or outside the annual quota. In both cases, a TCN will be issued a residence and work permit. The residence and work permits

179. Article 63, Aliens Act.
180. Article 62, Aliens Act.
181. Article 64, para. 1, Aliens Act.
182. Article 64b, para. 1, Aliens Act.
183. Article 65, Aliens Act.

are issued for the period necessary to perform the job or for the term of the employment contract or some other relevant contract, for up to one year. For some categories of TCNs, the permit can be issued with the term of validity for up to two years, unless a shorter validity period has been requested for the residence and work permit.[184] The annual quota for the employment of aliens is set by the Government of RoC, in accordance with the situation in the labour market. In order to be granted residence and work permit within the annual quota, a TCN has to provide: an employment contract or a written certificate of the conclusion of an employment contract or other relevant proof of employment, proof of the academic qualifications acquired and the skills, proof of the registration of a company, branch office, representative office, trade, association or institution in Croatia.[185] Similar conditions are set up for granting residence and work permit outside the annual quota, with the addition of an explanation of justification of employment of a TCN which contains information on the professional knowledge, qualifications and work experience, and the explanation why the working place cannot be filled by Croatian workers.[186] Other categories of aliens can also be granted residence and work permit. S*easonal workers* can work on residence and work permit for seasonal work up to ninety days or up to six months.[187] *TCNs in the framework of an intra-corporate transfer* (temporary secondment from the company located in the third country, to which the TCN is bound by a work contract, to a Croatian entity belonging to the same group of undertakings) can work on residence and work permit up to three years (managers and specialist) or up to a year (graduate trainee).[188] A temporary residence permit for the work can be granted to a *worker posted* for a limited period to work in Croatia by a foreign employer in the framework of the transnational provision of services, for a maximum period of one year.[189] TCNs who are *high-skilled workers* can reside in Croatia on the basis of the EU Blue Card which is at the same time regarded as approval for residence and work in Croatia. This temporary residence permit will be issued for up to two years. If the validity of the employment contract is shorter than two years, the permit is issued for a period which is three months longer than the validity of the employment contract, with a maximum of two years. Specific conditions for issuing permits are: higher education and an employment contract for the performance of a high-skilled job concluded for at least one year with a guaranteed salary of at least 1.5 times the average gross salary in RoC.[190] Temporary residence and work permit also be issued to a *TCN holding an EU Blue Card* who has resided in another EEA Member State for the last eighteen months on the basis of a Blue Card, provided that he or she meets the conditions for a residence of high-skilled workers. The application for a residence permit shall be submitted not later than one month after the date of entry into Croatia.[191]

184. Article 80, paras 2 and 3, Aliens Act.
185. Article 75, Aliens Act.
186. Article 77, para. 1, Aliens Act.
187. Article 75a, Aliens Act.
188. Article 79a, Aliens Act.
189. Articles 86 and 87, Aliens Act.
190. Article 191, Aliens Act.
191. Article 201, Aliens Act.

110. A *TCN's child born in the RoC* may be granted temporary residence for the period granted for temporary residence to one of his parents or the guardian, or up to one year if one of the parents or the guardian is an alien with permanent residence. The temporary residence application for the child has to be submitted before the child turns three months of age.[192]

111. A temporary residence can be granted for other purposes than listed above, but the Aliens Act does not give examples of those other reasons.

III. TCNs with a Permanent Residence Permit in Another EEA Member State

112. A TCN holding a permanent residence permit in another EEA Member State will be granted temporary residence in Croatia if he or she holds a valid travel document, sufficient means of subsistence for supporting himself and for supporting his family members and health insurance, provided that he or she meets other criteria for the approval of temporary residence in view of the purpose of residence.[193] When approving a temporary residence in Croatia to a TCN holding a permanent residence permit in another EEA Member State, the police administration or police station has to notify the competent body of that EEA Member State about the granted temporary residence permit.[194]

§2. Administrative Procedures and Documents for Temporary Residence

I. Application for a Temporary Residence Permit and Decision-Making

113. The main body for deciding on a temporary residence application is the MoI through the police administration or police station based on the place of temporary residence or intended stay of an alien.[195] In principle, a residence permit is issued upon request of an alien, while an application for the issuing of a stay and work permit may be submitted by the employer as well.[196]

114. TCNs who are not nationals of the countries whose nationals require a visa for entry to Croatia can submit temporary residence applications to the police administration or police station based on the place of their intended stay, the registered office (seat) of the employer or the place of work of the TCN. TCNs who

192. Article 51, Aliens Act.
193. Article 185, Aliens Act.
194. Article 189, para. 1, Aliens Act.
195. Article 50, Aliens Act.
196. Article 49, Aliens Act.

needs a visa for entry to Croatia have to submit an application for temporary residence in the diplomatic mission or consular office of the RoC in the country of origin or habitual residence, who will forward the application to the competent police administration or police station in the RoC. However, there are several exceptions:

- a TCNs who intends to study at Croatian university as a full-time student at undergraduate, graduate and postgraduate level;
- researchers;
- several categories of TCNs who can be granted a residence and work permit (TCNs working on the youth mobility programmes being carried out in cooperation with other states, scientific researchers and TCNs employed for scientific, scientific-teaching or other research workplaces in the scientific institution, university professors – native speakers of foreign languages, foreign-language instructors and other lecturers teaching at Croatian universities or registered foreign language schools, and TCNs working pursuant to an international treaty);
- members of the immediate family of previously mentioned groups;
- a member of the immediate family of a Croatian citizen;
- a TCN who is in a life partnership or informal partnership with the Croatian citizen.

Those categories can submit an application for the approval of the temporary residence at a police administration or police station in Croatia. If TCNs who can apply for residence permit while already staying at the territory of the RoC submit a temporary residence application before the expiration of short-term stay, they can stay in Croatia until the decision becomes enforceable.[197]

115. Together with the application for a temporary residence permit, a TCN has to submit the following documents: proof of means of subsistence, proof of health insurance, a copy of the valid travel document verified by the official, evidence justifying the purpose of stay, and a colour photo.

116. The procedure for the issuing of a residence and work permit is somewhat different than the one explained above (about the access to the labour market *see* more in Part VII).

117. A TCN with the temporary residence has to register at the police station or police administration his or her temporary residence and address at which he is staying and any change of his temporary residence and address at which he is staying within three days of entry in the RoC or of the day of changing his temporary residence or address.[198] If a TCN leaves the address at which he is staying or temporary residence, he or she has to cancel it at the latest within three days of the date of departing.[199]

197. Article 48, Aliens Act.
198. Article 148, Aliens Act.
199. Article 149, Aliens Act.

II. Refusal of the Application for Temporary Residence Permit

118. The application for a temporary residence permit is refused if a TCN does not meet any of the conditions required by the Aliens Act:

- if a TCN does not possess a valid travel document, appropriate health insurance[200] or sufficient means of subsistence,[201] cannot prove the purpose of temporary residence, and if he or she did not fulfil the other conditions required for the issuing of individual types of temporary residence permits;
- if a TCN is prohibited from entering the country;
- if there are serious reasons for suspicion that a TCN may pose a danger for public order,[202] national security[203] or public health;
- if the documentation supplied is fraudulently acquired, restored or forged;
- if there is evidence or serious and objective reasons for a TCN to reside in the RoC for purposes other than that for which he or she is applying for a temporary residence permit;
- if a warning is issued in the Schengen Information System for refusal of entry and residence.[204]

119. Possibilities for rejection of the application for residence and work permit and the EU Blue Card are explained in Part VII, Chapter 2, §3.

200. According to the judicial practice, 'the fact that the TCN did not meet the health insurance obligations is a sufficient reason to refuse her temporary stay'. The High Administrative Court, decision of 10 Apr. 2013 (cited in Frane Staničić, *supra*, p. 170).
201. According to the judicial practice, registration of a company in which a husband is a director cannot be considered evidence of the existence of sufficient means of subsistence as permanent income. 'This this Court finds that the proposed evidence (extract from the Register of Commercial Court) cannot be considered as proof of the means of subsistence in the sense of the aforementioned provisions of the Act because, in addition to the fact that it is not considered as evidence of the existence of the means of subsistence referred to in Article 6 paragraph 3 of the Ordinance on the Status and Work of Aliens in the Republic of Croatia, from the statement of the husband of the plaintiff, a director of that company, it is clear that the company is not active and has no regular monthly income.' The High Administrative Court, Usž-1140/15-2, a decision of 30 Sep. 2015.
202. According to the judicial practice, 'the alien will not be granted temporary residence if he or she is the perpetrator is a criminal offender, and rehabilitation has not occurred'. The High Administrative Court, decision of 29 Dec. 2011 (Cited in Frane Staničić, *supra*, p. 169). 'In accordance with the evidence provided during the judicial procedure, it clearly follows that the alien was legally punished for the criminal acts of robbery and heavy theft, which indicates that the conclusion that his behaviour presents a danger to the public order was correct. Furthermore, contrary to the plaintiff's allegations, and according to the evidence in the file, the plaintiff has also committed new criminal offences.' The High Administrative Court, Usž-1953/17, a decision of 19 Jul. 2017.
203. According to the Art. 5 of Aliens Act, security checks for the purpose of establishing national security reasons are conducted by the Security and Intelligence Agency. The decision rejecting or terminating the residence under the grounds of national security will only specify the legal provision, but the reasons for the decision will not the elaborated.
204. Article 54, Aliens Act.

III. Extension of a Temporary Residence Permit

120. A temporary residence permit can be extended. A TCN has to apply for the extension of temporary residence sixty days before the expiration of the valid temporary residence at the latest. The competent body is the police administration or police station based on the place of temporary residence of the TCN, the registered office (seat) of the employer, or the place of work of the TCN. A TCN who applied for the extension of temporary residence may remain in Croatia until the decision on his application becomes enforceable, while a police administration or police station has to issue a decision before the expiration of the term of validity of the previous temporary residence permit.[205]

IV. TCNs with a Permanent Residence Permit in Another EEA Member State

121. TCNs with a permanent residence permit in another EEA Member State and members of their family can submit an application for the approval of temporary residence, either to the police administration or police station if already staying in Croatia, or in a diplomatic mission or consular office of the RoC in an EEA Member State in which they have approved permanent residence. In general, a TCN with an approved permanent residence in another EEA Member State may stay in Croatia for up to three months or until the expiration of the term of validity of the visa or residence card which was issued by such other EEA Member State. If a TCN intends to stay in Croatia for a period of over three months, he or she has to submit an application for the approval of temporary residence to the police administration or police station before the expiration of the term of validity of the visa or residence card which was issued by another EEA Member State. The TCN who applied for the temporary residence in a diplomatic mission or consular office may enter the RoC before a decision on the application is issued. Upon entry to Croatia, a TCN must notify the police administration or police station. A TCN may stay in Croatia during the process of deciding on their application, based on the certificate on the submission of an application for the issuing of approval for temporary residence.[206]

§3. Legal Position of Residents

122. According to the Croatian Constitution, all persons in the RoC, including aliens, enjoy rights and freedoms and are equal before the law.[207] There are, however, certain exceptions as to the reach of human rights protection, such as the right to vote, or to participate in the conduct of public affairs and to have access to public services, which are reserved only for Croatian citizens.

205. Article 53, Aliens Act.
206. Article 188, Aliens Act.
207. Article 14, Constitution of the RoC.

123. TCNs having a residence permit may reside in Croatia only in accordance with the purpose for which the permit was issued. A TCN with a temporary residence permit can move without restrictions within Croatia and can choose his or her place of residence. However, he or she has to register his temporary residence with the police administration or police station within eight days from the approval of temporary residence.[208] The residence permit protects a TCN from deportation unless there are circumstances that justify a termination of the right to reside in Croatia (*see* Part IV on the loss of the right of residence). During his movement and stay in Croatia, a TCN has to comply with laws and regulations, and decisions of the state authorities.[209]

124. According to the Aliens Act, TCNs with temporary residence permit (a TCN who has been granted a residence and work permit, the EU Blue Cardholder[210] and a TCN granted temporary residence permit for the family reunification, a life partnership, on humanitarian grounds, as the autonomous residence, for research or study) are entitled to following rights:

- professional development;
- education and student scholarships;
- social welfare, rights arising from pension, health insurance and the right to child allowance;
- tax benefits;
- access to the market of goods and services;
- the freedom of association and the freedom to connect and to be a member in organisations representing employees or employers or organisations whose members are engaged in specialised professions, including to remuneration provided by such organisations;
- recognition of diplomas and professional qualifications as well as the counselling services provided by the employment bureaus in accordance with special regulations;
- working conditions (maximum duration of working hours and the minimum duration of rest; the minimum duration of paid annual leave; the minimum salary, including increased salaries for overtime; health and safety at work; protective measures for work of pregnant women, women who have recently given birth or are breastfeeding, and minors; prohibition of discrimination; conditions for assignment of workers through the employment agency).[211]

125. Primary education is compulsory for all children residing in Croatia, generally from six to fifteen years of age.[212] Children of TCNs with temporary residence permit who do not know or do not know the Croatian language sufficiently,

208. Article 141, Aliens Act.
209. Article 4, para. 1, Aliens Act.
210. Article 196, Aliens Act.
211. Article 85a, Aliens Act.
212. Article 4, para. 2, Primary and Secondary School Education Act (*Zakon o odgoju i obrazovanju u osnovnoj i srednjoj š*koli), OG 87/2008, 86/2009, 92/2010, 105/2010, 90/2011, 5/2012, 16/2012, 86/2012, 126/2012, 94/2013, 152/2014, 07/2017, 68/2018.

are entitled to preparatory or supplementary classes for effective integration into the system of education.[213] Aliens enter the study under the same conditions as Croatian citizens, but in accordance with the decision of the competent state authority or institution of higher education, they may be asked to pay part or the full costs of the study. Aliens may be restricted or denied enrolment in the case of studies related to military or police education or other studies that are of interest to national security.[214] Some Croatian higher education institutions might offer some financial aid or partial tuition fee waivers for international students.[215]

126. According to the Social Welfare Act, TCNs with the temporary residence permit are not entitled to social welfare rights. However, they may be granted the right to a one-off allowance and temporary accommodation under conditions prescribed by the legislation provided this is necessary because of the person's circumstances at the time.[216] The right to maternity and parental benefits can only be realised for persons with compulsory health insurance regulated by the Croatian Health Insurance Fund.

127. TCNs with temporary residence permit are entitled to certain rights during unemployment. A TCN can register with the Croatian Employment Service to claim unemployment benefits if he or she has lost his or her job without his or her fault or with his or her consent. However, they are excluded from other rights guaranteed during unemployment (pension insurance, financial assistance and cost reimbursement during the period of training, and one-time financial assistance and reimbursement of travel and relocation expenses). Once the benefits have been paid up or upon expiry of the temporary resident permit, a TCN will no longer be in the registry.[217]

128. TCNs with temporary residence permits are entitled to health insurance, which is compulsory in Croatia. The health insurance and healthcare of aliens are regulated by a special act – the Act on Health Insurance and Health Care of Aliens in the RoC.[218] Regardless of the purpose of the temporary residence permit, a TCN is obliged to apply for compulsory health insurance, provided that his or her right

213. Article 3, para. 1, Ordinance on conducting preparatory and supplementary courses for pupils who do not speak Croatian or do not speak it sufficiently well, and classes in their mother tongue and the culture of the country of origin of pupils (*Pravilnik o provođenju pripremne i dopunske nastave za učenike koji ne znaju ili nedostatno znaju hrvatski jezik i nastave materinskoga jezika i kulture države podrijetla učenika*), OG 15/2013.

214. Article 77, para. 8, Act on Scientific Activity and Higher Education (*Zakon o znanstvenoj djelatnosti i visokom obrazovanju*), OG 123/2003, 198/2003, 105/2004, 174/2004, 02/2007, 46/2007, 45/2009, 63/2011, 94/2013, 139/2013, 101/2014, 60/2015, 131/2017.

215. https://www.studyincroatia.hr/study-in-croatia/tuition-fees-and-scholarships/scholarships (accessed on 15 Apr. 2018).

216. Article 22, Social Welfare Act (*Zakon o socijalnoj skrbi*), OG 157/2013, 152/2014, 99/2015, 52/2016, 16/2017, 130/2017.

217. Article 15, Labor Market Act (*Zakon o tržištu rada*), OG 118/2018.

218. Act on Health Insurance and Health Care of Aliens in the Republic of Croatia (*Zakon o obveznom zdravstvenom osiguranju i zdravstvenoj zaštiti stranaca u Republici Hrvatskoj*), OG 80/2013, 15/2018.

to compulsory health insurance or healthcare is not secured on a different basis.[219] TCNs who are temporarily residing in Croatia with the purpose of secondary education or studying are exempted from the obligation to apply for compulsory health insurance, provided that he or she has proof of health insurance during the temporary residence. Those categories will bear the costs of healthcare in a public or private health provider. For a TCN whose temporary residence is approved for the purpose of secondary education, studying, specialisation or the scientific research as a scholar of Croatian state authority's scholarship, bodies of local and regional (regional) governments, associations or other legal or natural persons, the application is submitted by the provider of scholarships who is also a taxpayer of contributions for compulsory health insurance, unless the scholarship provides otherwise. A TCN at the temporary residence for the study who comes on the basis of the mobility programme of young framework programmes on student inter-university education and science exchange, if the listed programmes cover the health insurance, is not obliged to apply for the mandatory health insurance.[220] Application of compulsory health insurance is submitted to the regional or local office of the Croatian Health Insurance Fund. Compulsory health insurance rights, including rights related to injuries at work and occupational diseases, cover the right to healthcare and monetary benefits. The insured persons are obliged to participate in the costs of healthcare from compulsory health insurance, for services that are not fully insured at the expense of the Croatian Health Insurance Fund. If a TCN did not pay a compulsory health insurance contribution for at least thirty days, the scope of the right of compulsory health insurance would be limited to the right to emergency medical assistance, which includes diagnostic and therapeutic procedures that are necessary to eliminate imminent danger to life and health.[221]

129. TCNs employed in the territory of Croatia are entitled to pension insurance unless legal provisions of the EU on the coordination of social security systems or an international agreement on social security establishes otherwise.[222] After returning to their country of origin, aliens can access their social security and pension rights for which contributions have been paid in Croatia, provided that Croatia concluded a bilateral agreement on social insurance with that country. As of 2018, Croatia has concluded bilateral agreements with Australia, Bosnia and Herzegovina, Montenegro, Canada, Macedonia, Serbia (SR Yugoslavia), and Turkey.

§4. Position of Family Members of Temporary Residents

130. As explained before, family reunification is considered to be the valid purpose for applying for a temporary residence permit. Temporary residence permits for the family reunification are issued for a period of up to one year, or until the

219. Article 6, para. 1, Act on Health Insurance and Health Care of Aliens in the Republic of Croatia.
220. Article 6, paras 2, 9 and 10, Act on Health Insurance and Health Care of Aliens in the Republic of Croatia.
221. Article 8, Act on Health Insurance and Health Care of Aliens in the Republic of Croatia.
222. Article 9, para. 1, Pension Insurance Act (*Zakon o mirovinskom osiguranju*), OG 157/2013, 151/2014, 33/2015, 93/2015, 120/2016, 18/2018, 62/2018, 115/2018.

expiration of the temporary residence permit of the TCN with whom family reunification is sought. Also, if a family member had an uninterrupted temporary residence permit for the purpose of family reunification in the duration of at least two years, he or she can be granted a temporary stay for up to two years.[223] The right to family reunification is applicable to a TCN who is a member of the immediate family of a Croatian national, the TCN with approved permanent or temporary residence, the TCN granted international protection under the Act on International and Temporary Protection, and the TCN with a valid stay and work permit based on the annual quota provided that the TCN had temporary stay in Croatia granted for at least two years.[224] The same conditions apply to the temporary residence for the life partnership to a TCN who is in a life partnership or informal partnership with a Croatian national, a TCN who has been granted permanent or temporary residence or international or temporary protection.[225] Family members of seasonal, posted or daily migrant workers, TCNs granted temporary residence for other purposes, or service providers on behalf of a foreign employer, are not entitled to family reunification. Therefore they will not be granted a temporary residence permit.[226]

131. The Aliens Act stipulates that members of the immediate family include the following categories:[227]

– a spouse (in the case of a polygamous marriage, family reunification will be granted to only one spouse);
– non-marital partner, provided that both partners are unmarried and that a partnership lasts for at least three years, or less if a mutual child is born;
– the underage children of married couples and non-marital partners, their underage adopted children, and the underage children of each of them, who have not formed families of their own;
– parents or adoptive parents of underage children.

If there are special personal or serious humanitarian grounds, some other relatives may also be regarded as a member of the immediate family of a TCN granted temporary residence. If the spouse or non-marital partner is married or has a long-term relationship with another person family reunification will not be granted.

132. Temporary residence for the family reunification or a life partnership will not be granted if marriage is a marriage of convenience, which means any marriage concluded with a view to circumventing the requirements necessary for the entry and residence of aliens. Indications[228] that marriage is a marriage of convenience are as follows:

223. Article 59, Aliens Act.
224. Article 55, paras 1 and 2, Aliens Act.
225. Article 56b, Aliens Act.
226. Article 55, para. 3, Aliens Act.
227. Article 56, Aliens Act.
228. According to the judicial practice, ' … on the basis of the inconsistent statements of spouses, it is correctly established that they do not maintain the marriage union. It should be noted, however, that contradictions in statements do not (though they may) refer to basic information on spouses

– the spouses do not maintain their marital union;
– the spouses do not perform their marital obligations;
– the spouses have never met before the conclusion of the marriage;
– the spouses fail to provide consistent personal data;
– the spouses do not speak a language that they both understand;
– material assets were exchanged for the conclusion of the marriage unless the assets represent dowry, and the spouses come from countries where the presentation of dowry is a custom;
– there is proof of previous marriages of convenience on the part of any of the spouses either in Croatia or abroad.[229]

133. Some categories of family members can be granted a temporary residence permit on more lenient conditions. In the case of regulating temporary residence for the family member of a person granted international protection, he or she will not have to provide proof of means of subsistence and health insurance.[230] A member of the family of a Croatian citizen, besides proving of being a member of immediate family as a condition for a valid purpose of the stay, only needs to prove the fulfilment of the several general conditions for issuing a temporary residence permit (i.e., travel document, health insurance) but does not have to prove possession of means of subsistence. Exceptionally, a TCN does not have to fulfil the condition of having a valid travel document, if that document cannot be obtained at the embassy or consular office of his state in Croatia, and his or her identity can be undoubtedly determined on the other way.[231]

134. The spouse or non-marital partner and child who turned 18 years of age can be granted autonomous residence, provided that they have temporary residence for the purpose of family reunification in the uninterrupted duration of four years. If the person through whom they were granted temporary residence for the family reunification died, the condition for temporary residence is approved temporary stay for the family reunification in the uninterrupted duration of three years.[232]

135. A family member of a TCN with approved permanent stay in another EEA Member State who has approved temporary residence in Croatia will be granted temporary stay for the purpose of family reunification if he or she has approved stay in another EEA Member State and if he or she lived in a shared household with a TCN in a state in which the TCN has permanent residence. In this case, family members include the spouse; the underage children of married couples, their underage adopted children, and the underage children of each of them, who have not formed families of their own; parents or adoptive parents of underage children.[233]

---

and marital life. It is sufficient that there are differences in which it is apparent that the marital community is not maintained.' The High Administrative Court, Usž-1473/17, a decision of 27 Jul. 2017.

229. Article 57, Aliens Act.
230. Article 58, Aliens Act.
231. Article 56a, Aliens Act.
232. Article 60, Aliens Act.
233. Articles 186 and 187, Aliens Act.

136. Family members of a TCN to whom an 'EU Blue Card' was issued in the RoC are entitled to join him if they stayed with him legally in another EEA Member State. They have to submit an application for temporary residence for the family reunification within one month of the date of entry to the RoC, and include the following documentation:

- a valid travel document or visa, if required;
- a residence permit proving that as family members they legally resided in the territory of an EEA Member State;
- proof of health insurance;
- proof of means of subsistence.[234]

137. Aliens are granted temporary residence for family reunification, and an alien with autonomous residence have the right to education, professional development, work and self-employment under the provisions of the Aliens Act.[235]

234. Article 202, Aliens Act.
235. Article 61, Aliens Act.

Chapter 3. Long-Term Residence

§1. Conditions for Long-Term Residence

138. A permanent residence is granted for an indefinite period. A TCN who had approved temporary residence for an uninterrupted period of five years can acquire a permanent residence, if he or she satisfies conditions prescribed by the Aliens Act and if there are no reasons for refusing the application for a permanent residence permit. At the time of deciding about his permanent residence application, a TCN must have approved temporary residence in Croatia.[236] In addition, a TCN has to fulfil the following conditions:

- a valid foreign travel document;
- the means of subsistence;
- health insurance;
- knowledge of the Croatian language and the Latin script, and the Croatian culture and social system;
- a TCN does not pose a threat to public order, national security or public health.[237]

In order to acquire a permanent residence permit, an alien has to reside in the RoC according to the purpose for which his or her temporary residence was approved.[238]

139. One of the preconditions for acquiring a permanent residence in Croatia is the uninterrupted stay for five years in Croatia. In addition, 'the uninterrupted stay' also means the stay with multiple periods of absence from Croatia, up to ten months in total, or a one-time absence of up to six months, for five years.[239] However, there are some situations in which the residence in Croatia will not be included in the time required for granting permanent residence: the time spent serving a prison sentence and the period of residence based on the residence and work permit issued to seasonal workers, daily migrant workers, service providers on behalf of a foreign employer, posted workers, TCNs in the framework of an intra-corporate transfer and their family members, other necessary persons as defined in the Protocol on the Accession of the RoC to the Marrakech Agreement on the Founding of the World Trade Organization and their family members. If a temporary residence was issued

236. Article 92, Aliens Act.
237. Article 96, Aliens Act.
238. Frane Staničić, *supra*, p. 179.
239. Article 92, para. 2, Aliens Act. According to the judicial practice, the conditions for a permanent residence permit will not be met if an alien was absent from Croatia multiple times, and the total absence was longer than ten months. '… referring to the records of persons over whom border control has been carried out, whose management is within the competence of the Ministry of the Interior. In these records, it was found that in the last five years the claimant had a total of 83 entries and exits from the Republic of Croatia, and his absence from the Republic of Croatia was found to last for a period longer than ten months'. The High Administrative Court, Usž-640/17, a decision of 23 Mar. 2017.

to study, the time required for the approval of permanent stay includes only half of the time spent further to the temporary residence permit to study.[240]

140. The conditions for acquiring permanent residence in Croatia are more lenient in the case of asylees and aliens granted subsidiary protection. Asylum or subsidiary protection will be calculated as temporary residence permit, except if asylum or subsidiary protection were cancelled. To the time required for the approval of permanent residence, it will be added one half of the period of decision-making about asylum seeker's application for asylum, or the entire period if it is longer than eighteen months. Asylees and aliens granted subsidiary protection do not have to possess a valid foreign travel document,[241] as fulfilling this condition in many cases would be impossible due to persecution, war or human rights violations in the country of origin.

141. In certain cases, it is possible to acquire a permanent residence permit earlier than after five years of residing in Croatia. The Aliens Act envisaged four categories of aliens that could acquire permanent residence on more lenient conditions, with two categories of persons who are considered aliens as a result of the dissolution of former Yugoslavia and war events during the 1990s. The first group of aliens are those who had at least three years of uninterrupted temporary stay, and at least ten years of refugee status, which is demonstrated by a certificate of the competent state body for refugees. The second group are aliens who had residence in the RoC on 8 October 1991 (when Croatian Parliament decided to end relations and legal ties with other republics and provinces of Yugoslavia), and who were beneficiaries of the programme of return, reconstruction or housing care, as demonstrated by a certificate of the competent state body for refugees, and for whom it was established that he returned with the intention of living in the RoC permanently. The third category is a child living in Croatia, who can be granted permanent residence in the following situations:

- if both parents at the moment of his or her birth had approved permanent residence;
- if one parent at the moment of his or her birth had approved permanent stay (with the consent of the other parent);
- if one parent at the moment of his or her birth had approved permanent stay in Croatia, with the other parent being unknown, deceased, declared deceased, denied parental care or entirely or partially denied business capacity with respect to parental care.

The fourth category is an alien who was born and has been living in Croatia since his or her birth, but who did not have his residence regulated for justified reasons he or she was unable to affect. Those four categories of aliens can acquire a permanent residence even if they did not fulfil the condition of temporary residence for an

240. Article 93, Aliens Act.
241. Article 93, para. 3, Aliens Act.

uninterrupted period of five years.[242] Also, those categories have to fulfil only two general conditions: a TCN has to have a valid travel document and must not pose a threat to public order, national security or public health. In some cases, a lack of travel document will not present an obstacle for acquiring a permanent residence: if an alien cannot obtain it at the foreign diplomatic and consular office in the RoC and his or her identity can be undoubtedly determined in another way.[243]

142. The condition of staying in Croatia for an uninterrupted period of at least five years also applies to an EU Blue Cardholder. This condition can be met if he or she has resided in the EEA area for five years on the basis of an EU Blue Card, out of which he or she would have had to have resided in Croatia for at least two years before applying for a permanent residence permit. Absence from the EEA area for up to twelve consecutive or separately up to eighteen months will be considered the uninterruptedness stay and can be extended to up to twenty-four consecutive months if a TCN proves that he was absent due to employment or self-employment or that he or she performed volunteer work or studied in the country of his or her origin. An EU Blue Cardholder has to fulfil other general conditions for acquiring permanent residence permit (travel document, means of subsistence, health insurance, knowledge of Croatian language, and that a TCN is not considered a threat to public order, national security or public health).[244]

143. The Aliens Act also acknowledge the long-term resident status granted to TCNs who have permanent residence based on the legal residence for five years, means of subsistence and health insurance in Croatia or the other EEA Member State.[245]

§2. Administrative Procedures and Documents for Long-Term Residence

I. Competent Bodies and Procedure

144. The procedure for the issuing of a permanent residence permit is similar to the procedure for the issuing of temporary residence permit. A TCN has to submit an application for the issuing of a permanent residence permit to the police administration or police station based on the location of his or her temporary residence, while the MoI will decide upon the application.

145. In order to demonstrate knowledge of the Croatian language and the Latin script, a TCN will have to pass the test, apart from pre-schoolers, persons who finished primary, secondary or higher education in the RoC, and persons over the age of 65 if they are not employed. The testing may be conducted by higher education

242. Article 94, Aliens Act.
243. Article 96, paras 2 and 3, Aliens Act.
244. Article 199, Aliens Act.
245. Article 2, para. 1, Aliens Act.

institutions, secondary schools and institutions for adult education that organise Croatian language courses based on the permission of the Ministry of Education and Sciences. A TCN bears the costs of the testing.[246]

146. For aliens who had a residence in the RoC on 8 October 1991 and who were beneficiaries of the programme of return, reconstruction or housing care, it has to be established that he or she returned with the intention to live in the RoC permanently. This fact can be proved, for example, with the lease contract for the apartment concluded with the competent ministry, on the basis of the Conclusion on the way of providing housing care for returnees – former tenant right holders to apartments outside areas of special state concern, although during the two filed visits the plaintiff or his/her family members were not found in the apartment. Also, in such cases, the Aliens Act does not prescribe an ongoing physical presence of the alien in the RoC as a precondition for the approval of permanent residence.[247]

II. Refusal of Application for Permanent Residence Permit

147. The application for a permanent residence permit is refused if a TCN does not meet any of the conditions required by the Aliens Act: temporary residence for an uninterrupted period of five years, a valid travel document, health insurance, sufficient means of subsistence, knowledge of the Croatian language and the Latin script, and the Croatian culture and social system. Also, the application can be refused if there are serious reasons for suspicion that an applicant may pose a danger for public order,[248] national security or public health.

§3. Legal Position of Long-Term Residents

148. Aliens with a permanent residence permit have the right to reside in Croatia for an unlimited period. The permit does not have to be extended or renewed, such as a temporary residence permit. It means that a TCN does not have to prove the conditions in order to retain the residence permit. Therefore, the permanent residence permit provides a more secure legal status compared to temporary residence permit. The status of a permanent resident is equivalent to the status of a long-term resident introduced at the EU level.

149. A TCN with a permanent residence permit can move without restrictions within Croatia and can choose his or her place of residence. However, he or she has

246. Article 97, Aliens Act.
247. The High Administrative Court, Usž-1634/15-2, a decision of 15 Oct. 2015.
248. According to the judicial practice, if the applicant committed offences, the application can be refused based on the violation of the public order and legislation of the RoC: ' … committed many violations for which he was sentenced to court and fines, which is why it is estimated that by repeated misdemeanours he is not complying with the positive regulations of the Republic of Croatia and its legal order'. The High Administrative Court, Us-2411/2011-4, a decision of 12 Feb. 2015.

to register their residence at the police administration or police station within eight days after the approval of permanent residence,[249] who will issue a residence permit for the term of validity of five years.[250] Along with permanent residence, a TCN with a permanent residence may also register his or her temporary residence for a period of up to one year, at a place where he or she stays habitually but without the intention of settling there.[251]

150. In principle, a TCN who has been granted permanent residence has equal treatment concerning rights and obligations as Croatian citizens, unless the Constitution or the law reserves a right to nationals. During his stay in Croatia, a TCN with a permanent residence has to comply with laws and regulations, and decisions of the state authorities.[252] The residence permit protects a TCN from deportation unless there are circumstances that justify a termination of the right to permanently reside in Croatia (*see* Part IV on the loss of the right of residence). According to the Aliens Act, a TCN is entitled to the following rights: work and self-employment; professional development; education and student scholarships; social welfare, rights arising from pension, health insurance and the right to child allowance; tax benefits; access to the market of goods and services; the freedom of association and the freedom to connect and to be a member of organisations representing employees or employers or organisations whose members are engaged in specialised professions, including to remuneration provided by such organisations.[253] TCNs with a permanent residence can study under the same conditions as Croatian citizens, but in accordance with the decision of the competent state authority or institution of higher education, they may be asked to pay part or the full costs of the study. However, they may be restricted or denied enrolment in the case of studies related to military or police education or other studies that are of interest to national security.[254] Compulsory health insurance in Croatia is mandatory for all aliens with approved permanent residence,[255] who are, therefore, obliged to acquire health insurance according to one of the grounds of the insurance specified in the Compulsory Health Insurance Act. A TCN thus acquires the status of insured persons in compulsory health insurance and has the rights and obligations of compulsory health insurance. Compulsory health insurance covers only the most general and urgent healthcare services and examinations, while other services, such as specialist examinations or require additional payment or complementary health insurance. A TCN with a permanent residence permit can work in Croatia without a stay and work permit or a work registration certificate.[256] In the case of unemployment, they can register at the Croatian Employment Office. According to the Social Welfare Act, TCNs with the permanent residence permit are entitled to social welfare rights under the same conditions as Croatian citizens.

249. Article 141, Aliens Act.
250. Article 140, para. 2, Aliens Act.
251. Article 146, para. 3, Aliens Act.
252. Article 4, para. 1, Aliens Act.
253. Article 98, Aliens Act.
254. Article 77, para. 8, Act on Scientific Activity and Higher Education.
255. Article 5, Act on Health Insurance and Health Care of Aliens in the Republic of Croatia.
256. Article 73, para. 3, Aliens Act.

§4. Position of Family Members of Long-Term Residents

151. A TCN with a permanent residence permit has the right to reunification with their close family members, who can be issued a temporary residence permit for the family reunification.[257] The members of the immediate family are: a spouse; non-marital partner, provided that both partners are unmarried, and that a partnership lasts for at least three years, or less if a mutual child has been born; the underage children of married couples and non-marital partners, their underage adopted children, and the underage children of each of them, who have not formed families of their own; parents or adoptive parents of underage children. If there are special personal or serious humanitarian grounds, some other relatives may also be regarded as a member of the immediate family.[258] The same conditions apply to the temporary residence for the life partnership to a person who is in a life partnership or informal partnership with a TCN who has been granted permanent residence.[259] As in the case of family reunification with a TCN with a temporary residence permit, temporary residence for the purpose of family reunification or the purpose of a life partnership will not be granted if the marriage is a marriage of convenience, which means any marriage concluded with a view to circumventing the requirements necessary for the entry and residence of aliens.[260]

152. Aliens granted temporary residence for the family reunification with a TCN with a permanent residence permit have the right to education, professional development, work and self-employment.[261]

257. Article 55, para. 1, Aliens Act.
258. Article 56, Aliens Act.
259. Article 56b, Aliens Act.
260. Article 57, Aliens Act.
261. Article 61, Aliens Act.

Part III. Right of Residence for Specific Categories of Persons

Chapter 1. Nationals with Preferential Treatment

§1. EEA Citizens and Their Family Members

I. Short Stay of EEA Citizens and Their Family Members

153. As explained in Part II, EEA citizens have the right to reside in Croatia for up to three months from the date of entry, if they hold a valid travel document or identity card,[262] which means without a residence permit. If the EEA citizen intends to stay for more than three months, within eight days of the expiration of three months of his or her stay, he or she must apply for a temporary stay.[263]

154. Family members of EEA citizens have the right to reside in Croatia for up to three months from the date of entry if they hold a valid travel document or identity card.[264] The reasons to refuse entry permission to a family member of an EEA citizen are the same as the reasons to refuse entry to EEA citizens: lack of valid travel document, visa, or residence permit, a prohibition of entry, if he or she is considered to be a threat to public order internal security, public health or the international relations, or cannot justify the purpose and conditions of the intended stay and does not have sufficient means of subsistence.

II. Temporary Residence for EEA Citizens and Their Family Members

155. EEA citizens and their family members (including EEA citizens who are family members of Croatian citizens) are entitled to temporary residence in the RoC for work, studying or vocational training, family reunification, and other purposes. Regardless of the purpose of intended temporary residence in Croatia, EEA citizens and their family members need to have a valid identity card or a valid travel document, sufficient resources to support himself and members of his family so that during their stay they would not become a burden to the social welfare system, and

262. Article 155, Aliens Act.
263. Article 157, Aliens Act.
264. Article 155, Aliens Act.

health insurance. In evaluating whether the resources are sufficient for supporting oneself, the personal circumstances of EEA citizens and their family members have to be taken into account, and they will not be required to amount to more than the amount of money required for the realisation of rights under the social welfare system in the RoC.[265]

156. In order to be granted a certificate of the registration of temporary residence for the *work*, an EEA citizen must provide a certificate of employment or proof of self-employment. If an EEA citizen becomes unemployed, he or she will retain the status of the employee or self-employed person provided that he or she: is temporarily incapable of work due to illness or accident; has lost his or her job without their fault, which he or she performed for at least one year, and is registered as job-seeker with the competent service; and joins an occupational training programme. The occupational training programme must be linked to previous employment unless an EEA citizen lost his job without his or her fault. The status of an employee or self-employed person will be limited to six months in two situations: if the EEA citizen had worked based on the employment contract concluded for the period shorter than one year and lost the job without his fault and is registered as a job-seeker, or if in the first twelve months of work he or she lost his job without his fault and is registered as job-seeker. The same rules apply to EEA citizens who work as seasonal workers, and for those who are employed with an employer from another EEA Member State and provide services for a foreign employer in Croatia based on the contract concluded between a foreign contractor and a Croatian client.[266] For the issuing a certificate of the registration of temporary residence for the *study or vocational training*, the EEA citizen has to provide evidence of attendance of vocational training or enrolment in a higher education institution, or that he or she comes within the framework of student exchanges or youth mobility, or comes to professional practice through an authorised organisation or on the basis of international or inter-university agreements.[267]

157. Persons who can apply for family reunification with EEA citizens or Croatian nationals are:

- a spouse;
- non-marital partner or a partner in a long-term relationship provided that a partnership lasts for at least three years or less if there are circumstances that prove the stability of the relationship;
- descendants and adopted children of the EEA citizen or his spouse, a non-martial or cohabiting partner under the age of 21;
- descendants above the age of 21 and family members in the ascending line whom the EEA citizen or the Slovenian national supports or is obliged to support and supports them in practice;

265. Article 156, Aliens Act.
266. Article 159, Aliens Act.
267. Article 160, Aliens Act.

- another family member who has lived in another country in a shared household with an EEA citizen or a Croatian national, or whom the EEA citizen or the Croatian national supports as well as a family member who is dependent on the personal care of EEA citizen or the Croatian national because of serious health reasons.[268]

158. In addition to an identity card or travel document, a family member of an EEA citizen or a Croatian national who is an EEA citizen, with the application for temporary residence has to provide the following:[269]

- a document proving that he or she is a family member (such as a marriage certificate or a birth certificate);
- relevant documents proving that in view of his or her material and social situation in the country from which he or she arrived, he or she is dependent on the EEA citizen or a Croatian national in providing for his basic needs, or is a member of his household, or that in view of health-related serious reasons he or she requires special personal care by the EEA citizen or a Croatian national (such as medical documentation, proof of support or custody, etc.).

A family member has to register his or her temporary residence within eight days of the expiration of the three months of stay to the police administration or police station based on the place of stay.

159. Temporary residence will be issued for a family member who is not an EEA citizen if he or she is accompanying or joining an EEA citizen who meets the criteria for granting temporary residence. A family member will be issued the 'Registration Card for a Family Member of an EEA Citizen', provided that he or she:

- has a valid travel document;
- encloses a document proving that he or she is a family member;
- encloses a document issued by the competent body of the state from which he or she arrives, confirming officially that he or she is a dependent family member or a member of the household of the EEA citizen, or encloses proof that due to serious health-related reasons, special personal care of the EEA citizen is required;
- does not pose a threat to public order or national security;
- is not prohibited for entry and stay in the RoC.

The term of validity of the residence card for a family member is five years, or shorter if the EEA citizen intends to stay in Croatia for less than five years. Its validity will not be affected by the time of absence from the RoC for up to six months

268. Article 162, Aliens Act.
269. Article 163, Aliens Act and Art. 11, Ordinance on the Manner of Determining the Conditions for Entry and Residence in the Republic of Croatia of EEA Citizens and Members of their Families (*Pravilnik o načinu utvrđivanja uvjeta za ulazak i boravak u Republici Hrvatskoj državljana država članica Europskog gospodarskog prostora i članova njihovih obitelji*), OG 126/2012, 81/2013, 38/2015, 85/2015, 132/2017.

per year, or up to twelve months without interruptions for justified reasons, such as pregnancy, childbirth, serious illness, studies, professional development, posting to another state, or for military service.[270]

160. In the case of the death of an EEA citizen or leaving Croatia, the temporary residence permit of the family member remains valid without any restrictions. If the family member is not an EEA citizen, the residence permit will remain valid in the case of death of the EEA citizen, provided that they resided in Croatia for at least one year. Children of an EEA citizen and the other parent taking care of children, regardless of nationality, shall retain the right to the temporary residence if the EEA citizen dies or leaves Croatia, provided that the children are residing in Croatia and attending an educational institution, until completion of their education. In the case of a divorce or annulment of marriage, a family member of an EEA citizen shall retain the right to temporary residence. However, if the family member is not himself an EEA citizen, he or she may retain the right to temporary residence provided that:

- the marriage lasted for at least three years, where the spouses stayed in Croatia for at least one year;
- in the case of enforcement of parental rights concerning the children of an EEA citizen awarded to him for care or upbringing by agreement of the spouses or court decision;
- in the case of enforcement of parental rights with respect to underage children staying in Croatia and awarded for care or upbringing to the other parent by agreement of the spouses or court decision;
- it is justified by other particularly difficult circumstances, such as domestic violence.

In all cases, a family member has to prove that he or she is employed or self-employed or has resources for supporting himself and his family members and health insurance, or that he or she is a family member of an EEA citizen who died or left Croatia.[271]

III. Long-Term Residence for EEA Citizens and Their Family Members

161. EEA citizens can be granted permanent residence in Croatia after five years of uninterrupted residence in the RoC. The residence will be considered interrupted if the EEA citizens were absent from the RoC for up to six months per year, or up to twelve months without interruptions for justified reasons, such as pregnancy, childbirth, serious illness, studies, professional development, posting to another state, or for military service. The police administration or police station will issue a card confirming permanent residence of an EEA citizen, at his or her request, as

270. Article 169, Aliens Act.
271. Article 171, Aliens Act.

soon as possible after having verified the duration of stay.[272] The Aliens Act also stipulates that under certain conditions an EEA citizen will have a right to permanent residence if he or she did not reside in Croatia for five years:

- as an employed or self-employed person, he or she stopped working, and is eligible for an old-age pension in the RoC, provided that he was employed in Croatia for at least the preceding twelve months and that he or she resided without interruptions for more than three years;
- he or she retired early, and was employed in the RoC for at least the preceding twelve months and resided without interruptions for more than three years;
- as an employed or self-employed person, he or she stopped working due to permanent disability to work, and resided in Croatia without interruptions for more than two years;
- as an employed or self-employed person, he or she stopped working due to permanent disability to work, resulting from a work-related injury or occupational disease which is the ground for a disability pension, regardless of the duration of his or her residence in Croatia;
- as an employed or self-employed person, after three years of uninterrupted employment and residence in Croatia, he or she is employed in another EEA Member State but retains temporary residence in the RoC and returns daily or at least once a week.

The period of unemployment registered with the Croatian Employment Service, which occurred through no fault of the employee, and the period of temporary inability to work due to illness or injury, will be regarded as the period of employment.[273] An EEA citizen on a permanent residence will be issued with a residence card valid for ten years.[274]

162. The general condition for acquiring permanent residence for family members of an EEA citizen (who is not a citizen of the EEA Member State) is that they are residing in Croatia together, for an uninterrupted period of five years. Same as in the case of the EEA citizen, the residence will be considered uninterrupted if the family member was absent from the RoC for up to six months per year, or up to twelve months without interruptions for justified reasons or military service.[275] In some cases, the permanent residence can be acquired if the family member resided in Croatia for less than five years without interruptions. The first situation is when the EEA citizen dies during temporary stay for work which lasted for two years

272. Article 173, Aliens Act.
273. Article 174, Aliens Act.
274. Article 16, para. 3, Ordinance on the Manner of Determining the Conditions for Entry and Residence in the Republic of Croatia of EEA Citizens and Members of their Families.
275. Article 176, Aliens Act.

without interruptions prior to death or if his or her death was the result of a work-related injury or professional disease. The second is when the family member is the spouse who lost Croatian nationality by marriage to an employed or self-employed EEA citizen.[276]

The family member will be issued the residence card with a term of validity of up to ten years, which is automatically renewed. Stay of a family member outside the RoC for a period under two years without interruptions will not affect the validity of the permanent residence permit.[277]

163. EEA citizens and their family members on a permanent residence are protected from expulsion unless there are serious reasons for protection of public order or national security. If the EEA citizen resided in Croatia for the previous ten years or is a minor, he or she can be expelled from Croatia only for the necessary reasons for the protection of national security.[278]

276. Article 177, Aliens Act.
277. Article 178, paras 3 and 4, Aliens Act.
278. Article 180, Aliens Act.

Chapter 2. Students and Researchers

164. TCNs have the right to reside in Croatia for the study and research, as stipulated by the Aliens Act. The study or research are considered one of the purposes for which it is possible to acquire a residence permit in Croatia.

165. Temporary residence for the purpose of studies will be granted to a TCN who studies at a Croatian higher education institution.[279] Apart from the general conditions for issuing temporary residence permit (*see* above Part II, Chapter 2), a student has to provide evidence of enrolment into a higher education institution, of evidence of coming to Croatia within the framework of student exchanges or youth mobility, or to vocational practice through an authorised organisation or based on international or interuniversity agreements or youth mobility (if longer than ninety days), and proof of health insurance.

166. The temporary residence permit for the study will be issued for the term of validity of up to one year, that is, by the end of the academic year. If the student comes to Croatia under the EU programme or multilateral programme which includes mobility of students, or agreement between higher education institutions, he or she will be granted a permanent residence permit with a validity period of up to two years.[280]

167. The Aliens Act provides for an exception to the general rule that the students need to apply for a temporary residence. If the student holds a valid permit issued by another EEA Member State and comes to Croatia under an EU programme or multilateral programme which includes mobility of students, or agreement between higher education institutions, he or she will be able to spend part of his studies at a higher education institution in Croatia during a period of not more than 360 days without acquiring temporary residence permit. This right will not be exercised if a student is considered a threat to public order, national security or public health. A student has to inform the police administration or the station about the intention to study when registering for a short stay. If the student is not coming to Croatia under EU programme or multilateral programme which includes mobility of students, or agreement between higher education institutions, he or she must apply for temporary residence permit in order to spend part of studies at the higher education institution in the RoC.[281]

168. Temporary stay for the scientific research shall be granted to a TCN who concluded a hosting contract with a Croatian institution carrying out scientific research activities and who intends to stay in Croatia for longer than 180 days. Apart from the general conditions for issuing temporary residence permit (*see* Part II, Chapter 2), a researcher has to provide evidence that he or she concluded a hosting contract. A researcher will be issued a temporary residence permit with validity for

---

279. Article 63, Aliens Act.
280. Article 63, paras 2 and 3, Aliens Act.
281. Article 63, paras 5 and 6, Aliens Act.

up to one year, and if he or she is coming under the EU programmes or multilateral programmes which includes mobility of researchers, the residence permit will be issued for a period of up to two years. Family members of the researcher can also acquire temporary residence permits, under the conditions stipulated by the Aliens Act for family reunification.[282]

169. Students and researchers are granted the same rights as Croatian citizens concerning:

- working conditions, including wages and termination of employment, as well as safety requirements at the workplace;
- freedom to establish trade union or take membership in a trade union or any professional organisation; as well as the rights and privileges provided by such organisations, including the right to collective bargaining and concluding collective agreements;
- general and vocational education;
- recognition of educational and professional qualifications;
- measures of social security as defined by the EU regulations;
- tax relief, to the extent that a TCN is considered a resident in Croatia for tax purposes;
- access to goods and services and to the supply of goods and services made available to the public, including procedures for obtaining subsidised accommodation;
- counselling services provided by the Croatian Employment Office.[283]

282. Article 64, Aliens Act.
283. Article 64a, Aliens Act.

Chapter 3. Labour and Economic Migration

§1. Labour Employment

170. As explained, a temporary residence permit can be granted for the purpose of working in Croatia, as a residence and work permit, for the time period necessary to perform the job or for the term of the employment contract or some other relevant contract, up to one year or up to two years for some categories of TCNs.[284] TCNs can work in Croatia within the annual quota which is yearly set by the Government of RoC based on the situation on the labour market. For work outside the annual quota, it must be explained why the working place cannot be filled by Croatian workers.[285] TCNs who are high-skilled workers can acquire a temporary residence based on the EU Blue Card for up to two years. Temporary residence and work permit are also issued to a *TCN holding an EU Blue Card* who has resided in another EEA Member State for the last eighteen months based on a Blue Card, provided that he or she meets the conditions for the residence of high-skilled workers in Croatia. A TCN can work only on such jobs for which he or she has a residence and work permit or a work registration certificate, and only with the employer with whom he contracted employment. An employer may assign a TCN only to such jobs for which he or she has a residence and work permit or a work registration certificate.[286] For more detailed information, *see* Part VII on access to the labour market.

§2. Seasonal Workers and Temporary Workers

171. Seasonal workers can work based on the residence and work permit for seasonal work for up to ninety days or up to six months.[287] TCNs in the framework of an intra-corporate transfer (temporary secondment from the company located in the third country to which the TCN is bound by a work contract, to a Croatian entity belonging to the same group of undertakings) can work on residence and work permit up to three years (managers and specialist), or for a year (graduate trainee).[288] A temporary residence permit for the work can be granted to a worker posted for a limited period to work in Croatia by a foreign employer in the framework of the transnational provision of services, for a maximum period of one year.[289] For more detailed information *see* Part VII on access to the labour market.

284. Article 80, paras 2 and 3, Aliens Act.
285. Article 77, para. 1, Aliens Act.
286. Article 73, paras 5 and 6, Aliens Act.
287. Article 75a, Aliens Act.
288. Article 79a, Aliens Act.
289. Articles 86 and 87, Aliens Act.

§3. Independent Economic Activities

172. Independent economic activities and self-employment of TCN are regulated by the Aliens Act, the same as the other forms of employment of aliens. Therefore, the same regime of obtaining residence permits is also applicable for self-employed aliens.

§4. Investment Activities

173. The Aliens Act does not provide any special regime for obtaining a residence permit based on the investment activities of aliens. TCNs will be granted the stay and work permit outside the annual quota provided that they perform key activities in a company, or hold an ownership share in such company of at least 51%, and the company either benefits from incentives in accordance with a regulation on the award for incentives for investments, or performs strategic investment projects in Croatia.[290]

290. Article 79, para. 1, Aliens Act.

Chapter 4. Humanitarian Reasons

§1. Humanitarian Grounds

174. According to the Aliens Act, a temporary residence permit under humanitarian grounds can be grounded to:

- victims of trafficking who participate in an assistance and protection programme;
- abandoned minors or minors who are a victim of organised crime, or who remained without parental protection, guardianship or escort for some other reasons;
- TCNs who had the status of refugee for at least ten years or who were included in a reconstruction, return or housing care programme for refugees from Croatia;
- TCNs who cooperate with the competent bodies and their participation is crucial in the criminal proceedings conducted against the employer who employed them illegally;
- for other serious justified humanitarian reasons.[291]

For more detailed information on temporary residence, *see* Part II, Chapter 2.

§2. Unaccompanied Minor Children

175. The Aliens Act and the Act on International and Temporary Protection define an unaccompanied minor as a TCN or a stateless person younger than eighteen years of age who entered the RoC unaccompanied by an adult person responsible for him or her in the sense of parental care, until placed under the care of such a person, and includes all minors who are left unaccompanied after they entered the RoC.[292]

176. In principle, unaccompanied minors arrive in Croatia irregularly. When an unaccompanied minor is caught in the territory of the RoC, he or she will first be interviewed at the competent police station. When a police officer establishes that the child is an unaccompanied minor, the officer will immediately invite an expert employee of the competent Centre for Social Welfare who will be present during the police procedure. A police officer and an expert worker are obliged to inform the child about his rights as well as about the procedure to follow, and the Centre for Social Welfare will appoint a guardian. The guardian should be trained to work with children and cannot have a conflict of interest with the child. The guardian will not be appointed to an unaccompanied minor older than 16 years of age who is married, which can be understood that persons from the age of 16 have the capacity 'to perform procedural acts' on their behalf in procedures for international protection. A guardian must be present during transport to the social welfare institution. For

291. Article 65, Aliens Act.
292. Article 2, Aliens Act and Art. 4, Act on International and Temporary Protection.

identification, the unaccompanied minor over 14 is obliged to undergo taking fingerprints and photographing. Until recently, guardians were appointed among persons with whom the child entered RoC. This practice is generally not in the best interests of the child and carries certain risks for the child since it is almost impossible to determine whether such a person meets the legal requirements necessary to perform the duties of a legal guardian. This is because most children do not possess any personal documents or possess forged documents; therefore, it is impossible to determine their identity. However, it must be noted that this practice has changed. In addition, guardians of unaccompanied children were generally appointed among the social workers of the competent Centre for Social Welfare. Still, according to the available reports of Non-Governmental Organisations (NGOs), due to the work overload of social workers and the language barrier between the guardian and the client, their role was usually formal, and there was no active involvement in the procedure to protect the best interest of the child or other clients.[293]

177. In July 2018, the Government of the RoC adopted Protocol on the Treatment of Unaccompanied Children.[294] The previous Protocol was adopted in 2013 with the purpose to determine the actors/providers of the obligations and procedures for enabling identification, assistance and protection of unaccompanied minors, including those who seek asylum, for the purpose of timely and effective protection of their rights and interests, in order to ensure the safe return, family reunification or re-integration into Croatian society. Although the Protocol has contributed to the better treatment of unaccompanied children by competent institutions, its full implementation is not without difficulties. Therefore, a new and improved Protocol has been adopted.

178. Abandoned minors or minors who are a victim of organised crime or who remained without parental protection, guardianship or escort for some other reasons can be granted a temporary residence on humanitarian grounds (*see* Part II, Chapter 2). However, there are no publicly available data about the number of unaccompanied minors granted a temporary residence in Croatia based on Article 65 of the Aliens Act. Unaccompanied minors who entered Croatia irregularly can either apply for asylum (*see* Chapter 5 on Asylum) or will be deported from Croatia. If deportation is not immediately possible, they can also be detained in the reception centre, but only as a measure of last resort (for more information, *see* Part V on sanctions against unlawful stay or residence).

179. The MoI will terminate a temporary residence issued under humanitarian grounds if the purpose because of which temporary residence was granted to an

293. Croatian Law Centre, Legal Representation of Unaccompanied Children. Croatia. AIDA Report. http://www.asylumineurope.org/reports/country/croatia/age-assessment-and-legal-representation-unaccompanied-children-0 (accessed 20 Jul. 2018).

294. https://mdomsp.gov.hr/UserDocsImages/djeca%20i%20obitelj/Protokol%20o%20postupanju%20prema%20djeci%20bez%20pratnje.pdf (accessed 20 Jul. 2018).

unaccompanied minor terminates, or if required by the reasons of protecting public order, national security and public health.[295]

§3. Victims of Trafficking in Human Beings

180. Victims of trafficking who participate in an assistance and protection programme can be granted a temporary residence on humanitarian grounds (*see* Part II, Chapter 2), whether or not they decide to cooperate with the investigation or prosecution. Residence permits are valid for up to one year and are renewable. However, no foreign victims requested temporary residence status in 2017 (one in 2016).[296] In principle, the mobile team will request a residence permit on behalf of the victim, to the police which will transmit this request to the central services of the MoI.[297]

181. The MoI is in charge of identification of the victim in cooperation with civil society organisations and, if a victim is a minor, with the ministry competent for social welfare. After the identification of a victim, the national coordinator for combating trafficking in human beings from MoI immediately informs the victim of the responsible head of coordination of mobile teams. Mobile teams consist of specially trained representatives of the social welfare centres, Croatian Red Cross and civil society organisations which deal with combating human trafficking.[298] The mobile team will transfer the victim to the reception centre after identification where the victim will stay until decides about accepting the aid and protection programme.[299] The victim must decide whether or not he or she will accept the programme of aid and protection in sixty days from the day of identification. If the victim is a child, the child's guardian will decide on the child's participation in the assistance and protection programme within ninety days, with the consent of the Centre for Social Welfare, bearing in mind the best interests of the child and the child's opinion. However, this timeframe (sixty/ninety days) need not be complied with if it is established that the alien identified as a victim is not a victim or if he actively, voluntarily and on his initiative renewed his contacts with the perpetrators of the criminal offences or if required by reasons of protecting public order and national security. It is therefore not linked to a decision on whether to co-operate with the investigations and prosecutions of traffickers, but rather to benefit from

---

295. Article 71, Aliens Act.
296. US Department of the State, Trafficking in Persons Report 2018, https://www.state.gov/documents/organization/282798.pdf (accessed 20 Jul. 2018).
297. Report concerning the implementation of the Council of Europe Convention on Action against Trafficking in Human Beings by Croatia, GRETA (2015)33, https://rm.coe.int/CoERMPublicCommonSearchServices/DisplayDCTMContent?documentId=0900001680630e7c (accessed 20 Jul. 2018).
298. There are four mobile teams based in Zagreb, Rijeka, Split and Osijek, which cover the entire country. Local jurisdiction over the team is determined according to the place where the victim was identified.
299. Protocol on Identification, Assistance and Protection of Victims of Human Trafficking, 2017, https://pravamanjina.gov.hr/UserDocsImages/dokumenti/Protokol%20za%20identifikaciju,%20pomo%C4%87%20i%20za%C5%A1titu%20%C5%BErtava%20trgovanja%20ljudima.pdf (accessed 21 July 2018).

assistance measures available to victims of human trafficking. During this period (recovery and reflection period), victims benefit from the same rights as those having formally accepted to be assisted (safe accommodation, healthcare, psycho-social assistance, legal assistance and interpreters). They are also provided information about their rights.

182. The person shall lose the right to assistance and protection if he or she based their testimony on false facts if the circumstances under which he or she acquired the right to assistance and protection terminated or if he or she acts contrary to the rules laid down in the assistance and protection programme.[300] The aid and protection programme includes medical and psycho-social protection, safe accommodation, translation and interpretation services, legal assistance and a safe return to the country of origin.[301]

183. A victim granted temporary residence is entitled to safe accommodation, health protection, financial assistance, education and work.[302] According to the Protocol on Trafficking in Human Beings Victims Integration/Reintegration, several institutions are involved in the procedure for integrating/reintegrating the victim: the ministries competent for health (for health protection and insurance), social welfare (social welfare rights), science and education (inclusion into training programmes at all levels), Croatian Employment Service (employment mediation, professional orientation and training as per the labour market needs), and the civil society organisations.[303]

184. Temporary residence will terminate if the victim lost the victim status, if it is established that the victim is abusing his or her position, or if it is required for reasons of protecting public order, national security and public health. If a victim is a minor, when deciding on termination of a temporary residence, the MoI will have to consult the competent body for social welfare.[304]

185. The MoI is also in charge of the safe return of a TCN who has the victim status, considering victim's rights, safety and dignity. If possible, the return should be voluntary. Minors who are the victims of trafficking will not be returned to any state if, after an evaluation of the risks and safety, there are indications that the return would not be in the best interests of the minor. According to the Protocol on Procedures during Voluntary return of Victims of Human Trafficking, before deciding on return, a victim has to be timely informed about all the facts and legal consequences of return. From the moment of identification of a victim until victim's

---

300. Article 66, Aliens Act.
301. *Ibid.*
302. Article 68, Aliens Act.
303. Protocol on Trafficking in Human Beings Victims Integration/Reintegration, 2012, https://pravamanjina.gov.hr/UserDocsImages/arhiva/protokoli/Protocol%20on%20Trafficking%20in%20Human%20Beings%20Victims%20Integration_Reintegration.pdf (accessed 23 Jul. 2018).
304. Article 71, Aliens Act.

return to the country of return, risk assessment is done in order to determine the degree of victim's safety and safety of victim's family in the country of return, including:

- opportunities for a safe return to the location where the victim wishes to return;
- name of person or organisation that will take over the victim in the country of return;
- family and social circumstances of the victim;
- the possibility of safe accommodation (safe house or alternative accommodation);
- circumstances around the criminal offence and perpetrator;
- if necessary, other circumstances important for victim's return.

The MoI must assess risks and safety of return, in cooperation with competent state authorities, international and non-governmental organisations and the Croatian Red Cross. During the process of return, the MoI will provide the victim with the necessary travel documents if the victim does not have any and will also organise victim's trip and provide necessary accompaniment of police officers to the country of return. If necessary, the MoI will organise a health check of the victim in cooperation with the state administration body competent for health protection. If a victim is a child, accompaniment of guardian will be provided during the process of return.[305]

186. In practice, Croatia is increasingly becoming a country of origin as well as being a country of destination and transit for victims of human trafficking. In the period 2011 until June 2015, there were 118 identified victims. The majority of the identified victims were Croatian nationals, with only sixteen foreign victims, with the main countries of origin being Bosnia and Herzegovina, Romania and Serbia. However, it is acknowledged that the real scale of human trafficking is higher than the figures of identified victims suggest. Due to a low number of identified victims among aliens, including asylum seekers and aliens detained in the Reception Centre for Foreigners, one of the suggestions for the improvement is the continuous training on the identification of victims of trafficking should be provided to staff, including medical staff, of centres for asylum seekers and irregular migrants.[306] In 2016, thirty victims were identified, and twenty-nine in 2017. According to the latest reports, the government demonstrated increased efforts by working with NGOs to strengthen proactive victim identification efforts for first responders among large migrant flows and identifying more foreign victims within migrant flows.[307]

---

305. Protocol on Procedures during Voluntary return of Victims of Human Trafficking, 2017, https://pravamanjina.gov.hr/UserDocsImages/dokumenti/Protokol%20o%20postupanju%20pri%20dobrovoljnom%20i%20sugurnom%20povratku%20%C5%BErtava%20trgovanja%20ljudima.pdf (accessed 18 Jul. 2018).
306. Report concerning the implementation of the Council of Europe Convention on Action against Trafficking in Human Beings by Croatia https://rm.coe.int/CoERMPublicCommonSearchServices/DisplayDCTMContent?documentId=0900001680630e7c (accessed 18 Jul. 2018).
307. US Department of the State, Trafficking in Persons Report 2017, https://www.state.gov/reports/2017-trafficking-in-persons-report/ (accessed 18 Jul. 2018).

§4. Others

187. A temporary residence permit under humanitarian grounds can be grounded to a TCN who had the status of refugee for at least ten years or who was included in a reconstruction, return or housing care programme for refugees from Croatia (*see* more below).

Chapter 5. Asylum

§1. Conditions

188. Conditions for refugee status (including refugee status, subsidiary protection status and temporary protection status) are defined in the Act on International and Temporary Protection. From the moment when the intention to apply for international protection is expressed up until the final decision on the application (or until the moment of termination of the asylum procedure), the person is considered an applicant for international protection (asylum seeker).[308] When the decision by which asylum (refugee status) or subsidiary protection is granted, the person is considered a refugee (the Croatian legislation use the term 'asylee') or a foreigner under the subsidiary protection.

189. An asylum seeker (or applicant for international protection) is a TCN or stateless person who expressed the intention to lodge an application for international protection. Exceptionally, an applicant may also be a national of an EU Member State when this is prescribed by the provisions of Protocol 24 to the Treaty of Lisbon.[309]

I. Refugee Status

190. According to the Act on International and Temporary Protection, asylum is defined as the status recognised by a decision of the competent body if a person is meeting the conditions laid down in the Act.[310] Asylum is granted to persons who are outside the country of their nationality or habitual residence and have a well-founded fear of persecution owing to their race, religion, nationality, affiliation to a certain social group or political opinion, as a result of which they are not able or do not wish to accept the protection of that country.[311] The conditions for granting refugee status are aligned with the EU Qualification Directive. The elements important for the assessment of whether the conditions for refugee status are met are further defined by the law and elaborated in the following parts of this chapter.

191. In order to be regarded as persecution, an act must be:

- sufficiently serious or repeated, so that they constitute a serious violation of fundamental human rights, in particular, the rights from which derogation cannot be made under Article 15, paragraph 2 of the European Convention for the Protection of Human Rights and Fundamental Freedoms;[312] or

308. The terms 'applicant for international protection' and 'asylum seeker' are used as synonyms.
309. Article 4, Act on International and Temporary Protection.
310. *Ibid.*
311. Article 20, Act on International and Temporary Protection.
312. Includes the right to life, prohibition of torture, inhuman and degrading treatment or punishment, prohibition of slavery and servitude, and the prohibition of punishment without law.

- an accumulation of various measures, including violations of human rights, which is sufficiently severe as to affect an individual similarly as referred to in the previous subparagraph.

Moreover, the acts of persecution, among other acts, include:

- acts of physical or emotional violence, including sexual violence;
- legal, administrative, police and/or judicial measures which are discriminatory or are implemented in a discriminatory manner;
- judicial prosecution or punishment which is disproportionate or discriminatory;
- denial of judicial redress which leads to disproportionate or discriminatory punishment;
- court prosecution or punishment for refusal to undertake military service during conflicts, where the performance of military service would include criminal offences or acts which fall within the grounds for exclusion as set out in the Act on International and Temporary Protection;
- acts of a gender-specific or child-specific nature.[313]

Also, there have to be a connection (nexus) between the reasons for persecution and the acts of persecution and/or the absence of protection against such acts. In assessing whether a person has a well-founded fear of being persecuted, it is immaterial whether the person possesses the racial, religious, national, social or political characteristics which cause the persecution, provided that such characteristics are attributed to him or her by the perpetrator of persecution.

192. Actors of persecution or serious harm include:

- state bodies;
- parties or organisations that control the state or a significant part of the state territory;
- non-state actors, if it is shown that state bodies or parties, or organisations that control a significant part of the state territory, including international organisations, are unable or unwilling to provide protection against persecution or serious harm.[314]

193. Providers of protection in the country of origin, if they are able and willing to provide protection, include state bodies, parties and national or international organisations that control the state or a significant part of the state territory. When assessing whether parties and national or international organisations control a significant part of the state territory, MoI should take into account the official guidance provided in EU legislation. Ability to provide the protection presumes the existence of an effective legal system for the detection, prosecution and punishment of acts constituting persecution or serious harm, as well as the possibility of providing that protection for the complete removal of the grounds on which the person bases his

313. Article 23, Act on International and Temporary Protection.
314. Article 25, Act on International and Temporary Protection.

or her fear of persecution or serious harm.[315] The inclusion of parties and international organisations as possible providers of protection in the country of origin is questionable since non-state actors are not the party to international human rights treaties, so accordingly, they cannot be held liable for non-fulfilment of obligations from international human rights and refugee instruments.[316]

194. The Act on International and Temporary Protection adhere to the principle of 'sur place', and provides that a well-founded fear of being persecuted or a real risk of suffering serious harm can be based on the events which took place after the person left the country of origin, or the activities the person is engaged in after he or she left the country of origin, in particular where it is established that they constitute the expression and continuation of beliefs and/or orientation held in the country of origin. However, if the person submits a subsequent application for asylum, the well-founded fear of persecution or the real risk of suffering serious harm cannot be founded exclusively on the circumstances which the person created in order to meet the conditions for the approval of international protection.[317]

195. Grounds for persecution should be assessed by taking the following elements into account. *Race* refers in particular to skin colour, descent, and membership of a specific ethnic group. *Religion* refers in particular to theistic, non-theistic and atheistic beliefs, participation in or abstention from formal worship in private or public, either alone or in community with others, other religious acts or expressions of faith, or forms of personal or communal conduct founded on religious beliefs or which stem from them. *Nationality*, in particular, refers to membership of a group that is specific in terms of its culture, ethnic or linguistic identity, common geographical or political origins, or its relationship with the population of another state, which may also include citizenship. *Political opinion*, in particular, refers to an opinion, thought or belief about matters related to the potential persecutors and their policies or methods, irrespective of whether the applicant acted upon that opinion, thought or belief. *Specific social group*, in particular, refers to members who share innate characteristics or a common background that cannot be changed, or characteristics or beliefs that are so fundamental to identity or conscience that these persons should not be forced to renounce them, and where that group has a distinct identity in their country of origin because it is perceived as being different by the surrounding society. Depending on the circumstances in the country of origin, a particular social group may also include a group based on the common characteristics of sexual orientation. Sexual orientation cannot be deemed to include acts considered to be criminal according to the legislation of the RoC. Aspects related to gender, including gender identity, are given due consideration to determine membership of a specific social group or identifying the characteristics of such a group.[318]

---

315. Article 26, Act on International and Temporary Protection.
316. Goranka Lalić Novak, 2016, *supra*, p. 148.
317. Article 24, Act on International and Temporary Protection.
318. Article 22, Act on International and Temporary Protection.

196. The Act on International and Temporary Protection provides that the internal resettlement alternative should be established when assessing the application. It will be considered that it is safe to internally resettle to a specific part of the country of origin where the person does not have a well-founded fear of persecution or of suffering serious harm or could receive effective protection from persecution or from suffering serious harm. In addition, it will be considered that the internal resettlement is possible if the person can travel to that part of the country safely and lawfully, can gain admittance to that part of the country, and can be reasonably expected to settle there.

197. The Act on International and Temporary Protection includes the exclusion of asylum clauses, although it has been established that an alien meets the conditions for granting protection. Accordingly, refugee status is not recognised if:

- the person enjoys the protection of or is receiving assistance from a body or agency of the UN, other than the UNHCR;
- the person already has the approval of stay in a state in which, on the basis of that approval, he or she has the same rights and obligations as the nationals of that state;
- there are serious reasons for considering that the person committed, incited or in some other way participated in committing a crime against peace, a war crime or a crime against humanity as defined by the provisions of international instruments;
- there are serious reasons for considering that the person committed, incited or in some other way participated in committing a serious non-political crime outside the RoC, before his or her arrival in the RoC, also including particularly cruel acts, even if committed with an allegedly political objective;
- there are serious reasons for considering that the person committed, incited or in some other way participated in committing acts contrary to the purposes and principles of the UN as set out in the Preamble and in Articles 1 and 2 of the Charter of the UN.[319]

The last reason is not fully aligned with Article 1(F)(c) of the Geneva Convention and the Qualification Directive since it must be established that the alien is guilty of committing acts contrary to the purposes and principles of the UN.[320] If the protection or assistance from an organ or agency of the UN (other than the UNHCR) has ceased for any reason over which the person has no control and his/her status has not been finally resolved pursuant to the relevant resolutions adopted by the General Assembly of the UN, he or she will be granted asylum.[321]

319. Article 30, para. 1, Act on International and Temporary Protection.
320. Goranka Lalić Novak, 2016, *supra*, p. 193.
321. Article 30, para. 2, Act on International and Temporary Protection.

II. Subsidiary Protection Status

198. Subsidiary protection is granted to an alien who does not meet the conditions to be granted asylum if justified reasons exist to indicate that if returned to his or her country of origin, he or she would face a real risk of suffering serious harm and who is unable, or owing to such risk, is unwilling to avail themselves of the protection of that country. Act on International and Temporary Protection further stipulates the forms of damage or consequences that should be considered serious harm – the threat of death by penalty or execution, torture, inhuman or degrading treatment or punishment and serious and individual threat to the life of the civil population due to arbitrary generalised violence in situations of international or internal armed conflicts.[322]

199. As in the case of conditions for granting the asylum, Act on International and Temporary Protection stipulates who can be considered actors of serious harm. Those actors include: state bodies; parties or organisations that control the state or a significant part of the state territory; non-state actors if it is shown that state bodies or parties or organisations that control a significant part of the state territory, including international organisations, are unable or unwilling to provide protection against persecution or serious harm.[323]

200. Like in the case of asylum conditions, providers of protection in the country of origin, include state bodies, or parties and national or international organisations that control the state or a significant part of the state territory, provided that they are able and willing to provide protection, Ability to provide the protection presumes the existence of an effective legal system for the detection, prosecution and punishment of acts constituting persecution or serious harm, as well as the possibility of providing that protection for the complete removal of the grounds on which the person bases his/her fear of persecution or serious harm.[324]

201. Although an alien meets the condition for protection, subsidiary protection will not be granted in case if:

- there are serious reasons for considering that he or she has committed, incited or in some other way participated in committing a crime against peace, a war crime, or a crime against humanity as defined by the provisions of international instruments;
- there are serious reasons for considering that he or she has committed, incited or in some other way participated in committing a serious crime (a crime which, pursuant to the Croatian legislation, is punishable by imprisonment for five years or more);

322. Article 21, Act on International and Temporary Protection.
323. Article 25, Act on International and Temporary Protection.
324. Article 26, Act on International and Temporary Protection.

- there are serious reasons for considering that he or she has committed, incited or in some other way participated in committing acts contrary to the purposes and principles of the UN as set out in the Preamble and in Articles 1 and 2 of the Charter of the UN;
- if he or she constitutes a danger to the national security or public order of the RoC.[325]

III. Temporary Protection

202. According to the Act on International and Temporary Protection,[326] temporary protection is protection approved in an extraordinary procedure, in the case of a mass influx or an imminent mass influx of displaced persons from third countries who cannot be returned to their country of origin, especially if a risk exists that due to the mass influx it is not possible to conduct effectively the procedure for approval of international protection, for protecting the interests of the displaced persons and others who request protection. Mass influx means a large number of displaced persons who come from a specific country or geographical area, whether their arrival was spontaneous or aided.

203. Displaced persons are TCNs or stateless persons who have had to leave their country or region of origin, or have been evacuated, in particular in response to an appeal by international organisations, and are unable to return to safe and enduring conditions because of the situation prevailing in that country, who may fall within the scope of Article 1A of the Geneva Convention or other international or national instruments giving international protection. In particular, it is considered that displaced persons are persons who have fled areas of armed conflict or endemic violence, and persons at serious risk of, or who have been the victims of, systematic or generalised violations of their human rights.[327]

204. A TCN or a stateless person will be excluded from temporary protection if serious reasons exist from which it is believed that:

- he or she has committed a crime against peace, a war crime or a crime against humanity as defined by the provisions of international instruments;
- he or she committed, incited to or participated in a serious non-political crime outside the RoC before arriving in the RoC, also including particularly cruel acts, even if they were committed with an allegedly political objective;
- he or she has committed acts contrary to the purposes and principles of the UN as set out in the Preamble and Articles 1 and 2 of the Charter of the UN;
- a well-founded suspicion exists that he or she is a threat to national security;

325. Article 31, Act on International and Temporary Protection.
326. Article 78, Act on International and Temporary Protection.
327. Article 78, para. 2, Act on International and Temporary Protection.

– he or she has been convicted by a final judgment of a particularly serious criminal offence for which under the legislation of the RoC a prison sentence of five years or longer may be imposed.[328]

205. A decision on introducing temporary protection will be rendered by the Government of the RoC pursuant to a decision by the Council of the EU on the existence of a mass influx of displaced persons.[329] Until the end of 2018, no such decision has been rendered in RoC.

206. Temporary protection will be approved for one year, but the longest duration of temporary protection is three years. With the expiry of the time limit of one year, temporary protection may be extended for six months and up to no more than one year, unless the temporary protection has ended. It can be further extended for no more than one year based on a decision by the Council of the EU. Temporary protection can be ceased in two situations: when the maximum duration of temporary protection has been reached or by a decision of the Council of the EU.[330]

IV. Other

207. Croatian legislation in the field of asylum does not provide any other statuses for persons in need of protection.

§2. PROCEDURES

I. Asylum Procedure

208. There are three types of asylum procedures in RoC: the regular procedure, the accelerated procedure, and the procedure at border crossings or in transit zones. In addition, the MoI can dismiss the applications or subsequent applications for international protection and conduct the Dublin procedure.

A. Competent Authorities and Applicable Legislation

209. The competent body for deciding on applications for asylum is the MoI. Issues concerning aliens, asylum seekers and asylees lie under the competence of the Directorate for Administrative and Inspection Affairs, as part of which the Sector for Administrative Affairs, Foreigners and Citizenship was set up, and within that Sector, the Service for Foreigners and Asylum, with the following departments: Department for Status Issues of Foreigners; the Asylum Department; the Visa Department; and the Reception Centre for Asylum Seekers. The officers working in

328. Article 80, Act on International and Temporary Protection.
329. Article 78, para. 4, Act on International and Temporary Protection.
330. Article 79, Act on International and Temporary Protection.

the Department for Asylum decide on asylum applications. The decision makers conduct interviews of asylum seekers, and on the basis of the asylum seeker's application, the testimony presented during the interview, the presented evidence and available reports on the situation in the country of origin, they render decisions on asylum applications. Pursuant to the General Administrative Procedure Act, the autonomy of the official person in establishing relevant facts and circumstances and freely assessing them, or the autonomy of the official person in resolving administrative matters, is one of the fundamental principles of the administrative procedure.[331] Against the decision rendered by the MoI, an administrative dispute may be brought before the administrative court.[332]

210. Asylum procedure is by nature administrative procedures meaning that for procedural issues that are not regulated in the Act on International and Temporary Protection, the General Administrative Procedure Act should be used as a subsidiary source of law.

B. Activities in the Procedure

211. There are several steps that will be performed from the moment an alien expresses the intention to seek asylum in the RoC until his or her application has been finally rejected and a return decision has been rendered. The procedure is conducted in the Croatian language and the Latin script. If the alien does not understand Croatian, a translator/interpreter will be provided for a language which he or she may justifiably be presumed to understand and in which he or she can communicate. If possible, a translator/interpreter of the same sex will be engaged in order to ensure a full account of the reasons for the application or other justified reasons.[333]

212. An alien (a TCN or a stateless person) may express his or her intention to apply for international protection during border control at a border crossing. If already in the territory of the RoC, his or her expression of intention to apply for international protection can be made at the police administration, a police station or a reception centre for foreigners. Those bodies should register the alien in the records of the MoI no later than three working days from the day the alien expressed his or her intention. An intention to apply for international protection may also be expressed in the Reception Centre for Asylum Seekers in extraordinary circumstances in order to allow access to the procedure for approving international protection. In that case, the Reception Centre will register the alien in the records of the MoI within six working days from the day when he or she expressed their intention. The body which undertook registration shall issue a certificate of registration of the alien in the records of the MoI, and, as necessary, will set a time limit in

331. Article 9, General Administrative Procedure Act.
332. Articles 38, 39, 41, 42 and 43, Act on International and Temporary Protection.
333. Article 14, Act on International and Temporary Protection.

which the person must report to the Reception Centre to lodge an application.[334] For a minor, the intention to apply for international protection shall be expressed by a legal representative.[335] In the majority of cases in RoC, aliens who have unlawfully entered the country expresses the intention when apprehended by a police officer.

213. Aliens who wish to express their intention to apply for international protection should be provided by police officers with all necessary information on the procedure for the approval of international protection in a language which they may be expected to understand and in which they can communicate. The MoI should inform an asylum seeker within fifteen days from the expression of intention of how the procedure of approval of international protection is conducted, on the rights and obligations they have in that procedure, and the possibility of applying to representatives of the UNHCR and other organisations who work to protect the rights of refugees, and the possibility of receiving free legal assistance.[336]

214. In 2017 and 2018, there were warnings and reports of international and Croatian non-governmental organisations on expulsions of refugees and possible asylum seekers (push backs) from Croatia coupled with limited access to international protection. Group of NGOs warned on several occasions of the practice of mass returns of persons from Croatia to Serbia being caught while illegally crossing the State border. According to the reports, people not only from Afghanistan but also from Iraq, Pakistan, Syria and other countries were not given access to the asylum procedure, although some explicitly and repeatedly approached the Croatian police, expressing their wish to apply for international protection. Instead, they were, according to the reports, illegally expelled to Serbia from Croatian territory. The reports stressed that this was accompanied by violence and degrading treatment by the Croatian police.[337] Similar concerns were raised by Human Rights Watch, Save the Children and OXFAM.[338]

---

334. Article 33, Act on International and Temporary Protection.
335. Article 16, para. 1, Act on International and Temporary Protection.
336. Article 59, paras 1–2, Act on International and Temporary Protection.
337. *See*: Welcome Initiative and Are You Syrious?, A Report on Unlawful and Forced Expulsion of Refugees from the Republic of Croatia, 24 Jan. 2017 (http://welcome.cms.hr/wp-content/uploads/2017/01/Izvje%C5%A1taj-o-nezakonitim-i-nasilnim-protjerivanjima-izbjeglica-iz-RH-AYS-i-Inicijativa-Dobrodo%C5%A1li.pdf, accessed 1 Jun. 2018); Second Report on Unlawful and Forced Expulsion of Refugees from the Republic of Croatia, 7 Mar. 2017 (http://welcome.cms.hr/wp-content/uploads/2017/03/DRUGI-IZVJE%C5%A0TAJ-O-NEZAKONITIM-I-NASILNIM-PROTJERIVANJIMA-IZBJEGLICA-IZ-REPUBLIKE-HRVATSKE.doc, accessed 1 Jun. 2018); Report on the new wave of violence against refugees on Croatian borders, 29 May 2017 (http://welcome.cms.hr/wp-content/uploads/2017/05/REPORT-ON-THE-NEW-WAVE-OF-VIOLENCE-AGAINST-REFUGEES-ON-CROATIAN-BORDERS.pdf, accessed 1 Jun. 2018); Welcome Initiative! and Center for Peace Studies, Are You Syrious?, and No-name Kitchen, Fourth Report on Illegal Pushbacks of Refugees from the Republic of Croatia in the period from June 2017 to February 2018, 28 Feb. 2018 (http://welcome.cms.hr/wp-content/uploads/2018/02/Fourth-Report-on-Illegal-Pushbacks_01032018.pdf, accessed 1 Jun. 2018).
338. Human Rights Watch, 'Croatia: Asylum Seekers Forced Back to Serbia', 20 Jan. 2017 (http://bit.ly/2k9cLej, accessed 3 Jun. 2018); Save the Children, 'Refugee and Migrant Children Injured in Illegal Border Push-Backs Across Balkans', 24 Jan. 2017 (http://bit.ly/2jH4a2I, accessed 3 Jun. 2018); OXFAM, 'A Dangerous "Game": The Pushback of Migrants, Including Refugees, at

Croatian Ombudswoman issued a report to the State Attorney of the RoC (DORH) stating that MoI systematically works on covering up their mistreatment of refugees. As stated in the Ombudsman's report, there are two controversial police decrees. The order of the Illegal Migration Service, that is, the Police Directorate of 25 November 2016, according to which all irregular migrants, nationals of Afro-Asiatic countries, who entered the RoC illegally from the Republic of Serbia and were detained in the Police Administration of Zagreb (PUZ), are to be handed over to Police Station Tovarnik (at the border with Serbia) and handed over to the Chief Officer for further procedure. That order was further supplemented by the Police Directorate's order of 15 February 2017 on the treatment of irregular migrants found in the depths of the territory when all police administrations were ordered to transfer all irregular migrants to the police administration at the state border, with prior written notice, which is then responsible for determining the details and the circumstances of their entry and stay in Croatia. If a police administration who found irregular migrants in their jurisdiction considers that the transfer to the police station at the border would not be useful for strengthening the external border protection measures, the procedure can be conducted under the Aliens Act, by that police administration.[339] The EU Human Rights Agency (FRA) in its report pointed out that border crossings in some Member States, such as Croatia, France, and Poland, remain demanding for migrants, as they have been returned from these countries without the ability to seek international protection. Pushbacks and refusal to asylum seekers to enter are just some of the facing challenges for migrants trying to enter or travel across the EU.[340] MoI denied all accusations and stated that access to asylum has been thoroughly respected.[341]

215. Immediately following the expression of intention to apply for international protection, the officers will take fingerprints and photograph an asylum seeker, establish his or her identity, establish how he or she entered the RoC, the travel route, and personal circumstances of importance for assessing the private and procedural guarantees. Photographs and fingerprints may be taken from any asylum seeker over the age of 14. In the case of the temporary inability to take fingerprints for medical or other reasons which were not caused deliberately by the actions of the asylum seeker, the asylum seeker is obliged to provide fingerprints within the shortest possible period following the resolution of the reason why it was not possible to take fingerprints earlier. Otherwise, his or her fingerprints will be taken by police officers without consent.[342] If the asylum seeker has refused to give fingerprints, the MoI may decide on his/her application in the accelerated procedure.[343]

Europe's Borders', April 2017 (https://www.oxfam.org/en/research/dangerous-game-pushback-migrants-including-refugees-europes-borders, accessed 5 Jun. 2018).

339. https://www.ombudsman.hr/hr/pravobraniteljica-dostavila-dorh-u-sve-informacije-o-okolnostima-pogibije-madine-husseini/ (accessed 6 Jun. 2018).

340. http://fra.europa.eu/en/news/2018/migrant-border-crossings-remain-challenging-some-member-states (accessed 6 Jun. 2018).

341. https://mup.hr/novosti/5415/u-2017-u-hrvatskoj-odobreno-najvise-medunarodnih-zatita-do-sada (accessed 19 Jun. 2018).

342. Article 33, paras 5–8, Act on International and Temporary Protection.

343. Article 41, para. 1, Act on International and Temporary Protection.

216. An alien who has illegally entered the RoC, coming directly from the territory where he/she was persecuted, or has been exposed to serious harm will not be punished for his or her illegal entry or stay provided that they express an intention to apply for international protection without delay and shows good cause for his or her illegal entry or stay.[344]

217. After the completion of the described procedure conducted by the police, the asylum seeker is transferred to and accommodated in the Reception Centre for Asylum Seekers. Applications for international protection are lodged directly with the Reception Centre (orally for the record) within the shortest possible time, and no later than within fifteen days from registration of the intention to seek asylum. The application of a minor is covered by the application made by his or her legal representative. However, a minor older than 16 years of age who is married may take part independently in the procedure for the approval of international protection.[345] Currently, there are two Reception Centres: in the suburbs of Zagreb (capital city) and in Kutina (a small city located some 80 kilometres out of Zagreb). The total capacity of accommodation is 700 persons. Upon arrival at the Reception Centre, a hygienic examination of the asylum seeker is performed and then he or she is referred to a health examination, following the regulations on healthcare of aliens.[346] According to the MoI, out of the total number of international protection applicants during 2017, 77% of procedures were suspended because the asylum seekers left the RoC before the end of the procedure.[347]

218. During the interview, the asylum seeker should explain to the official from the MoI all the facts and circumstances of importance for the procedure to approve international protection. The asylum seeker should give credible and convincing explanations of the reasons on which he or she bases their application for asylum, present all the available evidence used to support the application, and reply truthfully to all asked questions. The asylum seeker is obliged to attend and participate in the interview in person regardless of whether he or she has a legal representative, a guardian *ad litem* and/or an attorney. If possible, the interview will be conducted by an official of the same sex in order to ensure a full explanation of the application or for other justified reasons. An official from the MoI may interview the asylum seeker several times in order to establish the facts of the case.[348]

219. There are several situations under which it is considered that there is no need to undertake an interview, including when:

- a decision may be rendered based on the evidence available to approve international protection;

344. Article 8, Act on International and Temporary Protection.
345. Article 16, paras 2–3, Act on International and Temporary Protection.
346. Ordinance on the Realisation of Material Reception Conditions, OG 135/2015.
347. https://mup.hr/novosti/5415/u-2017-u-hrvatskoj-odobreno-najvise-medunarodnih-zatita-do-sada (accessed 20 Jun. 2018).
348. Article 35, paras 1–3, 5 and 7, Act on International and Temporary Protection.

- the asylum seeker is unfit or unable to be interviewed owing to enduring circumstances beyond his or her control;
- the admissibility of a subsequent application is being assessed.

If there is no interview, the asylum seeker or a member of his or her family will be permitted to submit evidence and make statements relevant for a decision on his/her application.[349]

220. When assessing the application, the MoI will collect and consider all the relevant facts and circumstances, especially taking into consideration:

- the relevant statements and evidence presented by the asylum seeker, including information about whether he or she was or could be exposed to persecution or the risk of suffering serious harm;
- current facts about the country of origin and, if necessary, the country through which the asylum seeker travelled, including the laws and regulations of that country, and the manner in which they are applied, as contained in various sources, especially those of the UNHCR and the European Asylum Support Office and other organisations dealing with the protection of human rights;
- the position and personal circumstances of the asylum seeker, including factors such as gender or age, in order to assess on those bases whether the procedures and acts to which he or she was or could be exposed, would amount to persecution or serious harm;
- whether the asylum seeker's activities since leaving the country of origin were aimed at creating the essential conditions for the approval of international protection, in order to assess whether those activities would expose the asylum seeker to persecution or the risk of serious harm if returned to that country;
- whether the asylum seeker could receive the protection of a country of which he/she can prove nationality.[350]

221. The fact that the asylum seeker has already been exposed to persecution or serious harm, or the threat of such persecution or harm is a serious indication of the well-founded fear of persecution or risk of suffering serious harm unless good reasons exist to consider that such persecution or serious harm will not be repeated.[351]

222. The asylum seeker has to cooperate with the MoI and provide all available documentation, and present true and accurate information relating to his or her identity, age, nationality, family, country and address of the previous residence, former applications, travel routes, identification and travel documents and the reasons for applying for protection.[352]

349. Article 35, paras 8 and 9, Act on International and Temporary Protection.
350. Article 28, para. 2, Act on International and Temporary Protection.
351. Article 28, para. 3, Act on International and Temporary Protection.
352. Article 28, para. 1, Act on International and Temporary Protection.

223. The asylum seeker's statement will be considered to be credible in the part in which certain facts or circumstances are not supported by documentation (benefit of the doubt) if:

- the general credibility of the asylum seeker's statement has been established;
- the asylum seeker has made a real effort to support his or her application with documentation;
- all the relevant elements available to asylum seeker have been lodged, with a satisfactory explanation regarding the lack of other relevant elements;
- it is established that the asylum seeker's statements are consistent and convincing, and they do not contradict the specific and general information available which is relevant for deciding on the application; and
- the asylum seeker requested international protection as soon as possible or has justified why he or she did not do so.[353]

224. A decision on the application must be delivered in person to the asylum seeker in a language which he or she is expected to understand and in which he or she can communicate. If the MoI does not know where the asylum seeker is (e.g., if he or she has left the RoC and did not notify the MoI), and if the asylum seeker does not have a legal representative or attorney for receipt of documents, the decision will be displayed on the notice board of the Reception Centre. It will be considered executed after the passing of eight days from the day the document was placed on the notice board.[354]

225. Information on the asylum seeker will not be collected from his/her country of origin if the collection of that information could endanger the physical integrity of the asylum seeker and members of his or her family who have lodged an application together with them or the freedom and safety of members of the family who live in the country of origin. Personal and other information collected during the procedure to approve international protection, especially the fact that an application has been lodged, constitute official, classified information, and may not be sent to the country of origin or to other bodies that are not involved in the procedure. However, information on the name and surname, date of birth, sex, citizenship, family members, documents issued by the country of origin, last address in the country of origin, and fingerprints and photographs can be submitted to the country of origin or a third country for an asylum seeker whose application is refused by a final decision under the condition that that country agrees to accept them or the bodies of a third country for the purpose of implementing the Geneva Convention.[355]

353. Article 29, Act on International and Temporary Protection.
354. Article 36, Act on International and Temporary Protection.
355. Article 19, paras 4–6, Act on International and Temporary Protection.

C. Regular Procedure

226. In the course of a regular asylum procedure, the MoI as a competent body for asylum procedures must establish and assess all facts and circumstances of the case, including the objective and subjective elements of persecution, using the available and accessible country of origin information. An application which may be approved based on the facts that were established in the procedure has priority in decision-making. With its decision, the MoI may grant the alien asylum or subsidiary protection or reject the application if the asylum seeker does not meet the conditions for asylum or subsidiary protection; if the conditions are met for exclusion; or as manifestly unfounded if the asylum seeker does not meet the conditions for asylum or subsidiary protection, and there are circumstances for MoI to decide in accelerated procedure.[356] By granting asylum or subsidiary protection, the person acquires certain rights arising from the status (*see* below).

227. The MoI has to render a decision on the application within six months from the day of submission of a duly completed application or a duly completed and admissible subsequent application. Also, this time limit will run from the day the responsibility of the RoC is established for considering the application, or the day of the handover of the applicant to the RoC under the Dublin III Regulation.[357] The time limit may be extended for a further nine months if: the application includes complex facts and/or legal issues; many aliens are requesting international protection at the same time; the asylum seeker, through his or her actions, causes the time limit to be extended. The time limit may be extended for a further three months exclusively in order to ensure the complete consideration of the application. If no decision can be rendered within the time limits, the asylum seeker will be informed of this in writing and at his or her request shall be provided with information about the reasons for the failure to respect the time limit and about the time needed before which he or she may expect a decision. In addition, if it is expected that no decision will be rendered within all time limits on account of the temporary unsafe situation in the country of origin, the MoI will periodically verify the situation in the country of origin, and inform the asylum seeker and the European Commission within a reasonable time of the reasons for failure to render a decision. Only in this situation, a decision must be within twenty-one months from the day the application is lodged.[358]

356. Article 38, Act on International and Temporary Protection.
357. Regulation (EU) No. 604/2013 of the European Parliament and of the Council of 26 Jun. 2013 establishing the criteria and mechanisms for determining the Member State responsible for examining an application for international protection lodged in one of the Member States by a third-country national or a stateless person, OJ L 180, 29 Jun. 2013, pp. 31–59.
358. Article 40, Act on International and Temporary Protection.

228. In the asylum procedure, the asylum seeker has the right to information and counselling, interpretation and translation, the right to access UNHCR or organisations providing legal aid and to receive a written decision which will be delivered in a language which he or is expected to understand and in which he or she can communicate.[359]

229. The asylum seeker, at his or her request, will be provided with legal and procedural information on the approval of international protection, taking into account the circumstances of the specific case, in a language which it may be reasonably be presumed that they understand and in which they are able to communicate. The right to legal counselling is limited only to asylum seekers who have no financial resources or things of significant value that enable them to have an appropriate standard of living. The legal counselling should be provided by organisations working to protect the rights of refugees or by attorneys with whom the MoI concludes a contract on the provision of legal counselling.[360] However, until the end of 2018, the MoI did not conclude a contract on legal counselling. In procedures before MoI, legal assistance to asylum seekers is offered by civil society organisations as part of their regular activities, and not financed by the state budget. Free legal assistance is limited to the procedure before Administrative Courts.

230. The procedure to approve international protection will be terminated, which means that a decision on the substance on the asylum application is not issued, if the asylum seeker withdraws the application for international protection. The application is deemed withdrawn if the asylum seeker:

- withdraws the application;
- does not appear at the Reception Centre or avoids lodging an application and fails to justify this within two days of the time limit set for appearing at the Reception Centre, or for lodging an application;
- does not respond to the summons to an interview, and does not justify his or her absence within two days of the scheduled interview;
- leaves his or her place of residence for longer than two days without the consent of the Reception Centre.

Therefore, in addition to the situation when the asylum seeker withdraws the application, the asylum procedure can also be terminated under the circumstances from which the MoI is in a position to conclude that the applicant has not been sufficiently diligent or that the applicant has left RoC and does not intend to continue the asylum procedure.

231. If asylum seeker did not appear at the Reception Centre or avoided lodging an application and failed to justify it, the MoI will institute proceedings ex officio and render a decision on termination of the procedure. In the last two situations described above, the MoI may reject the applicant's application if, from the facts

359. Articles 14, 36 and 59, Act on International and Temporary Protection.
360. Article 59, paras 3–5, Act on International and Temporary Protection.

and circumstances established, it may be assessed that he or she does not meet the conditions for approval of international protection.[361]

D. Accelerated Procedure

232. The MoI will decide in an accelerated procedure if, in conducting the regular procedure, it is established that:

- the asylum seeker has presented only facts which were irrelevant for an assessment of the application;
- the asylum seeker has consciously misled the MoI by presenting false information or unreliable documents, or by not providing relevant information or by concealing documents which could have had a negative effect on the decision;
- the asylum seeker in bad faith has probably destroyed documents that establish identity or nationality to provide false information about his or her identity and/or nationality;
- the asylum seeker has presented inconsistent, contradictory, manifestly inaccurate or unconvincing statements contrary to the verified information on the country of origin, rendering his or her application unreliable;
- a subsequent application is admissible;
- the asylum seeker has already been living for a long time in the RoC and for no justifiable reason failed to express his or her intention to apply for international protection earlier;
- the asylum seeker expressed the intention to apply for international protection for the clear purpose of postponing or preventing the enforcement of a decision which would result in his or her expulsion from the RoC;
- the asylum seeker represents a risk for the national security or public order;
- it is possible to apply the concept of safe country of origin;
- the asylum seeker has refused to give fingerprints.

The MoI will inform asylum seeker that a decision is to be rendered on his or her application in an accelerated procedure. In the accelerated procedure, the MoI will render a decision within two months from the day the application or a subsequent admissible application is lodged. This time limit will run from the day the responsibility of the RoC is established for considering the application, or the day of the handover of the RoC under the Dublin III Regulation. If no decision can be made within two months, the MoI will decide on the application in a regular procedure. Against a decision rendered in an accelerated procedure, a claim may be brought before the Administrative Court within eight days from the day the decision is served.[362]

233. A subsequent application for international protection means the intention to apply for international protection expressed after a final decision has been taken on

361. Article 39, Act on International and Temporary Protection.
362. Article 41, Act on International and Temporary Protection.

a previous application, or a decision by which the procedure was terminated. The subsequent application must be comprehensible and contain relevant facts and evidence which arose after the finality of the decision or which the asylum seeker did not present during the previous procedure for justified reasons. The asylum seeker must submit an explanation of the subsequent application to the Reception Centre directly in writing, or orally if the person is illiterate. The MoI will decide on the subsequent application no later than within fifteen days from the day of receiving it. The admissibility of the subsequent application will be assessed by the facts and evidence it contains, and in connection with the facts and evidence already used in the previous procedure. The subsequent application will be dismissed if it is established that it is inadmissible. If the MoI established that the subsequent application is admissible, it would render a decision once again on the substance of the application, and the previous decision will be revoked.[363]

E. Procedures at Border Crossings or in Transit Zones

234. If the alien expresses the intention to lodge an asylum application or a subsequent application at a border crossing or in the transit zone of an airport, seaport or inland water, the MoI will render a decision on the application in a procedure at the border crossing or in the transit zone within twenty-eight days from the day the application is lodged. This procedure is possible only if the asylum seeker is provided with the material reception conditions (accommodation, food and clothing provided in kind, remuneration of the cost of public transport used for participation of the procedure for the approval international protection, and financial assistance), and if the application or subsequent application may be rejected as manifestly unfounded (when the asylum seeker does not meet the conditions for asylum or subsidiary protection, and there are circumstances for MoI to decide in accelerated procedure). If the MoI did not render a decision within twenty-eight days from the day the application is lodged, the applicant would be permitted to enter the RoC in order to conduct the procedure for the approval of international protection.[364]

235. The asylum seeker has a right to legal counselling, which are to be provided by organisations working to protect the rights of refugees and which based on an agreement with the MoI provide legal counselling. Those organisations should be provided with sufficient access to border crossings or transit zones in airports, seaports or inland water ports. Access to an applicant by an attorney or representative of an organisation that works to protect the rights of refugees, apart from the UNHCR, may be temporarily restricted when this is necessary for the protection of the national security or public order of the RoC.[365]

236. Against the decision on the application in a procedure at the border crossing or in the transit zone a claim may be brought before the Administrative Court

363. Article 47, Act on International and Temporary Protection.
364. Article 42, paras 1, 4, 5, Act on International and Temporary Protection.
365. Article 42, paras 2–3, Act on International and Temporary Protection.

within five days from the day the decision is served. The MoI will submit the case file no later than within eight days from the day of receipt of the decision by which the Administrative Court requests the case file. The Administrative Court shall render a judgment on the claim within eight days from the day of receipt of the case file.[366]

237. Currently, there are two transit reception centres, in Tovarnik (near the border with Serbia) and Trilj (near the border with Bosnia and Herzegovina), which can be used for the accommodation of asylum seekers whose application can be decided upon in a procedure at the border crossing or in the transit zone. However, for now, no such cases were reported by the MoI.

F. Dublin Procedure

238. The Dublin procedure is a procedure defined in accordance with the Dublin III Regulation, in which the MoI assesses which country is responsible for examining the application and not the fulfilment of conditions for international protection by an alien who expressed his or her intention to seek asylum. If the responsibility is established of another EEA Member state to consider the application, the MoI will dismiss an application. Until handed over to the other Member State, the applicant is accommodated in the Reception Centre. If an alien under transfer (to another EEA Member State) lodge a subsequent application, it will be considered in the responsible Member State, and a subsequent application lodged in the RoC will be dismissed as inadmissible.[367]

239. An alien under transfer will have the rights and obligations as all asylum seekers in the RoC until handover is effected to the responsible Member State.[368]

G. Dismissal of Applications or Subsequent Applications

240. The MoI will dismiss an application if:

- the applicant has been granted international protection in another EEA Member State;
- the applicant has been granted international protection in a third state whose rights he or she still enjoys, provided that he or she will be received back into that state;
- it is possible to apply the concept of a safe third country;
- it is possible to apply the concept of European safe third country;
- the responsibility is established of another Member State to consider the application;

366. Article 42, para. 6, Act on International and Temporary Protection.
367. Article 43, Act on International and Temporary Protection.
368. Article 52, para. 5, Act on International and Temporary Protection.

– the application was lodged by a national of an EEA Member State.

The subsequent application will be dismissed if the MoI assessed it as inadmissible. Against a decision to dismiss an application or subsequent application, it is possible to bring a claim before the Administrative Court within eight days of the day of service of the decision.[369]

H. *Safe Country of Origin, Safe Third Country and European Safe Third Country*

241. The Act on International and Temporary Protection defines the concepts of safe country of origin, safe third country and European safe third country.

242. Country of origin is the country whose nationality is held by a TCN or the country in which a stateless person previously had habitual residence. If the TCN has more than one nationality, the country of origin shall be each of the countries whose national he or she is.[370] A country is considered a safe country of origin if, based on the legal situation, the application of the law and the general political circumstances, it can be shown that there is generally and consistently no persecution, or risk of suffering serious harm. This can be established based on the information on relevant laws and regulations and their application, protection of the rights and freedoms as defined by the European Convention for the Protection of Human Rights and Fundamental Freedoms and UN human rights treaties, respect for the principle of *non-refoulement,* and the system of effective remedies.[371] The list of safe countries of origin has been adopted in 2016 and currently includes the following countries: Algeria, Bosnia and Herzegovina, Montenegro, Morocco, Albania, Kosovo, Macedonia, Serbia, Turkey and Tunisia.[372]

243. The MoI is obliged to establish for each application individually whether the conditions are met for the application of the concept of safe country of origin. A country included on the list of safe countries of origin can be considered a safe country of origin in a specific case only if the applicant has the nationality of that country or had his or her previous residence in that country as a stateless person and has not explained in a credible manner why that country of origin cannot be deemed to be a safe country of origin for them. The applicant will be informed in good time of the application of the concept of the safe countries of origin in order to enable him or her to challenge it, given the specific nature of their circumstances.[373]

369. Article 43, Act on International and Temporary Protection.
370. Article 4, para. 1, No. 10, Act on International and Temporary Protection.
371. Article 44, s. 1, Act on International and Temporary Protection.
372. Decision on the List of Safe Countries of Origin in Proceedings for Granting International Protection (*Odluka o listi sigurnih zemalja podrijetla u postupku odobrenja međunarodne zaštite*), OG 45/2016.
373. Article 44, paras 5–6, Act on International and Temporary Protection.

244. A safe third country is a country where the asylum seeker stayed before arriving in the RoC and where he could apply for asylum. A third country is considered to be safe if the applicant is protected from persecution, or the risk of suffering serious harm, where he or she enjoys the benefits stemming from the *non-refoulement* principle, and there is a possibility of access to an effective procedure of being granted protection, pursuant to the Geneva Convention. The fact that the conditions have been met to apply the concept of safe third country is established for each application separately, by assessing whether a country meets the conditions and whether a connection exists between that country and the asylum seeker, on the basis of which it may reasonably be expected that he or she could request international protection there, taking into account all the facts and circumstances of his or her application. The asylum seeker will be informed in good time of the application of the safe third country concept, so that he or she can challenge this, given the specific characteristics of their circumstances.[374] If it is possible to apply the concept of a safe third country, the application for international protection will be dismissed. Against a decision to dismiss an application, it is possible to bring a claim before the Administrative Court within eight days of the day of service of the decision.[375] In the case that the application is rejected as it is established that the asylum seeker came from a safe third country, the MoI will provide him or her with a document in the language of that country, informing the state bodies that the application has not been examined on merit in the RoC. If the third country refuses to accept the alien, the MoI will render a decision on merit.[376]

245. European safe third country is a country where the asylum seeker has stayed before arriving in RoC. A European country will be considered a safe third country if it has ratified and applies the provisions of the Geneva Convention and the European Convention for the Protection of Human Rights and Fundamental Freedoms, including standards on effective remedy, and has established an effective procedure for the approval of protection pursuant to the Geneva Convention. The MoI will determine whether the conditions have been met for the application of the concept of European safe third country for each application individually. The application of an alien who entered the territory of the RoC unlawfully from a European safe third country will be dismissed, taking into account the *non-refoulement* principle and the special circumstances of a humanitarian or political character, as well as the rules of international public law. The asylum seeker has to be informed in good time of the application of the European safe third country concept, so that he or she can challenge it, given the specific characteristics of their circumstances.[377] If it is possible to apply the concept of a safe third country, the application for international protection will be dismissed. Against a decision to dismiss an application, it is possible to bring a claim before the Administrative Court within eight days of the day of delivering the decision.[378] If the application is rejected being established

374. Article 45, Act on International and Temporary Protection.
375. Article 43, Act on International and Temporary Protection.
376. Article 45, Act on International and Temporary Protection.
377. Article 46, Act on International and Temporary Protection.
378. Article 43, Act on International and Temporary Protection.

that the asylum seeker came from a European safe third country, the MoI will provide him or her with a document in the language of the European safe third country, informing the state bodies of that country that the application has not been examined on merit in the RoC.[379]

I. Special Procedures and Reception Guarantees

246. The Act on International and Temporary Protection provides special procedural and reception guarantees for asylum seekers who, given personal circumstances, are not completely capable of exercising their rights or obligations without the appropriate support.[380] Those personal circumstances may be related, among others, to their age, gender, sexual orientation, gender identity, disability, serious illness, mental disorder, or as a consequence of torture, rape or other serious forms of psychological, physical or sexual violence. Therefore, there is a need to provide those persons with appropriate support for the use of the rights and obligations stipulated by the Act.[381]

247. The procedure of recognising the personal circumstances of asylum seekers in need of special procedural and reception guarantees should be conducted continuously by specially trained police officers, employees of the MoI and other competent bodies, from the moment of the expression of intention to apply for international protection to the service of the decision on the application. If it is not possible to provide the appropriate support to asylum seekers who need special procedural guarantees, especially victims of torture, rape or another form of serious psychological, physical or sexual violence, the MoI will neither conduct accelerated procedure nor the procedure at border crossings or in transit zones.[382]

II. Review of the Decision Rejecting the Application for Asylum

248. The decision rendered by the MoI in the regular or special procedure (accelerated procedure, the procedure at border crossings or in transit zones) may be challenged before the Administrative Court.

249. In 2010 the new system of Administrative Court adjudication had been established with the new Administrative Disputes Act. The Act established a two-instance system of administrative adjudication where administrative disputes are resolved by four first-instance administrative courts for the area of one or more counties with a seat in Zagreb, Split, Osijek and Rijeka, and the High Administrative Court of the RoC as a second-instance court. The Act determined the territorial

379. Article 46, Act on International and Temporary Protection.
380. Article 4, para. 15, Act on International and Temporary Protection.
381. Article 15, para. 1, Act on International and Temporary Protection.
382. Article 15, paras 2–3, Act on International and Temporary Protection.

jurisdiction of the administrative courts *in favorem* of the complainant. If the complainant does not have permanent residence, temporary residence or a seat in the RoC, the Administrative Court with territorial jurisdiction is the court in the area of which the body of public law has issued the decision or carried out an action in the first instance has its seat.[383] Therefore, the Administrative Court in Zagreb is most frequently the competent court dealing with asylum seekers' claims, as the MoI has its seat in Zagreb. In 2012, administrative courts decided in a panel of three judges, but with the amendments of the Act in December 2012, the provision on the composition of the court was changed, and it was determined that a sole judge is deciding in court proceedings.[384]

250. A claim brought before the Administrative Court will suspend the enforcement of the MoI decision, except in the case of:

- the dismissal of an application in the accelerated procedure;
- the dismissal of an application, when the asylum seeker has been granted international protection in another Member State of the EEA, or international protection in a third state whose rights he or she still enjoys, provided that he or she will be received back into that state;
- the dismissal of a subsequent application if the MoI assesses that the application is inadmissible.

The claim may contain a request for suspensive effect, pursuant to the regulations on administrative disputes, except if the applicant has already been living for a long time in the RoC and for no justifiable reason failed to express his or her intention to apply for international protection earlier. The MoI will submit the case file within eight days from the day of receipt of the decision by which the Administrative Court requests the case file, for a decision on the request for suspensive effect. The Administrative Court must decide on the request for suspensive effect within eight days of the day of delivery of the case file. An appeal against the first-instance judgment by the Administrative Court will not have suspensive effect.[385]

III. Unaccompanied Minor Asylum Claimants

251. An unaccompanied minor is a TCN or a stateless person younger than eighteen years of age who entered the RoC without an adult person responsible for him or her in the sense of parental care, until placed under the care of such a person, and includes all minors who are left unaccompanied after they entered the RoC.[386] According to the Act on International and Temporary Protection, all procedures should be conducted in line with the principle of the best interests of the child. The best interests of the child shall be assessed, considering:

383. Article 13, para. 2, Administrative Disputes Act.
384. Article 14, Administrative Disputes Act.
385. Article 51, Act on International and Temporary Protection.
386. Article 4, para. 17, Act on International and Temporary Protection.

- the welfare and social development of the child, and his or her origin;
- the protection and safety of the child, especially if the possibility exists that he or she is a victim of trafficking in human beings;
- the child's opinion, depending on his or her age and maturity;
- the possibility of family reunification, etc.[387]

252. When an unaccompanied minor is caught in the territory of the RoC, he or she will first be interviewed at the competent police station. When a police officer establishes that the child is an unaccompanied minor, they will immediately invite an expert employee of the competent Centre for Social Welfare who will be present during the police procedure and will appoint a guardian. A police officer and an expert worker are obliged to inform the child about his rights as well as about the procedure to follow. The guardian should be trained to work with children and cannot have a conflict of interest with the child.

253. An unaccompanied minor can express the intention to apply for international protection. Guardian will not be appointed to an unaccompanied minor older than 16 years of age who is married, which can be understood that persons from the age of 16 have the capacity 'to perform procedural acts' on their behalf in procedures for international protection. An unaccompanied minor must be informed immediately about the appointment of the guardian.[388] There is no time limit prescribed by law for the appointment of the representative of an unaccompanied minor, but it is obvious from the Act on International and Temporary Protection that a guardian has to be appointed before submitting an application for international protection. If that is in the best interests of the child, the guardian of an unaccompanied minor shall undertake all the necessary activities, including contact and cooperation with the competent ministries, other state and foreign bodies, and NGOs, in order to reunite the child with his or her family.[389] A guardian must be present during transport to the social welfare institution or the Reception centre for asylum seekers, depending on the decision on the accommodation of an unaccompanied minor. For the identification, the unaccompanied minor over 14 is obliged to undergo fingerprints and photography.

254. Until recently, guardians were appointed among persons with whom the child entered RoC. This practice is generally not in the best interests of the child and carries certain risks for the child since it is almost impossible to determine whether such person meets the legal requirements necessary to perform the duties of a legal guardian. Most asylum seekers do not possess any personal documents or have forged documents, therefore it is impossible to determine their identity. However, it must be noted that this practice has changed. Also, guardians of unaccompanied children were generally appointed among the social workers of the competent Centre for Social Welfare. From 2016, employees of the Croatian Red

387. Article 10, paras 1–2, Act on International and Temporary Protection.
388. Article 17, paras 1–3, Act on International and Temporary Protection.
389. Article 10, para. 3, Act on International and Temporary Protection.

Cross, as well as employees of some other organisations, were also appointed as guardians of unaccompanied asylum-seeking children.[390]

255. An unaccompanied minor will lodge an application for international protection in person in the presence of the guardian. However, a guardian can lodge an application on behalf of an unaccompanied minor if, in the return procedure, it is assessed that a minor needs international protection given his or her circumstances. The MoI officials trained to work with children will conduct the procedure.[391]

256. The unaccompanied minor is obliged to participate in person in the MoI interview in the presence of the guardian. The guardian must prepare the unaccompanied minor in good time for the MoI interview and provide him or her with information on the significance and consequences of the interview. The communication has to be conducted in a language which may justifiably be assumed that a minor understands and in which he or she can communicate. The MoI will bear the costs of interpretation. Applications of unaccompanied minors have priority in decision-making.[392]

257. As a rule, the MoI will not decide upon applications lodged by an unaccompanied minor in the accelerated procedure. The exception is possible only in cases when:

- a minor lodged a subsequent application that is considered admissible;
- a minor represents a risk for the national security or public order of the RoC;
- it is possible to apply the concept of safe country of origin.

The procedures at border crossings or in transit zones will not be applied to applications of unaccompanied minors.[393]

258. If in the procedure to approve international protection doubt arises regarding the age of an unaccompanied minor, a procedure to assess the minor's age will be conducted. In age-related assessment, the priority is given to non-medical methods, i.e., available data about the child, including professional opinions of persons involved in working with the minor. If the information available is insufficient, a medical examination will be conducted, with the prior written consent of the minor and the guardian *ad litem*. The medical examination will be conducted using a physical examination, x-ray of the teeth and/or hands, with full respect for the dignity of the unaccompanied minor. An unaccompanied minor will be informed in writing, in a language which he or she may justifiably be presumed to understand and in which he or she can communicate, about the manner of examination and its possible consequences for his or her health, the consequences of the results of the

---

390. Croatian Law Centre, Legal Representation of Unaccompanied Children. Croatia. AIDA Report. http://www.asylumineurope.org/reports/country/croatia/age-assessment-and-legal-representation-unaccompanied-children-0 (accessed 15 Jul. 2018).
391. Article 17, paras 4–6, Act on International and Temporary Protection.
392. Article 17, paras 7–9, Act on International and Temporary Protection.
393. Article 17, paras 10–11, Act on International and Temporary Protection.

medical examination for the application for asylum, as well as the consequences of unjustified refusal of consent. In the case of unjustified refusal of consent, the unaccompanied minor shall be deemed to be an adult applicant. The application cannot be refused exclusively based on the fact that consent to perform a medical examination was not given. During the medical examination, an unaccompanied minor who does not understand Croatian shall be provided with a translator/interpreter for a language which he or she may justifiably be presumed to understand and in which he or she is able to communicate. If following the results and report on the undertaken medical examination, there is still doubt regarding the age of the minor, the concept of benefit of the doubt shall be applied.[394] According to the available reports, until March 2017, the age assessment procedure has not been conducted. However, in the past, with some asylum seekers claiming that they were children, some Centres for Social Welfare had the practice of conducting age assessments on their own. In practice, in most of those cases, age assessment was conducted based on the physical appearance of the child and an interview.[395]

259. From 2009 to 30 September 2018, a total of 869 unaccompanied asylum-seeking children were registered in Croatia.[396] The majority were males of the age 16–17. Unaccompanied minors are accommodated in different facilities, based on their age. Children up to 14 years of age are accommodated in children's homes, children over the age of 14 in Residential Child Care Institutions (institutions for children with behavioural problems), while children older than 16 years who seek international protection are accommodated in Reception centres for applicants for international protection. In practice, reception facilities are not adequate to accommodate unaccompanied minors because accommodation conditions do not meet their specific needs. The professional workers in these institutions are not trained to work with foreign nationals, and they do not have necessary anamnestic records about children, including data about the living conditions in the country of origin and reasons for leaving the country, whether the child has been a victim of ill-treatment, etc. Language barriers are often an obstacle because children cannot express their needs and even nonverbal communication can be hampered by cultural differences, which is frustrating for both children and staff. Aggressive, self-aggressive and destructive behaviour of children is often a consequence of helplessness due to the situation in which children are found.[397] Very often, unaccompanied minors would like to continue their travel towards the Western EU countries and consequently leave the RoC before the end of the asylum procedure.

---

394. Article 18, Act on International and Temporary Protection.
395. Croatian Law Centre, Asylum Procedure: Identification. AIDA report. http://www.asylumineurope.org/reports/country/croatia/identification (accessed 20 Jul. 2018).
396. MoI, Statistical Indicators of Persons Granted International Protection in 2018 to 30 September, https://www.mup.hr/public/documents/Statistika/Statisti%C4%8Dki%20pokazatelji%20osoba%20kojima%20je%20odobrena%20me%C4%91unarodna%20za%C5%A1tita%20u%20Republici%20Hrvatskoj%20zaklju%C4%8Dno%20do%2030.09.2018..pdf (accessed 1 Oct. 2018).
397. Ombudsman for Children, Recommendations for protection of the rights and interests of unaccompanied children, Zagreb, January 2017, http://dijete.hr/preporuka-pravobraniteljice-o-zastiti-djece-stranaca-bez-pratnje/ (accessed 1 Aug. 2018).

IV. Procedure for Temporary Protection

260. Temporary protection is approved in an extraordinary procedure, in the case of a mass influx or an imminent mass influx of displaced persons from third countries who cannot be returned to their country of origin, especially if a risk exists that due to the mass influx it is not possible to conduct the procedure for approval of international protection effectively. A decision on introducing temporary protection by the Government of the RoC will follow a decision rendered by the Council of the EU on the existence of a mass influx of displaced persons.[398]

261. The MoI has to inform foreigners under temporary protection in writing and as soon as possible about their rights and obligations in a language which they may be expected to understand, and in which they can communicate.[399]

262. A foreigner under temporary protection has the right to lodge an application for asylum, and the MoI can complete the procedure even after the end of temporary protection.[400] However, a foreigner under temporary protection who lodged an application for asylum may not exercise the rights of an asylum seeker while the temporary protection lasts. If the foreigner under temporary protection is not granted international protection, he or she will continue to exercise the rights granted within the temporary protection status (*see* Part II) for the remaining period of temporary protection.[401]

§3. Legal Position

I. Legal Position of Asylum Seekers

A. Rights and Obligations of Asylum Seekers

263. Rights of asylum seekers are defined in the Act on International and Temporary Protection and include the right to a residence and documents; freedom of movement; provision of the appropriate material reception conditions; healthcare; elementary and secondary education; information, legal counselling, and free legal assistance; freedom of religion; and work.[402]

264. Asylum seekers and their family members who arrived together with them, have the right of residence from the day of expression of intention to apply for international protection until the decision on the application becomes final. If the asylum seeker lodges a subsequent application with the intention of postponing or

398. Article 78, Act on International and Temporary Protection.
399. Article 91, Act on International and Temporary Protection.
400. Article 92, Act on International and Temporary Protection.
401. Article 83, paras 3 and 4, Act on International and Temporary Protection.
402. Article 52, Act on International and Temporary Protection.

preventing enforcement of the decision on expulsion which was dismissed as inadmissible, he or she shall have the right of residence until the decision on the subsequent application becomes final. An asylum seeker who lodge a new subsequent application after a decision has already been rendered on a previous subsequent application, will not have the right of residence.[403]

265. The asylum seekers right to residence is confirmed with a card for applicants for international protection. The MoI will issue the card within three days of the day of lodging the application for asylum to asylum seekers and his or her family members. However, asylum seekers who lodged an application at a border crossing or transit zone will not have a right to a card. In any case, the card is not proof of identity.[404]

266. The MoI may retain asylum seekers' travel or other identification documents, as long as there are reasons to retain them if this is necessary for the establishment or verification of identity, or protection of the national security or public order.[405]

267. Generally, asylum seekers have the right to freedom of movement in the RoC. The freedom of movement may be restricted if, based on all the facts and circumstances of the specific case, it is deemed to be necessary for:

- establishing the facts and circumstances on which the application for international protection is based, and which cannot be established without restriction of movement, especially if it is assessed that there is a risk of flight;
- establishing and verifying identity or nationality;
- protection of the national security or public order;
- prevention of abuse of the procedure if, based on objective criteria, which include the possibility of access to the procedure of approval of international protection, there is a well-founded suspicion that the intention to apply for international protection expressed during the procedure of expulsion was aimed at preventing the procedure from continuing.[406]

268. The freedom of movement of asylum seekers can be prohibited outside a specific area, limited to the area of the Reception Centre for Asylum Seekers or limited by detention in the closed-type Reception Centre for Foreigners. In the Reception Centre for Asylum Seekers, the freedom of movement can be restricted by the prohibition of movement outside the Reception Centre, appearance in person at the Reception Centre at a specific time or handing over travel documents or tickets. The measure of restriction of freedom of movement will be imposed for as long as there are reasons for this, but for no longer than three months. As an exception, for justified reasons, the application of the measure of restriction of freedom of movement

403. Article 53, Act on International and Temporary Protection.
404. Article 62, Act on International and Temporary Protection.
405. Article 63, Act on International and Temporary Protection.
406. Article 54, paras 1–2, Act on International and Temporary Protection.

may be extended for no longer than three more months. A decision on restriction of the freedom of movement will be rendered by the MoI, the police administration or the police station. A decision should establish the type of measure and its duration, which is proportionate to the aim of the restriction of movement. Against the decision, a claim may be brought before the Administrative Court, within eight days of the day of service of the decision. The responsible body must submit the case file to the Administrative Court within eight days of the day of receipt of the decision by which the Administrative Court requests the case file. The Administrative Court should render a decision on the claim after a personal interview within fifteen days from the day of receipt of the case file.[407]

269. Detention in the Reception Centre for Foreigners will be imposed if, by individual assessment, it is established that other measures referred would not achieve the purpose of restriction of freedom of movement.[408] The Act on International and Temporary Protection does not require the authorities to use the principle of proportionality when imposing a detention measure (weighing the severity of the measure with the aims it seeks to achieve). It has to be noted, however, that this is in line with the Reception Conditions Directive.[409]

270. A member of a vulnerable group will be detained in the Reception Centre for Foreigners only if it is established that such a form of accommodation is suitable for the person's circumstances and needs, and especially for his or her health. An unaccompanied minor will be detained in the Reception Centre for Foreigners separately from adults, for the shortest possible duration, if it is established that this measure of restriction of movement is necessary. In each case, the possibility of detention has to be determined by individual assessment.[410]

271. The movements of a foreigner under transfer (within the Dublin system) will be restricted only in order to ensure the enforcement of handover to another Member State of the EEA if it is assessed that risk of flight exists. The risk of flight is assessed on the basis of all the facts and circumstances of the specific case, especially in the view of earlier attempts to leave the RoC, the refusal to submit to verification and establishment of identity, concealment of information or providing false information on identity and/or nationality, violations of the provisions of the house rules of the Reception Centre, the results from the Eurodac system, and opposition to transfer. The same measures that restrict the freedom of movement of asylum seekers explained in the previous paragraphs can be applied to the foreigner under transfer. The measure can be imposed until the enforcement of transfer, but for no

407. Article 54, paras 5, 9, 11 and 12, Act on International and Temporary Protection.
408. Article 54, para. 6, Act on International and Temporary Protection.
409. Directive 2013/33/EU of the European Parliament and of the Council of 26 Jun. 2013 laying down standards for the reception of applicants for international protection, OJ L 180, 29 Jun. 2013, pp. 96–116.
410. Article 54, paras 7 and 8, Act on International and Temporary Protection.

longer than six weeks from the establishment of the responsibility of another Member State of the EEA. If an administrative dispute has been initiated, the time limit of six weeks will be counted from the time the decision on dismissal becomes final.[411]

272. Asylum seekers have the right to accommodation in the Reception Centre for Asylum Seekers. According to the Ordinances on the Realisation of Material Reception Conditions, they are entitled to accommodation in the reception centre from the moment they express the intention to lodge an application for international protection until the final decision on the application. An asylum seeker who expresses the intention to apply for international protection in detention, prison, hospital or similar institution will remain in the said institution while there are reasons for it, and upon release, he will be provided with accommodation at the reception centre.[412] During the accommodation in reception centre, they have the right to basic care which includes food and clothing provided in kind, remuneration of the cost of public transport for participating in the procedure for the approval of international protection, and financial assistance.[413] Before the entry into force of the Act on International and Temporary Protection in 2015, according to the previous Law on Asylum, asylum seekers were entitled to the same level of material reception conditions during all asylum procedures and during both the first-instance procedure and the appeal stage. However, this has changed with the new Act, and material conditions may be restricted during the subsequent application procedure.

273. In Croatia, there are two reception centres for asylum seekers: in Zagreb (with a maximum capacity of 600 persons) and in Kutina, which is located 80 km from Zagreb (with a maximum capacity of eighty-two persons). Both reception centres are managed directly by the MoI. The Centre in Kutina is aimed at the accommodation of vulnerable asylum seekers, however, with the increase of asylum seekers during 2016, vulnerable asylum seekers were also accommodated in one part of the Reception Centre in Zagreb. From the end of 2017, the Centre in Kutina also provides accommodation for refugees resettled from Turkey.

274. During the day the asylum seekers can freely leave and enter the Centre but have to return by 11 pm. They can stay outside the reception centre for longer than twenty-four hours with the prior consent of the reception centre.[414] Asylum seekers in the reception centres share rooms. In Kutina, families share a room, and unaccompanied children and single women are accommodated separately in rooms, while in Zagreb a maximum of four persons can share a room. Families are accommodated in the same room, but in Zagreb, a family with more than six members are accommodated in two rooms, if possible. There are sufficient showers and toilets, and the facilities are cleaned regularly. In both centres, residents get three meals per

---

411. Article 54, paras 3, 4 and 10, Act on International and Temporary Protection.
412. Article 7, Ordinance on the Realisation of Material Reception Conditions (*Pravilnik o ostvarivanju materijalnih uvjeta prihvata*), OG 135/2015.
413. Article 55, para. 1, Act on International and Temporary Protection.
414. Article 56, para. 6, Act on International and Temporary Protection.

day and pregnant women, recent mothers and children up to 16 years are also provided with an afternoon snack.[415] Due to the problems with infrastructure (electrical equipment, the water supply and sewage installations were worn out, as was the woodwork which all led to problems connected with the heating), parts of the Centre in Zagreb are currently under renovation. Since mid-2016, asylum seekers accommodated in Zagreb may use public transport free of charge.

275. Asylum seekers are allowed to stay at any address in the RoC, subject to prior approval by the MoI, at their own expense. Upon arrival at the reception centre, a hygienic and medical examination of the asylum seeker is performed. After examinations and submitting a request for international protection, the asylum seeker can move to private accommodation. In that case, he or she must provide a certified copy of the real estate lease agreement or a verified statement of the property owner to agree with the housing of the asylum seeker and to provide him or her with appropriate living conditions.[416]

276. According to the Act on International and Temporary Protection, financial aid is part of material reception, and the reception centre decides on the right to financial assistance.[417] Asylum seekers are entitled to financial support from the day when they were accommodated in the Reception Centre, either if they do not hold possession of greater value or if they do not have secured funds for personal use monthly amounting to more than 20% of a minimum amount for social welfare support.[418] Asylum seekers are entitled to financial support if, in the month for which they ask for the support, they have been accommodated in the Reception Centre for at least twenty-five consecutive days. The only exception from this rule in relation to continuous accommodation is the situation when the person has been admitted to the hospital for treatment or if he or she has requested to be absent from the Centre and that the request has been approved. If the asylum seeker is unjustifiably absent from the Reception Centre when the cash benefit is paid out, the financial assistance will be paid out when the payment is made for the next month. The right to financial assistance will not be provided to the asylum seeker who, unjustifiably and without permission, leaves the Reception Centre for more than five days during the month for which financial assistance is paid.[419] The amount of support is HRK 100 (app. EUR 13) per month.[420] Monthly financial support to asylum seekers is very low, although the amount varies if there are dependent family members. The system granting material reception conditions to asylum seekers is separate from the general welfare system for nationals and is less favourable compared to nationals. Asylum seekers who are detained in the Reception Centre for Foreigners are not allowed financial support. Just those asylum seekers who have not secured an

415. Croatian Law Centre, Conditions in reception facilities, AIDA report. http://www.asylumineurope.org/reports/country/croatia/conditions-reception-facilities-0 (accessed 15 Aug. 2018).
416. Articles 9 and 10, Ordinance on the Realisation of Material Reception Conditions.
417. Article 55, para. 2, Act on International and Temporary Protection.
418. Article 23, paras 1–2, Ordinance on the Realisation of Material Reception Conditions.
419. Article 24, Ordinance on the Realisation of Material Reception Conditions.
420. Decision on the Amount of Financial Assistance for Applicants for International Protection (*Odluka o visini novčane pomoći tražiteljima međunarodne zaštite*), OG 135/2015.

adequate standard of living have a right to material reception conditions, and accommodation in the Reception Centre for Foreigners should be considered the adequate standard of living is secured.[421]

277. The material reception conditions may be restricted or denied if the asylum seeker:

- does not reside in the Reception Centre in which accommodation has been provided for him or her;
- stays outside the Reception Centre for longer than twenty-four hours without the prior consent of the Reception Centre;
- possesses means which provide him or her with an appropriate standard of living;
- violates the provisions of the house rules of the Reception Centre.[422]

Based on a case by case assessment, the Reception Centre will render a decision to restrict or deny some of the material reception conditions. A decision must be proportionate to the aim pursued, considering the needs of an asylum seeker who require special procedural and/or reception guarantees and maintaining the dignity of the standard of living. If the circumstances referred under above mentioned first two points cease to exist, the Reception Centre has to render a decision to revoke the decision entirely or partially. An appeal may be brought before the Administrative Court within eight days from the delivery of the decision. The MoI has the right to request repayment of the costs of accommodation, including material damage incurred, in the cases prescribed in above mentioned last two points.[423]

278. Asylum seekers have the right to emergency health services, which include the right to emergency medical assistance and necessary treatment of illnesses and serious mental disorders. Vulnerable asylum seekers who need special reception and/or procedural guarantees, especially victims of torture, rape or other serious forms of psychological, physical or sexual violence, should be provided with the appropriate healthcare related to their specific condition or the consequences of those offences.[424] In practice, however, there are many deficiencies in providing healthcare to asylum seekers in reception centres in Zagreb and Kutina. Also, the additional healthcare for vulnerable groups is not accessible on a regular basis, as a system and mechanism for addressing special needs of asylum seekers has not been established. Therefore, several international and national non-governmental organisations provide complementary support to healthcare activities[425]

---

421. Article 3, Ordinance on the Realisation of Material Reception Conditions.
422. Article 55, para. 5, Act on International and Temporary Protection and Art. 4, para. 1, Ordinance on the Realisation of Material Reception Conditions.
423. Article 55, paras 6–9, Act on International and Temporary Protection.
424. Article 57, Act on International and Temporary Protection.
425. Croatian Law Centre, Healthcare, AIDA report. http://www.asylumineurope.org/reports/country/croatia/health-care (accessed 16 Aug. 2018).

279. The right to education is a constitutional right for all children staying in the RoC. According to the Act on International and Temporary Protection, only child applicants (i.e., under 18) are entitled to primary and secondary education. Applicants who have begun to exercise the right to secondary education are allowed to continue secondary education even after they turned 18. The right to primary and secondary education is granted to child applicants under the same conditions as for Croatian nationals, and children can access education within thirty days of lodging an application for asylum. If a child does not speak Croatian or speaks it insufficiently, he or she shall be provided with preparatory classes or supplementary classes in the Croatian language, as well as supplementary classes in individual subjects.[426] In November 2011, the Programme of Croatian for preparatory classes for elementary and secondary school students who do not speak or speak Croatian insufficiently was adopted, which involves an intensive seventy-hour course of Croatian for a maximum of one academic year.[427]

280. According to the available reports, there are obstacles to accessing secondary education for asylum-seeking children. The major problem when accessing school is the language barrier, but there has been progress in the last few years. Problems arose mainly relating to the organisation of preparatory Croatian classes, lack of documentation on previous education as well as in relation to the expansion of the so-called e-matica system (centralised system of the Ministry of Science and Education with the data of the pupils), as asylum seekers do not have an individual identification number required for registration in this system.[428]

281. Before expressing their intention to apply for asylum, asylum seekers will be provided by police officers with all necessary information on the procedure for the approval of international protection. Additionally, the MoI will provide asylum seekers with the information on how the procedure of approval of international protection is conducted, on the rights and obligations they have in that procedure and the possibility of applying to representatives of the UNHCR and other organisations who work to protect the rights of refugees and receiving free legal assistance. This information should be provided within fifteen days of the expression of the intention to seek asylum. In practice, this information is given in writing during the submission of the asylum application. During the asylum procedure, asylum seekers have the right to receive legal and procedural information on the approval of international protection, considering the circumstances of the specific case. Providing legal and procedural information is limited to asylum seekers who have no financial resources or significantly valuable assets that enable them to have an appropriate standard of living. This type of information should be provided by

426. Article 58, Act on International and Temporary Protection.
427. Programme of Croatian for preparatory classes for elementary and secondary school students who do not speak or speak Croatian insufficiently (*Odluka o Programu hrvatskoga jezika za pripremnu nastavu za učenike osnovne i srednje škole koji ne znaju ili nedovoljno poznaju hrvatski jezik*), OG 151/2011.
428. Croatian Law Centre, Access to Education, AIDA report. http://www.asylumineurope.org/reports/country/croatia/access-education-0 (accessed 20 Aug. 2018).

organisations working to protect the rights of refugees or by attorneys with whom the MoI concludes an agreement on the provision of legal counselling.[429]

282. Asylum seekers and foreigners under transfer have the right to free legal assistance, at their request, if they do not possess enough financial resources or things of significant value. The legal assistance encompasses assistance in drawing up a claim, representation in the first-instance administrative disputes, and exemption from payment of the costs of first-instance administrative disputes. The providers of legal assistance are attorneys and lawyers from associations registered with the Ministry of Justice as providers of legal assistance. The list of providers of legal assistance is available online.[430] The MoI notifies the asylum seekers about the right to select the provider of legal assistance from the list and the consequences that may arise if he or she does not timely appoint the legal assistance provider, at the latest when delivering the first-instance decision.[431]

283. The Administrative Court decides about the right to free legal assistance and the cost of legal assistance. The Administrative Court shall not grant the user the right to free legal assistance if, based on the request for free legal aid, evidence of the financial state of the beneficiary or evidence obtained in the administrative dispute, determines that the beneficiary has sufficient financial means or assets value.[432]

284. The right of asylum seekers to work is limited. Only asylum seekers who have not been issued a first-instance decision within nine months, and only if they did not cause any delay, have the right to free access to the labour market. The asylum seekers can work without a residence permit or work permit, or a certificate on registration of work until the decision on the application for asylum becomes final. The MoI must issue a document to certify that the asylum seeker has acquired the right to work, at his or her request. If the MoI refused to issue that document, the asylum seeker could bring a claim before the Administrative Court, within eight days from the day the decision is served. The right to work in practice means that the asylum seekers may conclude an employment contract or may become self-employed solely on the basis of their legal status.[433]

285. Obligations of asylum seekers are defined in the Act on International and Temporary Protection, and includes the obligation to: respect Croatian Constitution,

429. Article 59, Act on International and Temporary Protection.
430. Ministry of Interior, List of Free Legal Aid Providers in the International Protection Approval Procedure – Administrative Court, https://mup.hr/public/documents/Javnost/Obrasci/Stranci/Lista%20pru%C5%BEatelja%20besplatne%20pravne%20pomo%C4%87i%20u%20postupku%20odobrenja%20me%C4%91unarodne%20za%C5%A1tite%20-%20Upravni%20sud.pdf (accessed 20 Aug. 2018).
431. Article 5, Ordinance on Free Legal Aid in the Procedure of Approval of International Protection (*Pravilnik o besplatnoj pravnoj pomoći u postupku odobrenja međunarodne zaštite*), OG 140/2015.
432. Article 8, Ordinance on Free Legal Aid in the Procedure of Approval of International Protection.
433. Article 61, Act on International and Temporary Protection.

laws and other regulations; cooperate with the state bodies and act in line with their measures and instructions; submit to verification and establishment of identity; undergo a medical examination; respect the house rules of the Reception Centre; appear at the Reception Centre within the set time limits; respond to a summons by the MoI for an interview, and cooperate throughout the entire procedure of approval of international protection; remain within the Croatian territory throughout the entire procedure of approval of international protection; report any change of residence to the MoI within two days of the day of the change; respect the instructions and measures of the MoI regarding restriction of movement.[434] Complying with these obligations can have an important practical implication for asylum seekers. For example, as explained before, the material reception conditions may be restricted or denied if an asylum seeker violates the house rules of the Reception Centre, or stays outside the Reception Centre for more than twenty-four hours without prior consent. Another example is if the asylum seeker did not respond to a summons by the MoI for an interview and did not justify his or her absence within two days of the scheduled interview, the MoI will assume that the asylum seeker has withdrawn his or her application and the procedure will be terminated. A similar situation will be in case if asylum seeker leaves his or her place of residence for longer than two days without the consent of the Reception Centre.

B. Interrelation of the Asylum and Migration Systems

286. Asylum seekers do not have the right to lodge an application for approval of stay pursuant to the provisions of the Aliens Act. Asylees and foreigners under subsidiary protection do not have the right to lodge an application for approval of temporary or autonomous stay pursuant to the provisions of the Aliens Act.[435]

287. Many asylum seekers express their intention to seek asylum after being apprehended by the police in Croatian territory. Most of them have illegally entered the RoC. However, they should not be punished for illegal entry or stay, if they expressed an intention to apply for asylum without delay and showed good cause for illegal entry or stay, and that they came directly from the territory where they were persecuted or has been exposed to serious harm.[436]

288. The person who has not been granted international protection, that is, whose application has been refused with a final decision and a person whose international protection status has ceased or has been revoked fall under the Aliens Act and can be deported from the RoC. A decision on a measure to ensure return pursuant to the provisions of the Aliens Act will be rendered together with a decision

434. Article 52, Act on International and Temporary Protection.
435. Article 3, para. 2, Act on International and Temporary Protection.
436. Article 8, Act on International and Temporary Protection.

on the application or a decision on the cessation or revocation of international protection. Priority will be given to voluntary departure, unless the application was dismissed as manifestly unfounded or if a subsequent application is dismissed as inadmissible.[437]

II. Legal Position of Refugees and Persons with Subsidiary Protection

289. An asylum seeker who meets the required conditions can be granted international protection (either asylum or subsidiary protection). A person who has been granted asylum is an asylee, which means a refugee within the meaning of the Geneva Convention. A person who has been granted subsidiary protection is a foreigner under subsidiary protection.[438] The status of asylee or foreigner under subsidiary protection is acquired on the day the decision granting international protection is served.[439]

290. Asylees and foreigners under subsidiary protection benefit from the same rights, with two exceptions. The first exception relates to a residence permit: a permit will be issued to an asylee for five years, and to a foreigner under subsidiary protection for a period of three years.[440] The second exception relates to the travel documents, as a foreigner under subsidiary protection can be issued with a travel document for foreigners, pursuant to the provisions of the Aliens Act.[441]

291. Asylees and foreigners under subsidiary protection have the following rights: residence in the RoC; family reunification; accommodation; work; healthcare; education; freedom of religion; free legal assistance; social welfare; assistance for integration into society; ownership of real property pursuant to the Geneva Convention; acquisition of Croatian citizenship pursuant to the regulations governing the acquisition of citizenship. Also, asylees or foreigners under subsidiary protection will be provided with general information on the rights and obligations acquired with the approval of international protection within eight days of the service of the decision.[442]

292. Asylees and foreigners under subsidiary protection have the right of residence from the day of the service of the decision approving international protection, which establishes the right of residence. The right of residence will be revoked if the asylee or foreigner under subsidiary protection moves out of the RoC or resides continually abroad for longer than six months without previously informing the MoI.[443] The request for issuing residence permit should be submitted to the

437. Article 37, Act on International and Temporary Protection.
438. Article 4, paras 1, 6 and 7, Act on International and Temporary Protection.
439. Article 64, para. 1, Act on International and Temporary Protection.
440. Article 75, paras 1, 2 and 3, Act on International and Temporary Protection.
441. Article 75, para. 8, Act on International and Temporary Protection.
442. Article 64, paras 2 and 3, Act on International and Temporary Protection.
443. Article 65, Act on International and Temporary Protection.

competent police administration, and the residence permit should be issued within thirty days from submitting the request.[444]

293. Asylees and foreigners under subsidiary protection have the right to accommodation if they do not possess financial means or property to support themselves, for a maximum period of two years from the date on which the decision approving international protection is served. The procedure for recognising the right to accommodation is initiated by the submission of a request to the social welfare centre in the place of domicile of the asylee and foreigner under subsidiary protection. The Centre will render a decision on the request, against which it is possible to lodge an appeal, and later a claim to the administrative court. If the asylee or foreigner under subsidiary protection generates the financial means or owns the property, he or she must participate in the payment of accommodation costs. After the end of the two years, the asylee or foreigner under subsidiary protection has the right to accommodation pursuant to the regulations governing the domain of social welfare of Croatian citizens.[445]

294. The right to accommodation of an asylee and foreigner under subsidiary protection will cease in the following cases:

(1) upon the expiry of the two-year time limit;
(2) upon personal request;
(3) if he or she refuses the accommodation provided;
(4) if he or she fails without justified reason to reside at the registered address for a period longer than thirty days;
(5) if he or she does not meet the conditions for recognition of the right to accommodation;
(6) if it is established that he or she fails to take due and responsible care of the accommodation provided;
(7) if it is established that he or she uses the accommodation provided contrary to its purpose.

Against a decision establishing the termination of the right to accommodation it is possible to lodge an appeal, and later a claim to the administrative court. In a case that a person cannot anymore participate in payment of accommodation cost by his or her financial means or own property, or the circumstances referred to in points 4 and 5 above cease to exist, as well as if the right to accommodation terminates upon personal request, the asylee and foreigner under subsidiary protection may re-submit a request.[446]

---

444. Article 10, para. 1 and Art. 12, para. 1, Ordinance on the Forms and Data Collections in the Procedure for International and Temporary Protection (*Pravilnik o obrascima i zbirkama podataka u postupku odobrenja međunarodne i privremene zaštite*), OG 85/2016.
445. Article 67, paras 1–7, Act on International and Temporary Protection.
446. Article 67, paras 8–11, Act on International and Temporary Protection.

295. After the amendments of the Act on International and Temporary Protection in 2017, the accommodation is provided by the Central State Office for Reconstruction and Housing Care and includes the process of finding, adapting, furnishing, maintaining, and the settlement of utility costs and leasing costs for the housing unit provided. The housing units can be a property of the RoC or at disposal to the Central State Office as per lease agreements concluded with other natural persons. The Central State Office for Reconstruction and Housing Care will sign a contract on lease or sublease of the housing unit with the asylee and foreigner under subsidiary protection. Funds for the costs of accommodation will be earmarked in the State Budget.[447]

296. Asylees and foreigners under subsidiary protection can work without a residence permit or certificate of registration of work. They have a right to adult training related to employment, vocational training and acquiring practical work experience, under the same conditions as Croatian citizens.[448] The Croatian Employment Service is responsible for the implementation of measures regarding foreigner employment with special emphasis on persons who have been granted international protection. The Ministry of Labour and Pension System and the Croatian Employment Service carry out active labour market measures aimed at encouraging employment, providing additional training for workers and maintaining workplaces. In the implementation of those measures' specific needs of certain groups of beneficiaries are taken into account. Nine different measures are being implemented. They are based on the National Guidelines for the Development and Implementation of Active Labour Market Policy in the RoC for 2015–2017.

297. Asylees and foreigners under subsidiary protection have the right to healthcare pursuant to the Act on Mandatory Health Insurance and Health Care for Foreigners.[449] The Act prescribes that asylees and foreigners under subsidiary protection are not health insured persons, but they have a right to healthcare, in the same scope as health insured persons under mandatory health insurance.[450] The costs of healthcare are paid from the State Budget under the item of the Ministry of Health. In practice, however, asylees and foreigners under subsidiary protection face obstacles in accessing healthcare. Besides language barriers which are the main problem in the exercise of any right, the fact that they are not health insured persons but use medical services with their identity card is confusing for doctors who do not know how to identify beneficiaries in the system or records.[451]

298. In the field of education, asylees and foreigners under subsidiary protection have the same rights as Croatian nationals regarding elementary, secondary and

447. Article 67a, Act on International and Temporary Protection.
448. Article 68, Act on International and Temporary Protection.
449. Article 69, Act on International and Temporary Protection.
450. Articles 17 and 21, para. 1, Act on Mandatory Health Insurance and Health Care for Foreigners in the Republic of Croatia (*Zakon o obveznom zdravstvenom osiguranju i zdravstvenoj zaštiti stranaca u Republici Hrvatskoj*), OG 80/2013, 15/2018.
451. Croatian Law Centre, Health Care for Beneficiaries, AIDA report. http://www.asylumineurope.org/reports/country/croatia/health-care-beneficiaries (accessed 12 Sep. 2018).

higher education, adult education, and recognition of foreign qualifications. For those persons, who for justified reasons are not able to provide the necessary documentation to prove their qualifications, an assessment shall be conducted of their prior learning. A decision to refuse an application for recognition of foreign vocational qualifications cannot be based exclusively on the fact that no official documents exist to prove a specific vocational qualification. If an asylee or foreigner under subsidiary protection does not have sufficient financial resources, the translation of foreign documents for the recognition of foreign qualifications shall be provided from the State Budget by the Ministry of Science and Education.[452] Schools are obliged to provide special assistance to children who are entitled to an education but do not speak Croatian or do not speak Croatian sufficiently.[453]

299. Asylees and foreigners under subsidiary protection have the right to social welfare under the Social Welfare Act[454] under the same conditions as Croatian nationals. They mostly use social benefits in kind, financial benefits and social services (providing information on the rights from the social welfare system and counselling and assistance services). Moreover, they often use the right to the guaranteed minimum benefit, one-off benefit, assistance for covering accommodation costs, assistance and care supplement, and assistance in getting heating material and meals in soup kitchens. Asylees and foreigners under subsidiary protection can use the right to child benefits pursuant to the Child Benefit Act[455] and the rights pursuant to the Act on Pregnancy and Parenthood Support.[456]

300. The Croatian Citizenship Act regulates requirements for the acquisition and termination of Croatian citizenship. An application for Croatian citizenship on the grounds of naturalisation should be submitted at the competent police administration at the regional level, or police station at the local level. An application can also be submitted at diplomatic missions or consular offices of the RoC abroad.[457] A foreign citizen who submits application for acquiring Croatian citizenship shall acquire Croatian citizenship by naturalisation if he or she:

- has reached the age of eighteen years and that his or her legal capacity has not been taken away;
- has had his or her foreign citizenship revoked or he or she submits proof that they will get a revocation if admitted to Croatian citizenship;

452. Article 70, Act on International and Temporary Protection.
453. Article 43, para. 2, Act on Primary and Secondary Education (*Zakon o odgoju i obrazovanju u osnovnoj i srednjoj školi*), OG 87/2008, 86/2009, 92/2010, 105/2010-correction, 90/2011, 5/2012-Government Regulation, 16/2012, 86/2012, 94/2013, 152/2014, 7/2017, 68/2018.
454. Article 22, Social Welfare Act.
455. Article 7, Child Benefit Act (*Zakon o doplatku za djecu*), OG 94/2001, 138/2006, 107/2007, 37/2008, 61/2011, 112/2012, 82/2015, 58/2018.
456. Article 8, Act on Pregnancy and Parenthood Support (*Zakon o rodiljnim i roditeljskim potporama*), OG 85/2008, 110/2008, 34/2011, 54/2013, 152/2014, 59/2017.
457. Article 24, para. 4, Croatian Citizenship Act.

- before submitting the application, he or she had a registered place of residence for eight years continuously on the territory of the RoC and has been granted permanent residence permit;
- is proficient in the Croatian language and Latin script and is familiar with the Croatian culture and social system, following successful completion of a proficiency verification;
- is deemed to respect the legal order and customs of the RoC.[458]

If asylees or beneficiaries under subsidiary protection are not able for objective reasons to obtain official documents from their country of origin necessary to acquire Croatian citizenship, official documents of the RoC shall be taken into account in the procedure to acquire Croatian citizenship, along with other documents they possess, on the basis of which it may be assessed whether they meet the conditions for the acquisition of Croatian citizenship. A decision to refuse an application for Croatian citizenship may not be based exclusively on the fact that the necessary official documents of the country of origin have not been submitted.[459]

301. The Anti-Discrimination Act[460] regulates the protection from discrimination including discrimination based on race, ethnicity or colour, language, religion, political or other convictions and national or social origin.

302. According to the Act on International and Temporary Protection, asylees and foreigners under subsidiary protection are obliged to attend a course in the Croatian language, history and culture (free of charge), for the integration into Croatian society. In the case of failure to fulfil this obligation, they should repay the costs of the course.[461]

303. Asylees and foreigners under subsidiary protection have the right to assistance for integration into society for no longer than three years from the service of the decision. The MoI provides assistance which covers: drawing up a plan of integration for asylees or foreigners under subsidiary protection given their individual needs, knowledge, abilities and skills; aiding asylees or foreigners under subsidiary protection for the realisation of the plan drawn up; and supervising the implementation of the plan.[462]

III. Legal Position of Foreigners under Temporary Protection

304. A foreigner under temporary protection has the right of a residence during the period of temporary protection, and a card which proves the right of residence in the RoC. A foreigner under temporary protection may work without a residence

458. Article 8, para. 1, Croatian Citizenship Act.
459. Article 77, Act on International and Temporary Protection.
460. Anti-Discrimination Act (*Zakon o suzbijanju diskriminacije*), OG 85/2008, 112/2012.
461. Article 74, Act on International and Temporary Protection.
462. Article 76, Act on International and Temporary Protection.

or work permit or certificate of registration of work. Foreigners under temporary protection shall exercise the right to adult education concerning employment, vocational training and acquisition of practical work experience. Healthcare for foreigners under temporary protection includes emergency medical assistance and, for vulnerable groups, appropriate medical and other assistance. They have the right to elementary and secondary education and re-training and additional training, under the same conditions as Croatian citizens. During the period of temporary protection, a foreigner under temporary protection will be provided with appropriate accommodation if he or she does not possess financial resources. Accommodation will also be provided for a foreigner whose temporary protection has come to an end if he or she does not possess his or her own financial resources and if, for serious health reasons, it is not possible to return him or her to the country of origin. They have the right to family reunification, and a family member who is reunited with a foreigner under temporary protection will be granted temporary protection as well. In cases where family members enjoy temporary protection in different Member States of the EU, when reuniting the family, the interests of the family shall be taken into consideration.[463] The obligations prescribed for asylum seekers will be applied to foreigners under temporary protection (*see* Part II).[464]

IV. Legal Position of Relocated and Resettled Refugees

305. Relocated refugees who are granted international protection and those that were resettled to the RoC have all rights and obligations granted to asylees and foreigners under subsidiary protection by the Act on International and Temporary Protection. They are accommodated in the Reception Centre in Kutina and provided with the crash course of Croatian language and society. In due time they are moved to other parts of the RoC, according to the available accommodation, or other factors, such as employment possibilities. The International Organisation for Migration provided support to the MoI in the resettlement of refugees to the RoC, with the aim to provide comprehensive resettlement and post-arrival orientation as well as early integration support, including capacity building and networking of relevant national and sub-national stakeholders.[465] Since December 2018, Jesuit Refugee Council has started to provide support in the integration of resettled refugees in Croatia.[466]

---

463. Articles 83–90, Act on International and Temporary Protection.
464. Article 83, para. 2, Act on International and Temporary Protection.
465. http://croatia.iom.int/projects/pilot-project-%E2%80%9Cproviding-refugee-resettlement-assistance-government-republic-croatia%E2%80%9D-0 (accessed 20 Sep. 2018).
466. https://www.mup.hr/novosti/6446/sporazum-o-suradnji-na-podrucju-integracije-preseljenih-osoba (accessed 20 Dec. 2018).

§4. POSITION OF FAMILY MEMBERS

306. According to the Act on International and Temporary Protection, family members of asylum seekers, asylees, foreigners under subsidiary protection and foreigners under temporary protection include:

- the spouse or unmarried partner under the regulations of the RoC, and persons who are in a union, which may be deemed to be a life partnership or informal life partnership;
- the minor child of the marital or unmarried partners; their minor adopted child; the minor child and minor adopted child of a married, unmarried or life partner who exercises parental care of the child;
- the adult unmarried child, who, due to his or her state of health is not able to take care of his or her own needs;
- the parent or another legal representative of a minor;
- a relative of the first degree in a direct bloodline, with whom he or she lived in a shared household if it is established that he or she is dependent on the care of the asylum seeker, asylee, foreigner under subsidiary protection or foreigner under temporary protection.[467]

307. A minor child of an asylee or foreigner under subsidiary protection who has not found their family shall follow the legal status of their legal representative, to whom international protection has been granted. Other family members have to regulate their residence pursuant to the provisions of the Aliens Act.[468]

308. A family member of an asylee or foreigner under subsidiary protection who is legally resident in the RoC has the same rights as an asylee or foreigner under subsidiary protection. A family member for whom reasons exist for exclusion and protection of the national security or public will not have the right of family reunification. In the case of family reunification of asylees and foreigners under subsidiary protection, and for a person who is unable to obtain official documents to prove a specific family relationship, circumstances shall be taken into consideration for which it may be assessed whether or not such a relationship exists. A decision to refuse an application for family reunification cannot be based exclusively on the fact that there is no official document which could prove a specific family relationship.[469]

---

467. Article 4, para. 1, No. 18, Act on International and Temporary Protection.
468. Article 66, paras 2 and 3, Act on International and Temporary Protection.
469. Article 66, paras 4–6, Act on International and Temporary Protection.

Chapter 6. Other Grounds

§1. Citizens of the Former Yugoslavia – Returnees to Croatia

309. A special category of persons who can acquire a temporary residence permit for humanitarian reasons under the Aliens Act is TCNs who had the status of refugee for at least ten years or who were included in a reconstruction, return or housing care programme for refugees from Croatia. The first category is the persons who came to Croatia from the republics of former Yugoslavia due to armed conflicts during the 1990s. The second category is the persons who, at the time when Croatia proclaimed its independence, did not have a registered residence in Croatia and had Yugoslav citizenship, and therefore were considered aliens. Also, this category includes persons who were born and lived in Croatia but had one of the parents originating from another Yugoslav republic and were not citizens of the former Socialist RoC. Many of them were of Serb origin and were registered as citizens of Bosnia and Herzegovina, Serbia or another former Yugoslav republic.

310. When the Act on Movement and Stay of Aliens came into force in 1991, persons who did not have Croatian citizenship, but had a registered residence in Croatia and were Yugoslav citizens, obtained the status of an alien with permanent residence. If the person stays abroad for more than a year without informing the MoI, permanent residence is terminated.[470] Those who did not meet the conditions were considered aliens on an extended stay, with a residence permit issued for one year, which had to be renewed.[471] In that way, the Act subjected non-Croat pre-conflict residents, whose permanent residence has been terminated by the MoI, to the same legal requirements as new immigrants. This regulation of the residence influenced the possibility of acquiring Croatian citizenship. The Citizenship Act distinguished between those who had a claim to Croatian ethnicity and those who did not. Ethnic Croats were eligible to become citizens, even if they were not citizens of the former Socialist RoC, as long as they submitted a written statement that they consider themselves Croats. Non-Croats had to satisfy stricter requirements to obtain citizenship through naturalisation after five years of registered residence. Even those who previously were lawful residents of the former Socialist RoC were compelled to provide proof of previous residence and citizenship that was not demanded of ethnic Croats.[472]

311. In 2003, the Aliens Act stipulated that only persons who acquired the status of an alien with permanent residence according to the previous Act on Movement and Stay of Aliens could regulate their status on more lenient conditions. The Aliens Act's transitional provisions were designed to enable former habitual residents to return and regularise their status. The Act stated that if they return within twelve

470. Article 47, Act on Movement and Stay of Aliens.
471. Article 79, Act on Movement and Stay of Aliens.
472. US Department of State, Country Reports on Human Rights Practices: Croatia, 25 Feb. 2004, sect. 5.

months, they would be reinstated into their pre-war status of former habitual residents without any further requirements and could subsequently apply for citizenship.[473] Those who did not regularise their status within the time limits were considered aliens applying for the residence permit for the first time and had to have sufficient means of subsistence, secured housing and health insurance.[474]

312. After the new Aliens Act came into force in 2012, returnees without Croatian citizenship who were returning to Croatia within the Programme of Return and Care for Refugees and Displaced Persons and the Programme of Housing Care and Reconstruction and who had registered residence in Croatia on the 8 October 1991, could immediately after return in Croatia submit a request for permanent residence.[475] After having obtained permanent residence, all who have the intention to stay in Croatia can acquire Croatian citizenship, under the condition of renouncing their primary citizenship (most frequently it was Bosnia-Herzegovina citizenship). However, in December 2012, a new Residence Act[476] stipulated the conditions for exercising the right to residence, which among other conditions, also include the obligation to regulate the residence status in Croatia in case of a longer stay abroad. Based on that regulations, several categories of persons were erased from the MoI's residence record: those who did not regulate the residence status and stayed abroad for a longer period of time, those who have never requested issuance of an ID card in Croatia, and had residence in Croatia before the war, as well as those whose ID card expired and those with residence registered at non-existent addresses (house number 0 or bb). Almost 260,000 persons were de-registered from the MoI's records by February 2015, of whom 37,234 persons of Serb nationality.[477] With the 2013 amendments to the Residence Act, the deadline for regulating residency was extended for two years (until 29 December 2014).

313. According to the Aliens Act, a TCN who had a residence in Croatia on 8 October 1991, and who was a beneficiary of the programme of return, reconstruction or housing care, and for whom it was established that he returned with the intention of living in Croatia permanently can acquire a permanent residence in Croatia.[478] However, the reports indicate that the process of obtaining evidence for granting permanent residence is rather long. Hence, the long-term procedure for obtaining residence permit results in a small number of approved permanent stays.[479]

---

473. Article 115, Aliens Act, OG 109/2003.
474. Article 49, Aliens Act, OG 109/2003.
475. Article 94, Aliens Act, OG 130/2011.
476. Residence Act (*Zakon o prebivalištu*), OG 144/2012, 158/2013.
477. https://snv.hr/sto-radimo/zastita-prava/statusna-prava (accessed 13 Sep. 2018).
478. Article 94, para. 1, Aliens Act.
479. People's Ombudsman, Izvješće pučke pravobraniteljice za 2013. godinu, Zagreb, 31. ožujka 2014. http://ombudsman.hr/hr/component/jdownloads/send/12-2013/55-izvjesce-pucke-pravobraniteljice-za-2013-po-prvi-puta-objedinjeno-izvjesce-o-stanju-ljudskih-prava-u-hrvatskoj-i-radu-ureda?option=com_jdownloads (accessed 14 Sep. 2018).

Part IV. Loss of Right of Residence

Chapter 1. Conditions under Which the Right of Residence Might Be Lost

314. Conditions under which the right of residence might be lost depend on the legal status of the person. According to the Alien Act, a short-term stay can be cancelled, while temporary and permanent residence can be withdrawn, in all cases by the MoI. In the casc of thc tcmporary rcsidence permit, the residence rights might be lost if the permit expired and it was not extended. The residence can be cancelled in the case of a short-term stay. While the previous Aliens Act has foreseen the possibility of the annulment of the residence permits, this is not the case with the current Aliens Act, except in the case of the residence and work permit issued to a TCN in the framework of an intra-corporate transfer. Residence and work permit for seasonal work can be revoked or annulled. There are two possibilities to terminate international protection: cessation and revocation of both asylum and subsidiary protection.

§1. Loss of Right to Short Stay

315. A short-term stay will be cancelled if a TCN:

- does not hold a valid travel document or another document used for crossing the state border;
- does not justify the purpose and conditions for entry and stay;
- does not have funds to support himself or herself during his or her stay in Croatia, and for returning to the state from which he or she came from or for travelling to a third country, and for those expenditures he or she also doesn't have a guarantee letter and/or other proof that the natural or legal person will bear the costs of their stay;
- does not settle the due financial obligations in the RoC;
- if there is a well-founded reason to believe that short-term stay was not used for the intended purpose.[480]

480. Article 46, para. 1, Aliens Act. According to the judicial practice, if an alien with a short-term stay, during the inspection supervision at the workplace, is caught while doing the job, there are justified reasons for cancelling his stay in the RoC since the short-term stay was not used in accordance with the intended purpose. 'Given the circumstances under which the plaintiff was caught during the

§2. Loss of the Right of Temporary Residence

316. According to Article 72 of the Aliens Act, a temporary residence will cease if the conditions for the approval of temporary residence cease to exist: if a TCN does not possess a valid travel document anymore, appropriate health insurance or sufficient means of subsistence, or cannot prove the purpose of temporary residence, and if he or she did not fulfil the other conditions required for the issuing of individual types of temporary residence permits. The other conditions for termination of a temporary residence permit are:

- if a TCN is prohibited entry and stay;
- if within thirty days after the approval of temporary stay a TCN fails to register his temporary residence with the police administration or police station;
- if a TCN moved out of the RoC or stays abroad without interruptions for a period over thirty days;
- if a TCN stays in the RoC contrary to the purpose of the temporary residence permit.

317. The Aliens Act provides two exceptions to the rule that the temporary residence will terminate: if a TCN moves out of the RoC or stays abroad without interruptions for a period of over thirty days. The first case refers to researchers and students, provided that they reside in another EEA Member State based on short-term or long-term mobility. The second case refers to the situation where a TCN had a justified reason for leaving Croatia, provided that he or she previously notified the police administration or police station about his or her leave. In the case that some extraordinary circumstances emerged after the TCN left Croatia, he or she has to inform the diplomatic mission or consular office of the RoC within thirty days from the onset of those circumstances.[481]

318. There are specific conditions for termination of a temporary residence on humanitarian grounds. Temporary residence for a victim of trafficking is terminated if the victim lost the victim status if it is established that the victim is abusing his or her status of the victim, or if it is required by reasons of protecting public order, national security and public health. Special protection is envisaged in the case of victims of trafficking who are minors as the police administration or police station when deciding on the termination of temporary residence should request the Centre for social welfare to issue its opinion. In case of other reasons for granting humanitarian temporary residence (abandoned minors or minors who are a victim of organised crime, or who remained without parental protection, guardianship or escort for some other reasons; TCNs who had the status of refugee for at least ten years or were included in a reconstruction, return or housing care programme for refugees

action of officers for illegal migrations and police officers, the first instance administrative court correctly ruled that the defendant (*Ministry of Interior*) had reason to reasonably suspect that the plaintiff's stay in the Republic of Croatia was not used in accordance with the purpose of short-stay.' The High Administrative Court, Usž-1282/17, a decision from 4 May 2017.

481. Article 72, Aliens Act.

from Croatia; TCNs who cooperate with the competent bodies and their participation is crucial in the criminal procedure conducted against the employer who employed them illegally; or other serious humanitarian grounds), it will be terminated if the purpose because of which temporary residence was granted was terminated, or if required by reasons of protecting public order, national security and public health.[482]

319. The Aliens Act regulates the conditions under which the right of residence might be lost if the residence permit is issued for work (residence and work permit). In addition to the general conditions for the cessation of temporary residence permit, a residence and work permit cease to be valid under the following conditions:

- on termination of the existence of conditions based on which it was issued;[483]
- if a TCN performs jobs for which the residence and work permit was not issued;
- if a TCN works for an employer for whom the residence and work permit was not issued;
- if a TCN or his or her employer do not respect regulations on employment, health and pension insurance and other regulations.[484]

For more information, *see* Part VII, Chapter 2, §3.

320. For EEA citizens and their family members, different conditions apply for the loss of their right of temporary residence. Temporary residence will terminate if an EEA citizen:

- is issued prohibition of entry and stay in the RoC;
- acquired temporary residence by having provided untrue information or having concealed the real aim and circumstances which were decisive for the registration of temporary residence;
- no longer meets the conditions for temporary residence;
- cancels his stay in Croatia.

Temporary residence of an EEA citizen and of a member of their family will not terminate if he or she does not have sufficient means of support, provided that he or she is employed or self-employed or that they have arrived with the intention of

482. Article 71, Aliens Act.
483. According to the judicial practice, the residence and work permit ceases to be valid, *inter alia*, by the termination of the conditions under which it was issued which, for a TCN holding key positions in companies, branch offices and representative offices, includes a condition that his or her gross salary is at least in the amount of an average gross salary paid in the RoC in the previous year. 'The court evaluates unfounded allegations in the plaintiff's appeal that he is a legally ignorant and does not know the Croatian language, which is why he did not understand the consequences of his conduct. In the administrative procedure, the plaintiff stated that he had been residing in the Republic of Croatia for a number of years, that he knows the Croatian language and Latin scripture and that he does not need a translator, and that he decided to reduce the salary due to financial difficulties.' The High Administrative Court, Usž-993/17, a decision of 24 May 2017.
484. Article 90, Aliens Act.

employment, and proves that he or she continues to seek a job actively, and it can reasonably be expected that they will find employment.[485] Termination of temporary residence of a family member of an EEA citizen who himself is not an EEA citizen will be possible under the same conditions as the residence of an EEA citizen, with one additional condition: if he or she stayed outside the RoC for more than six months per year during temporary residence. However, the residence will not cease to exist if he or she stayed outside the RoC because of the military service, or stayed outside of the RoC for up to twelve months without interruptions for justified reasons, such as pregnancy, childbirth, serious illness, studies, professional development or posting to another state.[486]

§3. Loss of the Right of Permanent Residence

321. According to the Aliens Act, the permanent residence will terminate in the following situations:

- if a TCN is prohibited from entering and staying in the RoC;
- if a TCN moved out of the RoC or stayed abroad without interruptions for over one year;
- if established that a TCN deliberately provided untrue information or deliberately concealed the aim and circumstances which were relevant for the approval of permanent residence;
- if required by the reasons of protecting public policy, national security or public health;
- at TCN's request;
- upon the annulment of asylum or subsidiary protection.[487]

322. The permanent residence of a TCN with long-term resident status can be terminated in cases similar to those described above (prohibition of entry and stay in the RoC, if required by the reasons of protecting public policy, national security or public health, at own request or upon the annulment of asylum or subsidiary protection) with the addition of the following:

- in the event of absence from the territory of the EEA for twelve consecutive months;
- in the event of absence from the RoC longer than six years;
- when such a status is granted in another EEA Member State;
- on detection of fraudulent acquisition of long-term resident status.[488]

485. Article 165, Aliens Act.
486. Article 172, Aliens Act.
487. Article 99, Aliens Act.
488. Article 99a, Aliens Act.

323. Permanent stay of a national of an EEA Member State (and family member of a national of an EEA Member State who himself is not a national of EEA Member State[489]) terminates if he or she is prohibited entry and stay in the RoC; is staying outside the RoC for over two years without interruptions; and cancels his residence in the RoC.[490]

324. More lenient conditions will apply in the case of permanent residence of a 'former EU Blue Cardholder', which will terminate if he or she is prohibited entry and stay in the RoC, or moved out or stayed abroad without interruptions for more than twenty-four consecutive months.[491]

§4. Loss of Refugee Status, Subsidiary Protection and Temporary Protection Status

325. A refugee (asylum) status can cease to exist either by the will of an asylee or due to changed circumstances in the country of origin. Asylum will be withdrawn if:

- the asylee voluntarily accepts the protection of the country of which he or she is a national;
- the asylee acquires the citizenship of the country whose protection he or she may enjoy;
- the asylee voluntarily returns and resides in the country they left or outside of which he or she has resided due to fear of persecution;
- the circumstances in the asylee's country of origin, on the basis of which international protection was approved, cease to exist;
- the asylee voluntarily re-acquires the nationality of his or her country of origin, which he or she had previously lost.

Subsidiary protection will be withdrawn if the circumstances from which it was recognised cease to exist, or are altered to such an extent that further protection is no longer necessary. International protection will cease by force of law when an asylee or alien under subsidiary protection acquires Croatian citizenship or on his or her death.[492]

326. International protection will be revoked if:

- reasons for exclusion are subsequently established;

489. Article 179, Aliens Act.
490. Article 175, Aliens Act.
491. Article 200, Aliens Act.
492. Article 49, Act on International and Temporary Protection.

- it is established that status was recognised on the basis of incorrectly presented or omitted facts, false presentation of important facts and circumstances, or the use of unreliable documents or other documents which were decisive for the approval of international protection;
- the person to whom international protection was granted represents a risk to the national security or public order of the RoC.

327. In the case that the international protection has been revoked due to a risk to the national security or public order of the RoC, and the person is still present in the territory of the RoC, certain rights set out in the Geneva Convention continue to apply, especially in relation to the prohibition of discrimination, freedom of religion, access to courts, education, non-punishment of illegal entry or stay, expulsion and respect of the *non-refoulement* principle.[493]

328. Temporary protection will come to an end when the maximum duration of temporary protection has been reached, or by a decision of the Council of the EU.[494]

493. Article 50, Act on International and Temporary Protection.
494. Article 79, Act on International and Temporary Protection.

Chapter 2. Legal and Administrative Procedures

329. The competent body for the issuing of decisions which result in the loss of residence rights is the MoI. In general, all procedures for the annulment, cancellation or revocation of the residence and stay for TCNs and EEA nationals are administrative procedures, which means that in addition to specific provisions on the administrative procedure defined in the relevant legislative acts the General Administrative Procedure Act has to be used as a subsidiary source of law.

330. The MoI, through competent police administration or police station, will decide on cancellation of the short-term stay, and if the decision is positive, a TCN will be prohibited from entering and staying in Croatia for a duration from one to three months. Against decision, the TCN can initiate an administrative dispute.[495]

331. The decision on termination of temporary residence is rendered by the MoI, at the proposal of the police administration or police station. In the procedure of termination of temporary residence, police administration or police station will interview a TCN. However, if the TCN was notified in advance of the procedure for termination of his temporary residence, the decision about the termination of the residence may be adopted without a preliminary interview with the TCN.[496] Against the decision of the police administration or police station on termination of the temporary residence, a TCN can file an appeal to the MoI Commission.[497]

332. The decision on termination of permanent residence of a TCN, including a TCN with long-term resident status, is rendered by the MoI, by the proposal of the police administration or police station. The decision can be adopted without a prior interview of a TCN. Against the decision, a TCN may initiate an administrative dispute.[498] In the case of termination of permanent residence of EEA Member State and family member of a national of an EEA Member State who himself is not a national of EEA Member State, a TCN may fill an appeal against the decision and the MoI's Commission shall decide about the appeal.

333. Security and Intelligence Agency conducts security checks for aliens to establish national security reasons for loss of residence rights. The decision will only specify the legal provision, where elaboration of the grounds decisive to adopt the decision is not to be included.[499]

334. The MoI will render a decision to revoke the decision approving international protection. After establishing that the circumstances related to the cessation of international protection have ceased to exist in a significant and permanent manner, the MoI will inform the asylee or alien under subsidiary protection accordingly

495. Article 46, Aliens Act.
496. Article 72, para. 3, Aliens Act.
497. Article 72, para. 5 Aliens Act.
498. Article 99, Aliens Act.
499. Article 5, Aliens Act.

and will allow him or her to make an oral statement for the record. The same is provided in the case of revocation of international protection, after establishing that circumstances have arisen relating to the revocation. Although no appeal is permitted against the decision on revocation or cessation of international protection, a claim may be brought before the Administrative Court within eight days of the day of service of the decision.[500]

335. An alien who does not have or no longer has a legal basis to stay in the RoC has to leave the country immediately, or within the time limit set by the MoI for leaving the country (*see* Part V, Chapter 2 on sanctions against unlawful stay or residence).

500. Articles 49–50, Act on International and Temporary Protection.

Part V. Sanctions

Chapter 1. Sanctions

§1. Administrative Sanctions

336. Administrative sanctions in migration legislation mainly relate to the work of aliens in Croatia. According to the Act on State Administration System, administrative sanctions can be imposed during the inspection supervision of legal and natural persons, performed by the central state administration organisations or deconcentrated state administration. In accordance with a special regulation, such as the Aliens Act, inspection consists of the insight into the general and individual acts and the conditions or the manner of work of the legal and natural persons concerned. The inspectors are entitled to inspect the premises, business documents, buildings, objects, goods and other items of the persons concerned, hold hearings of individuals in administrative proceedings, inspect the documents on the basis of which the identity of persons can be established, and perform other activities in accordance with the purpose of inspectional oversight. If he or she finds that the legislation has been violated, the inspector has the right to order that the deficiencies or irregularities be eliminated within a given time, which is an administrative measure. Also, the inspector can report a criminal offence to the competent state body or impose a misdemeanour sentence and take other measures and perform other activities for which he or she is authorised under special regulations.[501]

337. According to the Aliens Act, the MoI is in charge of inspection supervision relating to the obligation to register the staying of aliens. Inspection supervision relating to the work of aliens, the conditions of work and the rights of posted workers and accommodation of seasonal workers is performed by inspectors and civil servants of state administration bodies, each within their competence, in accordance with special regulations.[502] From April 2019, the main body in charge of inspectional supervision of work and work conditions will be the State Inspectorate.[503] In terms of protection of the rights and obligations from the employment contract and the conditions of work, regulated by the Labour Act[504] and the Occupational Health

501. Articles 24, 27 and 29, Act on State Administration System (*Zakon o sustavu državne uprave*), OG 150/2011, 12/2013, 93/2016, 104/2016.
502. Article 207, paras 1 and 2, Aliens Act.
503. State Inspectorate Act (*Zakon o državnom inspektoratu*), OG 115/2018.
504. Labour Act (*Zakon o radu*), OG 93/2014, 127/2017.

and Safety Act,[505] the inspector can impose administrative measures and fine/penalty on the employer (*see* Part VI, Chapter 3).

§2. Penal Sanctions

338. If an alien does not meet the entry requirements, he or she will be refused to enter Croatia and a border police officer will issue a decision on refusal of entry. Against the decision on refusal of entry an appeal can be filed through the competent diplomatic mission or consular office of the RoC. The Commission of the MoI decides on the appeals. However, the appeal does not postpone the enforcement of decision.[506] In such cases, there are no penal sanctions envisaged against the alien.

339. The penal sanctions for unlawful entry into Croatia are prescribed by the State Border Protection Act. There are two situations in which an alien will be fined: first, if the alien crosses or attempt to cross the state border beyond border crossing points or over the border crossing but beyond fixed opening hours, and second, if he or she avoid border control or leave the border-crossing area until border control has yet been carried out. In both cases, the alien will be fined up to thirty days in prison or with the financial a fine in the amount of HRK 2,000–HRK 10,000 (app. EUR 267–EUR 1,315).[507]

340. According to the Aliens Act, the offences committed by the alien in regard to unlawful entry or stay in Croatia can be categorised into two groups depending on the severity of the act which are considered either as a smaller offence, for which the fine is monetary or as a more serious offence, for which the fine is either imprisonment or monetary.

341. The police will impose a fine of HRK 500–HRK 5,000 (app. EUR 67–EUR 667) on the alien who:

- uses a travel document which he did not use to enter Croatia or fails to leave with a travel document used to enter;
- fails to apply for the temporary residence for a child before the child turns three months of age;
- fails to apply for an extension of the temporary residence permit within sixty days of the expiration of the validity period of temporary residence;
- does not inform the police administration or the police station about the cessation of the conditions under which mobility (of student or researcher) is permitted;
- is staying in Croatia contrary to the purpose for which temporary residence was granted,

505. Occupational Health and Safety Act *(Zakon o zaštiti na radu)*, OG 71/014, 118/2014, 154/2014, 94/2018, 96/2018.
506. Article 38, Aliens Act.
507. Article 42, State Border Protection Act.

- fails to notify the police administration or the police station on the changes of the accommodation (for seasonal workers) within eight days;
- fails to notify the police administration or police station that the grounds based on which the stay and work permit was issued no longer exist;
- does not report at the border crossing when leaving Croatia or at the diplomatic mission or the consular post of the RoC after leaving the EEA, as stipulated by the return decision;
- at the request by an official, fails to provide for review a valid travel document or identity card, residence permit or another public document containing the photograph;
- fails to obtain a residence permit within the eight days;
- fails to apply for the replacement of his residence permit within the eight days;
- fails to return his or her residence permit;
- fails to report the loss, disappearance or theft of his documents;
- does not register his accommodation within two days (for aliens on a short-term stay);
- does not include full and accurate information in the application form for accommodation during the short-term stay in Croatia or fails to report any changes occurred;
- fails to register his or her residence, the place where he stays habitually and the address at which he or she is staying;
- fails to cancel the address at which he is staying, temporary residence or permanent residence;
- during his stay in Croatia, wears a foreign military, police or customs uniform contrary to conditions prescribed by the Aliens Act.[508]

342. The alien who illegally stays in Croatia will be fined HRK 500–HRK 7,000 (app. EUR 67–EUR 933).[509] There are several situations in which it is considered that an alien is staying in Croatia illegally: if the alien is not on short-term stay, if he or she does not have a valid temporary or permanent residence permit, if he was not granted asylum, subsidiary or temporary protection, or if he is not an asylum seeker. Also, an alien who moves outside the area in which his or her movement is limited on the basis of a bilateral international agreement will be also considered staying illegally. However, there are several categories of aliens which will be considered to legally reside in Croatia until the decision concerning the application for residence becomes enforceable: an alien who submitted a temporary or permanent residence application before the expiration of short-term stay/temporary residence; an alien who by the date of submitting the application had at least three years of uninterrupted temporary residence and at least ten years of refugee status; an alien who had a residence in Croatia on 8 October 1991 and who is a beneficiary of the programme of return, reconstruction or housing care and for whom it was established that he returned with the intention of living in Croatia permanently.[510] The

508. Article 220, para. 3, Aliens Act.
509. Article 222, para. 2, Aliens Act.
510. Article 102, Aliens Act.

exceptions are also persons who have expressed the intention to apply for international protection and who should not be sanctioned for unlawful entry or residence in Croatia. A TCN or stateless person who has illegally entered Croatia, coming directly from the territory where he or she was persecuted, or has been exposed to serious harm will not be punished for his or her illegal entry or stay provided that he or she expresses an intention to apply for international protection without delay and shows good reason for their illegal entry or stay.[511]

343. For more serious offences, the police will issue the sanction of imprisonment in the duration of up to sixty days or a fine from HRK 3,000 to HRK 7,000 (app. EUR 400 to EUR 933) against any alien who:

- is staying longer than specified in the border area, as determined by a bilateral international agreement on the basis of which a border pass or a one-time crossing permit is issued;
- leaves the centre for foreigners without approval or fails to abide by the house rules of the centre;
- fails to comply with the obligations assigned to him;
- obstructs removal (forced return);
- at the request of an official, does not present a travel document or other document used to cross the state border;
- does not carry on him or her an identity document and does not present personal data at the request of a police officer;
- allows other persons to use his documents or uses invalid documents or another person's documents as his own.[512]

344. A specific regime is in place for EEA citizens and TCNs who are EU Blue Cardholders and their family members. With a fine ranging from HRK 500 to HRK 5,000 (app. EUR 67 to EUR 667), the police sanction an EEA citizen or his or her family member who either stays in during the prohibition of entry and stay, or fails to register temporary residence or the place where he stays habitually. EEA citizens and their family members will be fined HRK 500 if they fail to return the residence card. The same fine will be issued to a family member who himself is not an EEA national or who fails to submit an application for issuing a new residence card. A fine of HRK 200 (app. EUR 27) will be issued against a TCN who fails to register his or her temporary residence, or, at the request of an official, fails to provide for review a valid travel document or identity card, residence permit or other public document containing the photograph, or to carry the documents with him. The same fine will be issued against the family member of EEA national who fails to submit an application for issuing a residence card or, at the request of an official, fails to provide for review a valid travel document or identity card, residence permit or other public document containing the photograph or to carry the documents with him.[513]

---

511. Article 8, Act on International and Temporary Protection.
512. Article 222, para. 1, Aliens Act.
513. Article 221, paras 3, 5, 6, 7, 8, Aliens Act.

345. A fine from HRK 500 to HRK 3,000 (app. EUR 67 to EUR 400) will be issued against a TCN who is an EU Blue Cardholder who:

- failed to notify the police administration or police station of the termination of the work contract or criteria based on which the stay and work permit, the 'EU Blue Card', was issued;
- failed to apply for the extension of his stay and work permit, the 'EU Blue Card', within thirty days before the expiration of the deadline of the valid stay and stay permit;
- failed to apply for the residence and work permit, the 'EU Blue Card', within eight days;
- failed to notify the police administration or police station of the change of employer.[514]

346. The Criminal Code does not recognise criminal offences that explicitly address unlawful entry or stay of aliens in Croatia. The Code, however, contains the offence of the unlawful entry into, movement or residence in the RoC, another EU Member State or signatory of the Schengen Agreement, which refers to assisting in illegally entering, moving or residing (*see* more in the next parts of this chapter). There is no criminal offence if a person (without any assistance) is illegally entering, leaving, moving or staying in the RoC, but it is a misdemeanour for which the person shall be held accountable as described before.

§3. Detention

I. Reasons and Time Limits

347. Detention is usually justified on the basis that categories of aliens are 'illegal' either in entering a state's territory without authorisation or staying after they have been ordered to leave. It is broadly used in order to facilitate impending expulsion or where there is a concern that the individual may abscond. In Croatia, an alien may be arrested and detained for up to twenty-four hours if necessary, to issue a decision on refusal of entry or a decision relating to the return, or in the case of forced removal. However, it has to be established that there is a danger an alien may abscond. Detention can be prolonged for a maximum of forty-eight hours if forced removal or departure from the border crossing to a third country cannot be effected within twenty-four hours. Again, detention will be considered justified only if it is reasonably expected that return or departure can be executed within forty-eight hours. An alien should be released immediately upon cessation of reasons for arrest and detention, at the latest until the expiration of the time limit (twenty-four or forty-eight hours), except when activities for removal are ongoing or a decision on accommodation in the reception centre for aliens was adopted.[515]

---

514. Article 221, para. 4, Aliens Act.
515. Article 130, Aliens Act.

II. Less Coercive Measures

348. In order to enforce return, the police administration or the police station can impose to an alien less coercive measures than detention. Those measures include:

- deposit of travel documents, travel papers and travel tickets;
- deposit of certain funds;
- obligation to stay at a particular address of accommodation;
- regular reporting to the police station at a particular time.[516]

Although there are no absolute maximum time limits foreseen for the application of less coercive measures in the Aliens Act, it can be concluded that measures may be imposed as long as and to the extent that they can still be considered a 'necessary measure' to enforce return.

III. Detention in the Reception Centre for Aliens

349. An alien can be detained in the reception centre for aliens for up to six months only if considered necessary for ensuring the forced removal or departure, and only if the same purpose cannot be achieved by applying less coercive measures. A person can be detained only as short a period as possible and only maintained as long as removal arrangements are in progress and executed with due diligence.[517] Detention may be extended by not more than twelve months if an alien refused to provide personal or other information and documents required for forced removal, or he or she provided false information or prevented or in some other way caused delay of forced removal, or it is justifiably expected to receive travel and other documents required for forced removal, which were requested from another state.[518] Police administration or police station will issue a decision on accommodation in the centre, while the MoI will issue the decision on extending the accommodation.[519]

350. An alien can be detained only if there is a risk of absconding to leave the EEA or the RoC. The Aliens Act enumerates a number of criteria that might indicate that there is a risk of absconding, such as lack of documentation proving the identity, lack of registered residence or reliable address accommodation, lack of sufficient financial resources, illegal entry into the territory of the EEA or Croatia, expression of intent of non-compliance with return-related measures, non-compliance with previously issued return decision, existence of conviction for a criminal offence in another EEA Member State, ongoing criminal investigations and proceedings or sentence for a criminal offence in Croatia, non-compliance with the requirement to go immediately to the territory of another EEA Member State, and

516. Article 132, Aliens Act.
517. Article 131, Aliens Act.
518. Article 134, Aliens Act.
519. Article 135, paras 1 and 2, Aliens Act.

prior conduct of a TCN which indicates that there is a risk of absconding. In addition, a risk of absconding is presumed in the following situations: refusing to provide personal data and documents or providing false data, using false or forged identity documents, destroying or otherwise disposing of existing identity documents, refusing to provide fingerprints, opposing violently or fraudulently the return procedure, not complying with a less coercive measure aimed at preventing the risk of absconding, not complying with an existing entry ban or unauthorised secondary movement.[520]

351. An alien can also be held in detention under stricter police supervision if he or she does not comply with the house rules on residing in the centre. The Aliens Act listed criteria for stricter police supervision, which include, for example, leaving without permission the centre, physical attack on other detainees, police officials or other employees, intentional damaging the technical and other equipment in the centre, etc. Stricter police supervision includes the restriction of movement of an alien inside the centre, for up to seven days. The centre has to send a case file on stricter police supervision to administrative court immediately after the decision has been issued by the MoI. The court has to decide on the next working day to either annul the decision or to continue with the stricter police supervision. An alien is not allowed to appeal against the decision on stricter police supervision.[521]

352. In 2017, a total of 645 aliens were detained in the Reception Centre for Aliens in Ježevo. Five most frequent nationalities were from Kosovo (174), Turkey (174), Albania (65), Afghanistan (42) and Pakistan (29).[522]

IV. Detention of Minors

353. Unaccompanied minors and families with minors will only be detained as a measure of last resort only if forced removal cannot be ensured in some other way and for the shortest appropriate period.[523] In general, an unaccompanied minor is accommodated in different facilities under the auspices of the Ministry for Demography, Family, Youth and Social Policy, based on their age. Children up to 14 years are accommodated in children's homes and children over the age of 14 in Residential Child Care Institutions (institutions for children with behavioural problems).

354. Detained minors are accommodated in the centre separately from other aliens. Stricter police supervision cannot be imposed on a minor. Minors should

---

520. Article 133, paras 2–3, Aliens Act.
521. Article 138, Aliens Act.
522. Ministry of Interior, Survey of Basic Safety Indicators of the 2017 the Republic of Croatia, January 2018. https://mup.hr/public/documents/Statistika/Statisti%C4%8Dki%20pregled%20temeljnih%20sigurnosnih%20pokazatelja%20i%20rezultata%20rada%20u%202017.%20godini.pdf (accessed 21 Mar. 2018).
523. Article 138b, paras 1 and 2, Aliens Act.

have the possibility to engage in leisure activities, including play and recreational activities appropriate to their age.[524] Detained minors have the right to education and healthcare.[525]

§4. Expulsion and Removal

355. An alien who has no legal basis for staying in Croatia is considered to be staying illegally and has to leave the country without delay.[526] The measures for leaving the RoC include:

- the restriction of the freedom of movement (detention) as explained above;
- the voluntary departure;
- the ban on entry and stay;
- less coercive measures, as explained above;
- forced removal;
- other measures prescribed by the Aliens Act.

However, those measures will not be applied if a TCN is detected near the border during or immediately after the unlawful entry, for TCNs to be denied entry at the border crossing, and TCNs to be extradited on the basis of an international treaty.[527]

356. At the time of applying measures for leaving Croatia, including the voluntary departure, safeguards should be respected. Those include protection of the best interest of minors and the needs of other vulnerable persons (minors, persons with disability, elderly people, pregnant women, single parents with minor children, victims of torture, rape or other serious forms of psychological, physical or sexual violence and people with mental disabilities), family circumstances and the health condition of an alien.[528]

I. Return Decision

357. In the case of a TCN illegally residing in Croatia or whose legal stay is to be terminated by a decision of the national body, the MoI will issue a decision on return, with the following elements: statement that a TCN is illegally residing or ceases to legally reside in Croatia, a time limit for leaving EEA (voluntary departure), announcement of forced removal if a TCN does not voluntarily leave the EEA, and obligation to report at the border crossing when he or she leaves Croatia or at the diplomatic mission or consular post of the RoC after leaving the EEA.[529] In several cases the MoI is not obliged to issue a return decision:

524. Article 138b, paras 3, 5, 6, Aliens Act.
525. Article 101, para. 3, Aliens Act.
526. Article 102, para. 2, Aliens Act.
527. Article 100, paras 1, 3, Aliens Act.
528. Article 101, paras 1, 2, Aliens Act.
529. Article 103, Aliens Act.

- if there is a risk of absconding;
- if an application for a legal stay has been dismissed as manifestly unfounded or fraudulent;
- if a TCN may be forcibly deported to the other EEA Member State on the basis of a readmission agreement which entered into force before 13 January 2009;
- if a TCN concerned poses a risk to public order or national security.[530]

In those cases, an alien will be expelled from Croatia (*see* further in this chapter).[531]

358. If a TCN staying illegally in Croatia is the subject of a pending procedure for acquiring a temporary residence, the MoI can consider refraining from issuing a return decision.[532]

359. The amendments of the Aliens Act in 2018 introduced the possibility of issuing a decision on the return or expulsion of a TCN who illegally resides or illegally cross or attempts to cross the state border without conducting a misdemeanour procedure (except in the case of a TCN to be extradited on the basis of an international treaty),[533] which in practice gave more powers to the MoI in conducting the administrative procedure of return of aliens.

II. Voluntary Departure

360. Voluntary departure is considered one of the return measures, which means compliance with the obligation to return within the time limit fixed for that purpose in the return decision. The length of the period for voluntary departure will be determined with due regard to the specific circumstances of the individual case, taking into account, in particular, the prospect of return, which may not be shorter than seven days or longer than thirty days. In some circumstances, the length of the period for voluntary departure might be shorter than seven days: if there is a risk of absconding; if an application for a legal stay has been dismissed as manifestly unfounded or fraudulent; if a TCN poses a risk to public order or national security.[534] In justified cases, the length of the period for voluntary return might be longer than thirty days, but not longer than a year.[535]

361. If a TCN is issued with a decision on expulsion or a decision that terminates his or her legal residence, voluntary departure will be set up with this decision, and not with the return decision.[536]

530. Article 104, para. 1, Aliens Act.
531. Article 109, para. 1, Aliens Act.
532. Article 104, para. 2, Aliens Act.
533. Article 105, para. 3, Aliens Act.
534. Articles 103 and 104, para. 1, Aliens Act.
535. Articles 103 and 107, Aliens Act.
536. Article 105, para. 2, Aliens Act.

III. Expulsion

362. There are two situations in which an alien can be subjected to expulsion from Croatia: because of the illegal stay or due to increased social danger, in which cases the MoI will issue a decision on expulsion.[537] The decision will determine whether a TCN is illegally residing or ceases to legally reside in Croatia, whether he or she is required to leave the EEA, the length of the ban of entry and stay in EEA.[538] When deciding, the MoI hast take into account the vulnerability of an alien, length of his or her residence in Croatia, age, health, family and economic connections, the level of social and cultural integration in Croatia, and his or her ties to the country of origin.[539]

363. For illegal stay, a TCN will be expelled under the following conditions:

- if he or she did not leave the EEA or the RoC within the time limit set by the decision;
- if he or she arrived at the EEA or the RoC before the expiration of the ban on entry and stay;
- where is no obligation to issue a return decision, as explained above;
- and very generally, for an illegal stay or illegal cross or attempt to cross the state border for other than the previously mentioned reasons.[540]

The ban of entry and stay stipulated by decision on expulsion on the ground of illegal stay in Croatia cannot be shorter than three months or longer than five years.[541]

364. For a reason of increased social danger, the Aliens Act differentiate between the situation when the alien will be expelled and when he or she might be expelled.[542] The first situation covers the following:

- if an alien was, pursuant to a legally effective judgment, sentenced to unconditional imprisonment in the duration over one year because of a criminal offence committed with intention;
- if an alien was repeatedly sentenced over the period of five years, pursuant to a legally effective judgment, to imprisonment in the duration of three years, because of a criminal offence committed with intention;
- if an alien was sentenced to unconditional imprisonment, because of committing a criminal offence against the values protected by international law;
- if an alien poses a danger to national security.

537. Articles 108 and 109, Aliens Act.
538. Article 111, para. 1, Aliens Act.
539. Article 110, para. 1, Aliens Act.
540. Article 109, Aliens Act.
541. Article 111, para. 6, Aliens Act.
542. Article 108, Aliens Act.

Only if those circumstances exist, an alien with permanent residence, with temporary residence for an uninterrupted period of ten years, or with temporary residence and married to a Croatian national or an alien with approved permanent residence for three years, may be expelled from Croatia.[543] The MoI might expel an alien who:

- assists in unlawful entry, transit or stay;
- concludes a marriage of convenience;
- violates the regulations about the employment and work of aliens, the prevention of riots at sporting events, public order, weapons, narcotics abuse or custom and tax obligations;
- commits a criminal offence for which he or she is prosecuted ex officio or small offence with elements of violence;
- repeats offences.

The ban of entry and stay stipulated by decision on expulsion on the ground of increased social danger cannot be shorter than three months or longer than twenty years.[544]

365. Under certain conditions, the entry and stay ban may be revoked or the period may be shortened: if the grounds for expulsion ceased to exist, under humanitarian grounds, or if it is in the interest of the RoC. An application for revocation or shortening the period of the ban may be submitted on the expiration of half of the time of the issued ban of entry and stay, and in any case on the expiration of three years. If an alien expressed the intention to seek asylum, the decision on expulsion remains valid, but it will not be enforced by the end of the status determination.[545]

IV. Forced Removal

366. Forced removal means the enforcement of the obligation to return, namely the deportation from Croatia under police supervision, regardless of TCN's permission. An alien will be deported in two situations: if he or she failed to leave the EEA or the RoC before the deadline, or if the MoI is not obliged to issue a return decision. Deportation will be carried out to a TCN's country of origin, country of transit from which he or she arrived in Croatia, to another third country with his or her consent, or EEA Member State on the basis of a readmission agreement which entered into force before 13 January 2009 or under the Dublin procedure. If a decision on return contains a voluntary return period, a TCN will not be deported before the expiry of that period, unless it is established that at the time of the enforcement of

543. Article 110, para. 2, Aliens Act.
544. Article 111, para. 5, Aliens Act.
545. Article 113, Aliens Act.

the decision on return there was a risk of absconding or that risk appeared after issuing a decision on return. A TCN to be denied entry at the border crossing will be returned to the country of an entrance to Croatia.[546]

367. The MoI will also deport an alien against whom the EEA Member State has issued a legally effective decision on expulsion in the following cases:

- if he or she was sentenced to imprisonment in the duration of at least one year, because of a criminal offence;
- due to suspicion to have committed or intended to commit a serious criminal offence;
- due to violations of the regulations on the entry and residence of TCN.[547]

368. It is prohibited to deport an alien to a state where his or her life or freedom would be threatened on account of his race, religion or nationality, membership of a particular social group or political opinion, or where he or she might be exposed to torture or inhuman or degrading treatment or punishment or a death penalty might be executed against him or her, and to a state where he would be in danger of being deported to such a state. An unaccompanied minor can be deported only if it has been established that he or she shall be returned to a member of his or her family, a nominated guardian or adequate reception facilities in the state of return.[548] In both cases, deportation will be postponed, as well as if the court postponed the enforcement of the return decision or decision on expulsion. Deportation can be postponed due to lack of identification of a TCN, lack of transport capacity, serious health issues that could emerge during deportation, or other reasons that prevent TCN from deportation. Deportation can be postponed for a maximum of one year.[549] The postponement will cease with the expiry of the time limit, with the annulment of a decision on temporary postponement of deportation, and if an alien legalise his or her residence in Croatia.[550]

369. In 2017, there were 1,223 forced removals of aliens. Five most frequent nationalities were from Kosovo (549), Albania (209), Turkey (160), Bosnia (88) and Serbia (54). If compared with 2016, there was an increase of 28.2% of forced removals in 2017.[551]

V. Expulsion and Removal of EEA Citizens and Their Family Members

370. EEA citizen and a member of his family may be denied the right of entry and residence in the RoC if they pose a threat to public order, national security or public health (except if public health-threatening disease occurred three months

546. Article 122, Aliens Act.
547. Article 124, para. 1, Aliens Act.
548. Article 126, Aliens Act.
549. Article 138e, Aliens Act.
550. Article 138g, Aliens Act.
551. MoI, Survey of Basic Safety Indicators of the 2017 the Republic of Croatia.

after entering the RoC), based on their behaviour which constitutes a real, immediate and serious threat to the fundamental interests of society and in accordance with the principle of proportionality. A previous conviction for a criminal offence cannot be considered as such risk, neither can the circumstances not closely related to a particular case or the reasons for the purpose of general prevention. The ban cannot be based on economic grounds.[552]

371. EEA citizens and their family members can be deported from the RoC only on the grounds of protecting the public order, national security or public health. When deciding, the MoI has to take into account the length of his or her residence in Croatia, age, the state of health, family and economic connections, the level of social and cultural integration in Croatia, and his or her ties to the country of origin. If granted permanent residence, an EEA citizen and a member of his family can be deported only due to serious reasons for the protection of public order or national security. Even more restricted are the conditions for deportation of EEA citizens who have been legally residing in Croatia for an uninterrupted period of ten years or who is a minor – those categories can be deported only for the necessary reasons for the protection of national security, and for minors if it is in the best interest of the child. Deadline for leaving Croatia shall not be less than thirty days.[553]

552. Article 179a, Aliens Act.
553. Article 180, Aliens Act.

Chapter 2. Sanctions Against Persons Helping Illegal Entry and Residence

§1. Human Smuggling

372. Human smuggling is regulated by the Aliens Act as a misdemeanour offence and the Penal Code as a criminal offence. The difference between the two is based on the severity of the act: human smuggling will be considered a criminal offence if the perpetrator is helping in illegal entry and residence for personal gain.

373. According to the Aliens Act, it is forbidden to assist and to attempt to assist a TCN in the unauthorised entry, transit and residence in Croatia. The following activities will not be considered facilitation of unauthorised entry, transit and residence:

- providing free legal aid to aliens, as regulated by the Aliens Act (*see* more in Part VI);
- assisting the illegal crossing of the state border to save lives, prevent injuries, provide emergency medical assistance and provide humanitarian aid;
- assisting in unlawful residence for humanitarian reasons and without the intention to prevent or delay the execution of return measures.[554]

A person who assists or attempts to assist a TCN in unauthorised entry, transit and residence in Croatia will be punished by imprisonment for up to sixty days, and a fine of HRK 23,000 (app. EUR 3,067) for each assisted TCN. Higher sanctions are foreseen for legal persons: the legal person will be fined in the amount of HRK 50,000 (app. EUR 6,667), and responsible person in organization with a fine of HRK 23,000 (app. EUR 3,067) for each assisted TCN. In addition, the MoI can issue a protective measure of confiscation of items and a protective measure of prohibition of the performance of an activity.[555]

374. Sanctions for unlawful entry or stay of aliens can also be imposed on carriers as penalties given to transport companies if they carry improperly documented passengers. Carriers are obliged to take a TCN whose entry was refused, away from the border crossing point or from RoC without any delay. Carriers are also obliged to bear the cost of such transport, or to find some other way of transportation and to bear the cost of such transportation. If some other way of transportation shall not be possible immediately, the carrier shall assume the costs incurred during the residence and return of a foreigner.[556] The sanctions against the carrier include:

- for a carrier who transported a TCN who does not have a valid travel document or other document used to cross the state border, a valid visa or stay permit – a fine of HRK 23,000 (app. EUR 3,067) for each transported TCN;

554. Article 43, Aliens Act.
555. Article 225, paras 3–5, Aliens Act.
556. Article 41, Aliens Act.

- for a carrier – natural person who failed to transport a TCN from a border crossing point or Croatia at his own cost or failed to assume the costs of the TCN's return – a fine of HRK 23,000 (app. EUR 3,067) for each transported TCN;
- for a carrier – legal person – a fine of HRK 50,000 (app. EUR 6,667), and responsible person in the legal person with a fine of HRK 23,000 (app. EUR 3,067) for each assisted TCN.[557]

375. The Penal Code regulates the criminal offence of illegal entry, movement and residence in the RoC, another EU Member State or Signatory of the Schengen Agreement. The criminal offence exists in the event that the perpetrator for personal gain allows or helps another person to illegally enter, leave, move or reside in the RoC or another EU Member State or signatory of the Schengen Agreement. For this criminal offence, a prison sentence of one to eight years is prescribed. A more severe sanction is foreseen in cases of specific (qualified) forms of this criminal offence: if during the commission of the crime life or body of a person who illegally enters, moves or resides in the RoC or another EU Member State or signatory of the Schengen Agreement was endangered, or the person was subjected to inhuman or degrading treatment, or if an official person has committed a criminal offence in the performance of official duty. In such cases, the perpetrator shall be punished by imprisonment for three to twelve years.[558]

§2. HUMAN TRAFFICKING

376. According to the provisions of the Penal Code,[559] a criminal offence of 'Human trafficking' provides that who, by force or threat, deception, fraud, kidnapping, abuse of power or of a situation of hardship or dependence, or of the giving or receiving of payments or other benefits to achieve the consent of a person having control over another person or by any other means recruits, transports, transfers, harbours or receives a person, or exchanges or transfers control over a person for the purpose of exploiting his or her labour by means of forced labour or servitude, slavery or a relationship similar thereto, or for the purpose of exploitation for prostitution of the person or of other forms of sexual exploitation, including pornography, or of unlawful or forced marriage, or of taking parts of the person's body or of using the person in armed conflicts or of committing an unlawful act, shall be punished by imprisonment from one to ten years. The same punishment will be imposed on whoever recruits, transports, transfers, harbours or receives a child, or exchanges or transfers control over a child for the purpose of exploiting his or her labour by means of forced labour or services, slavery or a relationship similar thereto, or for the purpose of exploitation for prostitution of the child or of other forms of sexual exploitation, including pornography, or of unlawful or forced marriage, or of illegal

557. Article 225, paras 1, 2 and 4, Aliens Act.
558. Article 326, Penal Code (*Kazneni zakon*), OG 125/2011, 144/2012, 56/2015, 61/2015, 101/2017, 118/2018.
559. Article 106, Penal Code.

adoption, or of taking parts of a child's body, or of using the child in armed conflicts. Also, the same punishment shall be imposed on those who use the services of a victim through forms of exploitation, knowing that the person is a victim of trafficking. Those who allow the commission of the offence of trafficking, maintain, suspend, conceal, damage or destroy the passport or the identity document of another person or those who try to commit the offence will be punished with imprisonment not exceeding three years. The Penal Code further foresees aggravated forms of the crime of human trafficking punishable by imprisonment from three to fifteen years: if the offence is committed against a child or a juvenile, or by an official in performing his or her duties, or if it is committed against a larger number of persons or has caused the death of one or more persons.

Part VI. Legal Remedies and Procedural Safeguards

Chapter 1. Legal Remedies in Case of Refusal of Right to Enter, Stay or Reside

§1. General Framework

377. Decisions of competent authorities concerning the refusal of the right to enter, stay or residence of aliens are by its legal nature administrative acts and therefore fall under the scope of the General Administrative Procedure Act. It is a general law applicable to all proceedings in all administrative matters. However, it is possible that specialised laws regulate some procedural issues differently from the Act, but only under strictly regulated conditions: only particular issues of administrative procedure can be regulated differently, specific regulation is necessary for proceedings in a particular administrative area which cannot be contrary to the basic provisions and purpose of the General Administrative Procedure Act.[560] Therefore, the General Administrative Procedure Act has to be respected and used as a subsidiary source of law in all issues which are not regulated by specialised legislation in the field of migration and asylum: the State Border Protection Act, the Aliens Act and the Act on International and Temporary Protection.

378. The right to legal remedy is one of the basic legal principles of the General Administrative Procedure Act, which stipulates the appeal (*žalba*) and the complaint (*prigovor*) as the main legal remedies in administrative procedure.[561] There are four types of complaints: (1) complaint against a notice to the applicant of petition or notification; (2) complaint due to non-fulfilment of an administrative contract by the public law authority; (3) complaint for protection from the actions of public law authorities on which the decision is not made; and (4) complaint for protection from the actions of public service providers.[562] An appeal may be filed against a decision on the complaint made by the first-instance body, while an administrative dispute may be instituted against a decision on the complaint made by the body of the second instance. If there is no second-instance body, an administrative

560. Article 3, para. 1, General Administrative Procedure Act.
561. Article 12, General Administrative Procedure Act.
562. Articles 42, 154–158, General Administrative Procedure Act.

dispute may be instituted against the decision on the complaint.[563] Appeals shall be filed within fifteen days following the day of the decision's delivery.[564] The same timeline is stipulated for filing the complaint.[565] However, other laws can set a different (shorter or longer) period for the appeal or complaint.

379. The General Administrative Procedure Act also stipulates two so-called extraordinary legal remedies (ex officio interventions), which can be used even after the expiration of the period of the appeal: annulment and revocation of an unlawful act, and revocation of a lawful act according to which a party has acquired certain rights. Also, it is possible to declare the act null and void. The unlawful administrative act can be annulled, all effects produced by the act have to be annulled, and everything that has been received by the parties has to be restored (the *ex tunc* effect). If revoked, legal consequences of the act are not removed, but the act has no effect in future (the *ex nunc* effect).[566] If the party has received certain rights, the act can be annulled only if it has been issued by a public body without jurisdiction, without the approval of the other authority if such approval is legally prescribed, or if there is another legally effective decision in the same matter. If the act represents a severe breach of material law, the public authority may choose whether it wants the act to be annulled or revoked. If the administrative matter involves two or more parties with opposing interests, the decision can be revoked only with the consent of the opposing party.[567] Lawful act can be revoked provided that: the revocation is permitted by law, or the administrative act contains a reservation of revocation when the party has not fulfilled his or her obligation established by the administrative act, or the said obligation has not been fulfilled before the deadline, or the revocation is necessary in order to prevent serious and immediate danger to human life and health or public safety, and this cannot be done by other means which would interfere with the attained rights to a lesser degree.[568] Annulment and revocation of the act can be done by the issuing body, by the second instance body, or by the authority supervising the body which has issued the act. It can be initiated by the party, an authorised state body or ex officio. Unlawful decisions may be annulled within two years and revoked within one year following the date of delivery to the party.[569] Finally, the administrative act can be declared null and void in case of the most severe errors, such as if it constitutes a criminal offence. There is no time limit for declaring the act null and void, and it can be done by the body which has issued the act or by the supervising authority, at the request of the party or ex officio.[570]

380. In cases in which there is no appeal against the administrative decision (such as against the decision of the MoI's Commission, which is a second instance

563. Article 122, para 4, General Administrative Procedure Act.
564. Article 109, General Administrative Procedure Act.
565. Article 122, General Administrative Procedure Act.
566. Ivan Koprić, Polonca Kovač, Vedran Đulabić & Jasmina Džinić, *Legal Remedies in Administrative Procedures in Western Balkans* (Regional School of Public Administration, 2016), p. 130.
567. Article 129, General Administrative Procedure Act.
568. Article 130, General Administrative Procedure Act.
569. Article 131, General Administrative Procedure Act.
570. Article 128, General Administrative Procedure Act.

body), there is a possibility to initiate an administrative dispute (*upravni spor*) before the administrative court. A claim to the court should be filed within thirty days from the delivery of the administrative decision. If an individual decision in the part with the instruction about a legal remedy takes a longer period to initiate an administrative dispute than the time limit of thirty days, the claim may be filed within the time limit specified in the instruction about a legal remedy.[571] Only if prescribed by the relevant legislation, the claim will postpone enforcement of the administrative decision. In addition, the court may decide that the claim will postpone the enforcement of decision if its enforcement would cause a claimant damage that could be difficult to repair, and the postponement is not contrary to the public interest.[572]

381. The system of administrative justice has been organised as a two-tier system with four administrative courts of the first instance and the High Administrative Court of the RoC. According to the Administrative Disputes Act, administrative courts rule on: actions against individual decisions of bodies governed by public law; actions against the actions of bodies governed by public law; actions for failing to adopt individual decisions and/or failure on the part of a body governed by public law to act within a statutory deadline; actions taken against administrative agreements and the execution of administrative agreements; other cases prescribed by law. The High Administrative Court rules on appeals against judgments of the administrative courts and appealable decisions, on the legality of general acts, on conflicts of jurisdiction between administrative courts, and in other cases prescribed by the law.[573] According to the amendments to the Administrative Disputes Act of December 2014, a claim against a judgment by an administrative court to the High Administrative Court postpones its enforcement.[574]

382. Any breaches of human rights guaranteed by the Croatian Constitution fall under the jurisdiction of the Constitutional Court. The Court decides on constitutional complaints (*ustavna tužba*) against the individual decisions of state bodies, bodies of local and regional self-government and legal persons with public authority when these decisions violate human rights and fundamental freedoms. Citizens and legal entities may initiate a proceeding before the Constitutional Court only after exhaustion of ordinary legal remedies, in the allotted period of thirty days. If it pertains to a judicial act, the Constitutional Court appears to be the court of the fourth instance (an instance above the Supreme Court) but with exclusive jurisdiction to confirm or deny the decision's validity.

571. Article 24, Administrative Disputes Act.
572. Article 26, Administrative Disputes Act.
573. Article 12, Administrative Disputes Act.
574. Article 66, para. 5, Administrative Disputes Act.

§2. Refusal of the Right to Enter

383. Conditions for entry into and exit from Croatia are regulated by the Schengen Borders Code and the Aliens Act. A TCN who does not fulfil all entry conditions will be refused entry to Croatia, except in some specific circumstances, including the right to seek asylum. The decision stating the reasons for the refusal should be given in the standard form and handed to a TCN, who has to acknowledge receipt of the decision to refuse entry.[575] The decision is printed in Croatian and English and can be printed in other languages understood by TCNs.[576] Against the decision on refusal of entry, an appeal can be filed through the competent diplomatic mission or consular office of the RoC. The Commission of the MoI decides on the appeals. However, the appeal does not postpone enforcement of a decision which in practice means that a TCN should wait for a decision outside of the territory of the RoC.[577] An alien is not entitled to the right to free legal assistance in this procedure.

384. Concerning the refusal of entry to an EEA citizen and a member of his family, the decision to refuse entry cannot be appealed, but an EEA citizen or a family member can initiate an administrative dispute.[578]

§3. Refusal of a Visa Application

385. Against a decision on refusing, annulment or revocation a visa, a TCN can file an appeal within fifteen days from its delivery through the competent diplomatic mission or consular office of the RoC abroad. The MFEA decides on appeals, but the appeal does not postpone enforcement of the decision.[579] In 2017, thirty-three appeals were lodged against decisions to refuse a visa, and the MFEA rendered twenty-eight decisions dismissing appeals on the merits, three appeals by the parties were partially granted and applications were remanded to the first-instance body (diplomatic missions and consulate offices) for a new decision, one was dismissed, and in one case, the procedure was suspended. None of the appeals was successful.[580]

386. In the case of a negative decision about the visa extension, a TCN is entitled to appeal within fifteen days from delivery of this decision, through the competent diplomatic mission or consular office. The MFEA will consider the appeal. Again, an appeal will not postpone the enforcement of the negative decision.[581]

575. Article 14, paras 1–2, Schengen Borders Code.
576. Article 12, para. 5, Ordinance on Treatment of Third-Country Nationals.
577. Article 38, Aliens Act.
578. Article 179a, para. 8, Aliens Act.
579. Article 31, paras 3–4 and Article 33, paras 5–7, Aliens Act.
580. Croatian Law Centre, The Croatian asylum system in 2017 – National report, http://www.hpc.hr/wp-content/uploads/2018/10/National-Report-2017-Asylum-System.pdf (accessed 15 Dec. 2018).
581. Article 30, Aliens Act.

§4. Refusal of Application for Temporary Residence

387. As a rule, the main body for deciding on temporary residence application is the MoI through the police administration or police station based on the location of temporary residence or intended stay of an alien. Against the decision, an alien can appeal to the MoI's Commission.[582] The same legal remedy is foreseen regarding the appeal against the decision on refusal of residence and work permit issued by the police administration or police station.[583] The Aliens Act additionally specifies that an appeal to the MoI's Commission can be filled in the following cases:

- refusal, revocation and annulment of stay and work permit application for seasonal workers;[584]
- refusal and annulment of stay and work permit application for long term mobility of TCNs in the framework of an intra-corporate transfer;[585]
- annulment of stay and work permit of TCNs in the framework of an intra-corporate transfer;[586]
- cessation of stay and work permit.[587]

However, an appeal is not permissible against a decision refusing the issuing of a residence and work permit if the annual quota is full, or if the annual quota for extension new employment or seasonal employment was not set. In such case, an alien can initiate an administrative dispute before the administrative court.[588]

388. Concerning the temporary residence of an EEA citizen and a member of his family, they can appeal a decision of the MoI issued throughout police administration or police station rejecting the issuance of a certificate of the registration of temporary residence or a residence card for a member of the family of an EU citizen. The MoI's Commission will decide about the appeal.[589] The same legal remedy is provided regarding the decision on cessation of temporary residence of EEA citizens and their family members,[590] including the family member who is not an EEA citizen.[591]

389. Temporary residence and work permit for TCNs who are *high-skilled workers* (EU Blue Cardholders) can be refused by police administration or police station under the conditions stipulated by the Aliens Act. The appeal can be lodged against

582. Article 50, paras 1 and 2, Aliens Act.
583. Article 80, para. 1 and Art. 81, para. 2, Aliens Act.
584. Article 75a, para. 10 and Art. 75c, para. 6, Aliens Act.
585. Article 79c, para. 7 and Art. 79e, Aliens Act.
586. Article 79e, Aliens Act.
587. Article 90, para. 3, Aliens Act.
588. Article 50, para. 3, Aliens Act.
589. Article 170, Aliens Act.
590. Article 165, para. 2, Aliens Act.
591. Article 172, para. 3, Aliens Act.

a decision to the MoI's Commission.[592] Against a decision on the termination of the EU Blue Card, an appeal can be filed to the MoI's Commission.[593]

§5. Refusal of Application for Permanent Residence

390. A TCN has to submit an application for the issuing of a permanent residence permit to the police administration or police station based on the place of his or her temporary residence, and the MoI will decide upon the application. An appeal is not permissible against a decision of the MoI, but a TCN can initiate an administrative dispute before the administrative court.[594] The same legal remedy is provided in case of cessation of permanent residence,[595] and cessation of permanent residence of TCNs with long-term resident status.[596]

391. Against a decision on refusal of permanent residence, or more precisely, on issuing a residence card confirming permanent residence, an EEA citizen and a member of his family can lodge an appeal. The MoI's Commission will decide about the appeal.[597] The appeal can be lodged against the decision on cessation of permanent residence of EEA citizens and their family members,[598] including the family member who is not an EEA citizen.[599]

§6. Refusal of Application for International Protection

392. There is no possibility to appeal against the first-instance decision on an asylum application issued by the MoI on an asylum application. However, an asylum seeker does have the right to initiate an administrative dispute. Until the beginning of 2012 Commission for Asylum used to decide in the asylum procedure as a second-instance body. From 1 January 2012, this function was assumed by the Administrative Court. Namely, according to the EU Common Position in Chapter 24: Justice, Freedom and Security of September 2009, one of the benchmarks for the provisional closing of pre-accession negotiations in this Chapter was also related to the area of asylum, and included ensuring access to fully functioning asylum procedures for all third-country applicants wishing to apply for international protection. To meet this benchmark, it was necessary to establish a completely independent appellate body and an effective legal remedy. From the beginning of 2012, the administrative court was introduced as a second-instance body in asylum procedures.

592. Article 192, para. 4, Aliens Act.
593. Article 197, para. 4, Aliens Act.
594. Article 95, Aliens Act.
595. Article 99, para. 5, Aliens Act.
596. Article 99a, para. 4, Aliens Act.
597. Article 173, Aliens Act.
598. Article 175, para. 2, Aliens Act.
599. Article 179, para. 2, Aliens Act.

393. As a general rule, a claim brought before the administrative court will suspend the enforcement of the decision on the application for the international protection rendered by the MoI. Exceptions to that rule are provided in the following cases:

- the dismissal of an application in the accelerated procedure;
- the dismissal of an application pursuant to the fact that an applicant has been granted international protection in another EEA Member State or that the applicant has been granted international protection in a third state whose rights he or she still enjoys, provided that an applicant will be received back into that state;
- the dismissal of a subsequent application assessed as inadmissible;
- approving of the application and granting the right to international protection.[600]

The claim may contain a request for suspensive effect, pursuant to the regulations on administrative disputes, apart from the case when the applicant has already been living in Croatia for a long time, and for no justifiable reason failed to express his or her intention to apply for international protection earlier. The MoI shall submit the case file, no later than within eight days from the day of receipt of the decision by which the administrative court requests the case file, for a decision on the request for suspensive effect. The administrative court shall decide on the request for suspensive effect within eight days from the day of delivery of the case file. An appeal against the first-instance judgment by the administrative court to the High Administrative Court of the RoC will not have suspensive effect.[601]

394. Against a decision to terminate the procedure, a claim may be brought before the Administrative Court within eight days from the day the decision is served.[602] The same is provided in the case of revocation of international protection.[603]

600. Article 51, Act on International and Temporary Protection.
601. *Ibid.*
602. Article 39, Act on International and Temporary Protection.
603. Article 50, Act on International and Temporary Protection.

Chapter 2. Legal Remedies in Case of Expulsion and Detention

§1. Legal Remedies in Case of Expulsion and Removal

395. In the case of a TCN illegally residing in Croatia or whose legal stay is to be terminated by the decision of the national body, the MoI will issue a decision on return.[604] If a return decision is the only decision issued (and not in parallel a decision on expulsion) to a TCN who illegally resides in Croatia or is on a short-term stay, an administrative dispute may be initiated against such decision.[605]

396. If a TCN is issued with a decision on expulsion or with a decision that terminates his or her legal residence, voluntary departure will be set up with this decision. In such case, depending on the circumstances, the length of the period for voluntary departure can be challenged by a legal remedy provided against the expulsion decision (an administrative dispute), or against the decision on termination of the legal residence (appeal in the case of temporary residence and administrative dispute in the case of permanent residence).[606] Against a decision on extending the period for voluntary departure parties can initiate an administrative dispute.[607]

397. Against the expulsion decision issued to a TCN who illegally resides in Croatia or who is on a short-term stay, an appeal is not allowed, but an administrative dispute may be initiated.[608] The Aliens Act also stipulates that administrative dispute can be also initiated against the following decisions of the MoI:

- on the ban of entry and stay, and the decision to revoke the ban on entry and stay, if a TCN has a residence permit in another EEA Member State and a decision on expulsion has been issued;[609]
- a negative decision on the application for revocation or shortening the period of the entry and stay ban;[610]
- on the forced removal of a TCN who have been granted international protection in the other EEA Member State, or forced removal before the expiration of the period for voluntary departure,[611] or a TCN against whom the EEA Member State has issued a legally effective decision on expulsion.[612]

398. An appeal to the MoI's commission can be lodged against the decision on expulsion of EEA citizens and their family members.[613]

---

604. Article 103, Aliens Act.
605. Article 106, para. 2, Aliens Act.
606. Article 106, para. 1, Aliens Act.
607. Article 107, para. 5, Aliens Act.
608. Article 112, para. 1, Aliens Act.
609. Article 111, para. 4, Aliens Act.
610. Article 113, para. 4, Aliens Act.
611. Article 122, para. 8, Aliens Act.
612. Article 124, para. 6, Aliens Act.
613. Article 180, para. 11, Aliens Act.

§2. Legal Remedies in Case of Detention

399. Police administration or police station will issue a decision on accommodation in the centre (detention), while the MoI will issue the decision on extending the accommodation. Against both decisions, an alien can initiate an administrative dispute. The MoI has to send a case file on detention to administrative court immediately after the decision has been issued. The court has to decide whether an alien is to be released from the centre within ten days from the delivery of the case file. The administrative court may either annul or confirm the decision on the extension of detention, within five days from the delivery of the case file.[614] The Aliens Act adopted in 2011 envisaged that the administrative court would decide about a complaint lodged against the decision on detention after an oral hearing of an alien. With the amendments of the Aliens Act in 2018, the obligation of the holding of oral hearing of the alien has been narrowed only to minors.[615]

400. An additional safeguard is provided in the form of regular ex officio judicial review of the lawfulness of extension of detention decisions. The MoI has to deliver to the administrative court the case file on detention at the latest ten days before the expiration of the first and every three months from the day of extension of detention. The administrative court has to decide, within ten days from delivery of the case file, whether an alien is to be released from the centre.[616]

401. Against the decision on the application of less coercive measures, an administrative dispute can be initiated.[617]

614. Article 135, paras 1–4, Aliens Act.
615. Article 135, para. 7, Aliens Act.
616. Article 135, paras 5 and 8, Aliens Act.
617. Article 132, para. 4 Aliens Act.

Chapter 3. Procedural Safeguards

402. The specific laws guarantee procedural safeguards of the importance for aliens seeking residence right in Croatia, in particular, the Act on International and Temporary Protection and the Aliens Act (as *lex specialis*), but also by the General Administrative Procedure Act.

§1. General Administrative Procedure Act

403. When the administrative body in an administrative procedure decides on the rights, obligations or legal interests of legal and natural persons, including aliens, the General Administrative Procedure Act is applicable. The procedural safeguards are listed in the procedure principles of the Act and include:

- *A Principle of Legality*, which means that administrative bodies decide administrative matters on the basis of laws. If an administrative body is authorised by law to decide administrative matters according to its discretion, a decision has to be rendered within the limits of the authorisation and under the purpose for which the authorisation was provided.
- *A Principle of Proportionality in Protection of Rights of Parties and Public Interest*, which means that the right of a party may be limited by the action of an administrative body only where so anticipated by the law and if such action is necessary for achieving the purpose determined by the law and proportionate with the aim that is to be achieved. If a party has certain obligations under the law, more favourable measures should be, if, by such measures, the purpose of law may be achieved. In conducting procedures, administrative bodies are obligated to ensure that parties realise the protection and acquisition of their rights in the easiest possible way, taking care that the realisation of their rights is not at the expense of other person's interests or contrary to public interest.
- *A Principle of Assistance to a Party*, which means that when in the course of the procedure an official becomes aware or evaluates that a party has ground for the realisation of a specific right, the official will inform such a party thereof, as well as warn the party of the consequences of his actions or omissions in the procedure. The official has to take care that the lack of knowledge and ignorance of a party are not at the expense of the rights entitled under law.
- *A Principle of Establishment of Substantive Truth*, which means that in a procedure, an actual state of affairs has to be determined, and for that purpose, all facts important for lawful and correct adjudication of the administrative matter have to be determined.
- *A Principle of Independence and Free Assessment of Evidence*, which means that an official establishes facts and circumstances independently, and on the basis of facts and circumstances, decides in the administrative procedure.
- *A Principle of Efficiency and Cost-effectiveness*, which means that administrative procedure has to be as simple as possible, expeditious and with as few costs as possible, but also appropriate to establish all important facts and circumstances.

- *A Principle of Access to Data and Data Protection*, which means that administrative bodies are obligated to enable access to the necessary data and to provide the parties with other information, advice and professional assistance. Personal and classified data must be protected in the procedure.
- *The Right to Legal Remedy*, which means that a party has the right to an appeal against a first-instance decision, as well as when the administrative body has not adjudicated an administrative matter within a specific term unless provided otherwise by law. An administrative dispute can be initiated against a second-instance decision, or against a first-instance decision against which appeal is not allowed.
- *A Principle of Protection of Acquired Rights of Parties*, which means that a decision against which an appeal may not be lodged or administrative dispute initiated (final order), and by which a party acquired certain rights, or by which a party was obligated to perform certain obligations, may be annulled, revoked or changed only in the cases provided by law.
- *Usage of Official Language and Alphabet*, which means that an administrative procedure is conducted in the Croatian language and Latin alphabet. An administrative procedure can also be conducted in another language or alphabet officially used by the administrative body conducting the procedure.[618]

§2. Procedural Safeguards Provided by the Aliens Act and the Act on International and Temporary Protection

404. Procedural safeguards in the asylum procedure and procedures for obtaining residence permits relating to the right of every person to be heard before any individual measure which would affect him or her adversely is taken, the obligation of the administrative body to examine carefully and impartially all the relevant aspects of the particular case, the obligation of the administrative body to give reasons for its decisions and the right to data protection were addressed in detail in previous parts of this book. The right to legal remedy has been elaborated in the first chapter of this part of the book. In this chapter, two procedural safeguards will be addressed in more detail, the right to interpretation, and the right to free legal aid.

§3. Right to Interpretation

405. The administrative procedure for obtaining residence in Croatia and for the approval of international protection is conducted in the Croatian language and the Latin script. However, due to specific circumstances of aliens and lack of knowledge of the Croatian language, it is essential to provide them with the possibility to follow the procedure in a language they can understand, which includes the right to interpretation.

618. Articles 5–14, General Administrative Procedure Act.

406. If the asylum seeker does not understand Croatian, a translator/interpreter shall be provided for a language which he or she may justifiably be presumed to understand and in which can communicate. If possible, applicants will be provided ex officio with a translator/interpreter of the same sex to ensure a full account of the reasons for the application or other justified reasons. If the applicant does not have sufficient financial resources, the MoI will provide for the translation of a foreign document which is established to be a document of importance for the rendering of a decision.[619]

407. According to the Aliens Act, in the procedure of adopting all types of decisions relating to return of an alien staying illegally and an alien on short-term stay (i.e., return decision, entry-ban decisions, removal decisions, detention order, etc.), if an alien does not understand the Croatian language, he or she will be provided with a translation into the language that he or she understands. At the request of the alien, the decision relating to return will be translated.[620]

§4. Right to Free Legal Aid

408. Asylum seekers are entitled to the right to information and the right to counselling during the administrative procedure before the MoI, and to free legal assistance in the judicial proceedings before the administrative court. The right to information and the right to counselling includes providing all necessary information to an alien who wishes to express their intention to apply for international protection on the procedure for the approval of international protection, by police officers. The MoI has to inform applicants within fifteen days from the expression of intention of how the procedure of approval of international protection is conducted, on the rights and obligations they have in that procedure, and the possibility of applying to representatives of the UNHCR and other organisations who work to protect the rights of refugees, and the possibility of receiving free legal assistance. Asylum seekers will, at their request, be provided with legal and procedural information on the approval of international protection, by organisations working to protect the rights of refugees, or by attorneys with whom the MoI conclude an agreement on the provision of legal counselling.[621] Free legal assistance refers to the assistance in drawing up a claim, representation in the first-instance administrative disputes and exemption from payment of the costs of first-instance administrative disputes. The administrative court decides on the right to free legal and the amount of the expenses of legal assistance. The providers of legal assistance are attorneys and lawyers from associations registered with the Ministry of Justice to provide legal assistance.[622]

619. Article 14, Act on International and Temporary Protection.
620. Article 115, Aliens Act.
621. Article 59, Act on International and Temporary Protection.
622. Article 60, Act on International and Temporary Protection.

409. According to the Aliens Act, an alien staying illegally and an alien on the short-term stay is entitled to free legal aid in the procedure of adopting decisions relating to return against which there is no appeal, but the administrative dispute can be initiated. Free legal aid includes free legal advice and legal aid in making the complaint and representation before the administrative court. The legal aid in the judicial procedure is limited to aliens born in Croatia, aliens who were residing in Croatia for at least one year, the member of alien's close family who is Croatian citizen or granted temporary or permanent residence, and vulnerable persons. The legal aid before the court will not be provided to an alien who has sufficient financial means, who has already used the legal aid in the other procedures relating to the return, and in the judicial proceedings before the High Administrative Court. Free legal aid is provided by attorneys and lawyers from associations registered for the provision of legal aid, which have concluded a contract with the Ministry of Justice. The alien has to apply for free legal aid to the MoI. If the MoI refuses the application, an alien could initiate an administrative dispute. If an alien is granted free legal aid, he or she will be exempt from bearing the costs of an administrative dispute.[623]

623. Article 117, Aliens Act.

Part VII. Access to the Labour Market

Chapter 1. Overview of Applicable Legislation

410. Employment in Croatia is regulated by the Constitution, international conventions, treaties, the Community acquis of the EU, Labour Act, collective contracts and employment agreements. According to the Constitution of the RoC everyone shall have the right to work and to freedom of work; the free choice of vocation and employment; equal access to jobs and post under equal conditions; remuneration enabling workers to ensure a free and decent life; weekly rest period and paid annual leave; participation in decision-making in their places of employment; social security and social insurance; rights related to childbirth, maternity and childcare.[624] Forced and compulsory labour is explicitly prohibited.[625]

411. The central legislation in the field of labour law is the Labour Act of 2014, which regulates employment relationships in the RoC unless otherwise provided by another law or a published and valid international agreement, as concluded and ratified in accordance with the Constitution of the RoC.[626] The Act provides general rules of labour law, prohibits direct and indirect discrimination, regulates employment agreements, the age for employment, leaves, maternity leaves, salaries, strikes, etc. Before the new Act entered into force, there was a lack of flexibility in the Croatian labour market due to the country's employment protection regulation.[627] The main changes introduced by the Labour Act include easier termination of employment contracts in certain cases, changes in temporary employment through agencies, encouragement of atypical forms of employment, greater flexibility in working hours, etc.

412. The Aliens Act regulates access to the labour market for aliens. Until 2003, the access was regulated by the Act on Employment of Aliens.[628] Depending on

624. Articles 55–57, Constitution of the RoC.
625. Article 23, Constitution of the RoC.
626. Article 1, Labour Act (*Zakon o radu*), OG 93/2014, 127/2017.
627. *See*, for example, World Bank, *Employment Protection Legislation and Labour Market Outcomes: Theory, Evidence and Lessons for Croatia*, Zagreb (2011).
628. Act on Employment of Aliens (*Zakon o zapošljavanju stranaca*), OG 19/1992, 33/1992, 89/1992, 26/1993, 52/1994.

their status, aliens can work with a work and residence permit or a work registration certificate, either within the annual quota or outside the annual quota, or, in some cases prescribed by the law, without the work permit or the work registration certificate.

413. According to the Aliens Act, the annual quota set out the activities and occupations in which employment is permitted, and the number of work permits for each of the activities and occupations. The quota for seasonal employment can also be determined. Each year in December, the Government of RoC decides on the annual quota for the employment of aliens. The quota system is applied to non-EU workers and subdivided into quotas per sector. It is based on recommendations by various business associations and serves as an indicator of the shortage of workers. The ministry responsible for labour affairs makes a proposal for the annual quota for employment of aliens based on the opinion of Croatian Employment Institute, Croatian Chamber of Economy, Croatian Chamber of Crafts and representatives of social partners, and is determined in accordance with the migration policy and taking into account conditions on the labour market.[629]

414. Due to the demographic situation in Croatia (*see* more in the introductory part) and the growing needs for workers in several areas, especially in tourism and construction, in the last few years there is a steady growth in the number of work permits for aliens within the annual quotas (*see* Table 1).

Table 1 Annual Quotas in the Period 2010–2019

Year	*2010*	*2011*	*2012*	*2013*	*2014*	*2015*	*2016*	*2017*	*2018*	*2019*
Quota	6,948	566	3,988	2,329	2,256	1,730	3,115	9,079	38,769	65,100

Source: Government Decrees.

For 2019, the annual quota includes 65,100 work permits, out of which 15,000 permits are intended for existing permit renewals for aliens already working in Croatia within the previous annual quotas; 41,810 permits for new employment; 6,540 permits for seasonal jobs in tourism, farming, and forestry, and 250 permits for intra-corporate transfers. The greatest demand for foreign labour has been registered in the construction industry, which needs as many as 17,800 workers, tourism and hospitality (10,611), transport (2,314), the metal industry (2,200), economy and market (2,200), and agriculture and forestry (1,990).[630]

415. As a part of the Government Action Plan for Reducing Administrative Burden on the Economy, at the beginning of 2017, the new Regulation on the

629. Article 74, Aliens Act.

630. Decision on Establishing the Annual Quota for Employment of Foreigners for The Calendar Year 2019 (*Odluka o utvrđivanju godišnje kvote dozvola za zapošljavanje stranaca za kalendarsku godinu 2019.*), OG 116/2018.

Administrative Fee Tariff entered into force. It amended amounts of administrative fee tariffs, including fees for the issuance of residence permits to TCNs, that was reduced by 30%.[631]

631. Regulation on the Administrative Fee Tariff (*Uredba o tarifi upravnih pristojbi*), OG 8/2017, 37/2017, 129/2017.

Chapter 2. Conditions for Entitlement to Work in the Country as an Employed Person

§1. GENERAL CONDITIONS

416. Aliens can work in Croatia either with the work (and residence) permit or without the permit. The work permit is requested for TCNs, who can obtain it either within the annual quota or outside the annual quota, with some exceptions provided by the Aliens Act (*see* below). A TCN can work only on such jobs for which he or she was issued a stay and work permit or a work registration certificate, and only with the employer with whom he contracted employment. An employer may assign a TCN only to such jobs for which he or she was issued a stay and work permit or a work registration certificate.[632]

I. Work Permits within the Annual Quota

417. Within the annual quota, as explained in the previous chapter, aliens will be granted work (and residence) permit only for the activities and occupations in which the employment of TCNs is permitted. TCNs have to fulfil general conditions for obtaining residence and work permit (*see* Part II, Chapter 2) In addition, in order to be granted residence and work permit within the annual quota, a TCN has to provide an employment contract or a written certificate of the conclusion of an employment contract or other relevant proof of employment; proof of the acquired academic qualifications and the skills; proof of the registration of a company, branch office, representative office, trade, association or institution in Croatia.[633]

II. Work Permits outside the Annual Quota

418. The following categories of TCNs can work outside the annual quota in Croatia:

- daily migrant workers under the condition of reciprocity;
- key personnel, providers of services, workers and their family members, whose status is regulated by the Stabilisation and Association Agreement between the European Communities and their Member States and the RoC;
- TCNs holding key positions in companies, branch offices and representative offices;
- other necessary persons as defined in the Protocol on the Accession of the RoC to the Marrakesh Agreement establishing the World Trade Organization;
- TCNs who are self-employed in a company they own or in a company in which they hold a share of more than 51% or their craft;

632. Article 73, paras 5 and 6, Aliens Act.
633. Article 75, Aliens Act.

- a worker performing the activities of providing services on behalf or for a foreign employer not entitled to the right of establishment in an EEA Member State;
- teachers and lecturers at educational institutions in the language and script of a national minority;
- professional athletes or sports workers working in Croatia;
- artists working in cultural institutions in Croatia;
- TCNs employed in foreign associations registered as a foreign association in the RoC and at least three other states;
- TCNs who are members of the trust bodies of the representative offices of foreign trusts and foundations registered in the Register of the Representative Offices of Foreign Trusts and Foundations in the RoC;
- TCNs working on youth mobility programmes carried out by the RoC in cooperation with other states;
- scientific researchers and TCNs employed for scientific, scientific-teaching or other research workplaces in scientific institutions;
- professors – native speakers of foreign languages, foreign-language editors and other lecturers who teach at Croatian universities or registered foreign language schools;
- TCNs working pursuant to an international treaty;
- long-term residents in another EEA Member State;
- TCNs in the framework of an intra-corporate transfer for the long-term mobility;
- TCNs who come for a certain period to perform certain tasks in accordance with agreements concluded by the Government of the RoC with third countries;
- TCNs who are on specialisation in the area of healthcare.[634]

Besides, the work permit outside the annual quota may be granted to a TCN who:

- performs key activities in a company, or holds an ownership share in that company of at least 51%, and the company benefits from incentives in accordance with a regulation on the award for incentives for investments or performs strategic investment projects in accordance with the regulation on Strategic Investment Projects of the RoC;
- performs jobs or carries out projects in Croatia pursuant to international treaties on professional and technical assistance, which the RoC concluded with the EU, some other state or an international organisation.[635]

419. For obtaining permit for work (and residence) outside the annual quota, it has to be explained why the working place cannot be filled by Croatian workers,[636] except for some categories of aliens (e.g., for teachers and lecturers at educational institutions in the language and script of a national minority, TCNs working on youth mobility programmes carried out by the RoC in cooperation with other states, etc.).[637]

634. Article 76, para. 1, Aliens Act.
635. Article 79, para. 1, Aliens Act.
636. Article 77, para. 1, Aliens Act.
637. Article 77, para. 2, Aliens Act.

III. Work Registration Certificate

420. A work registration certificate is a permit for work for a certain number of days (ninety, sixty or thirty days) a year. In those cases, TCNs are not required to obtain a residence and work permit. This type of work permit is intended for work which can be performed in a shorter period.

421. The following TCNs can work in Croatia for up to ninety days a year based on the work registration certificate:

- procurators, key personnel and members of the supervisory board of a company, performing jobs for the company, who are not employed;
- service providers in tourism, tourist agents or entertainers;
- scientists on scientific and professional development, scientists-representatives of international organisations, and scientists who are to participate in the implementation of scientific projects important for the RoC;
- administrative staff, experts, teachers and lecturers at foreign cultural, educational and scientific institutions performing a job in Croatia as part of a cultural and educational cooperation programme, and administrative staff, experts, teachers and lecturers at foreign cultural, educational and scientific institutions having branch offices in the RoC, provided that they are coming from the home institution;
- civilian and military officials of the governments of other states coming to Croatia to work further to a cooperation agreement with the Government of the RoC;
- foreign correspondents, accredited in the RoC, or foreign media reporters;
- representatives and the staff of religious communities performing jobs exclusively related to religious or charitable service;
- TCNs who are working in diplomatic or consular missions accredited in the RoC;
- volunteers who are volunteering in a host organisation in the RoC, or based on programmes of international exchange and cooperation of volunteers;
- TCNs performing the activities of supervision and inspection of overhaul and shipbuilding and TCNs performing the activities of supervision or inspection of the production, assembly of equipment, machinery and other facilities under an export or order contract for a foreign client;
- TCNs working on vessels and who are included in the manifest of the crew;
- TCNs carrying out professional practice, training or volunteer work within the EU or international programmes;
- experts in the area of cultural heritage protection, library and archives science;
- TCNs carrying out professional training, development or education of workers employed in the RoC;
- TCNs engaged in activities related to the delivery, assembly or service of machinery and equipment, whose work is a condition for exercising warranty rights or is related to the delivery of machinery or equipment;
- TCNs attending professional training at a legal person with its registered office in Croatia which is organisationally linked to the foreign employer;

- TCNs on internship;[638]
- artists, authors, technical and other staff involved in recording high-budget films;
- TCNs registered for performing funeral activities;
- tourist representatives of foreign tourist agencies based on a contract for the provision of services with a tourist agency in the RoC.[639]

422. Several categories of TCNs can work up to sixty days a year based on a work registration certificate: providers of auditing and consulting services; lecturers taking part in organised professional gatherings and seminars; artists and technical staff participating in opera, ballet, theatre, concert, visual arts and other cultural events, and authors and performers in film and television arts; workers employed in circuses and amusement parks. Up to thirty days a year can work: musical, music-and-stage and dancing arts authors and performers, as well as accompanying reporting, organisational and technical staff; accompanying reporter, organisational and technical staff at sports events and competitions; TCNs on shooting fashion editorials or advertising campaigns; TCNs participating in fairs and exhibitions where their employers are exhibitors.[640]

423. A work registration certificate has to be obtained before the actual start of the work, from the police administration or police station based on the location of the performance of activities. Based on the work registration certificate, a TCN may work for the same employer or service recipient throughout the territory of the RoC.[641] The employer must have a contract or other relevant certificate signed with the TCN or the external employer who is sending the TCN to work in Croatia, except for TCNs participating in sports events and competitions in Croatia as the representatives of foreign teams, clubs or national teams.[642]

IV. Aliens Who Do Not Require Work Permit or Work Registration Certificate

424. As a rule, in order to be allowed to work in Croatia, a TCN has to obtain a work and residence permit or a work registration certificate. However, several categories of TCNs have free access to the labour market, e.g., can work in Croatia without a work and residence permit or a work registration certificate. Those include TCNs with:

- permanent residence;
- granted asylum or subsidiary protection and asylum seekers under the conditions prescribed by the Act on International and Temporary Protection;

638. Residence and work permit are issued to a trainee with a validity period of up to six months, and it can be extended for a maximum of six more months, if necessary, for completion of the internship (Art. 82, para. 9, Aliens Act).
639. Article 82, para. 1, Aliens Act.
640. Article 83, Aliens Act.
641. Article 84, Aliens Act.
642. Article 85, paras 1 and 3, Aliens Act.

- temporary residence for the family reunification or life partnership with a Croatian national, an alien on a permanent stay, an asylee and an alien who was granted subsidiary or temporary protection;
- temporary residence granted under humanitarian grounds;
- granted an autonomous stay;
- the status of a full-time pupil or student where they perform their work through authorised agents, without contracting employment;
- temporary residence for scientific research and family members of researchers;
- temporary residence for study for the regular student provided that he or she is self-employed up to twenty hours per week.[643]

425. A more lenient regime is provided in the case of EEA citizens and their family members, including EEA citizens who are family members of Croatian citizens. Those categories can work in Croatia without the work permit and will be granted a certificate of the registration of temporary residence for the purpose of work if holding a certificate of employment or proof of self-employment.

§2. Conditions for Employment of Specific Categories of Aliens

I. High-Skilled Workers and Holders of an EU Blue Card

426. High-skilled workers can work in Croatia based on the EU Blue Card, which is considered residence and work permit. Specific conditions for issuing permits are: employment contract for the performance of high-skilled job concluded for at least one year with a guaranteed salary of at least 1.5 times the average gross salary in RoC, and proof of university education or completed university or vocational studies. The EU Blue Card is issued for up to two years. If the validity of the employment contract is shorter than two years, the permit is issued for a period which is three months longer than the validity of the employment contract, with a maximum of two years.[644] The police administration or police station may refuse the issuing of the EU Blue Card if the employer is in breach of employment regulations or if the TCN is in breach of the provisions of the Aliens Act relating to the entry, stay and work of aliens.[645] The EU Blue Cardholder may work only on such jobs for which the stay and work permit was issued and only for an employer with whom he contracted employment.[646] However, if the EU Blue Card holder changes the employer within the first two years of stay in Croatia, he or she has to submit an application for the issuing of a new EU Blue Card within eight days from the date of termination of employment with the initial employer. After two years, the EU Blue Cardholder must notify the police administration or police station of the

643. Article 73, para. 3, Aliens Act.
644. Article 191, Aliens Act.
645. Article 192, para. 2, Aliens Act.
646. Article 193, para. 1, Aliens Act.

change of job within eight days of the change and submit the new employment contract or another relevant contract with the new employer.[647]

427. Temporary residence and work permit will also be issued to an EU Blue Cardholder who has resided in another EEA Member State for the last eighteen months on the basis of a Blue Card, provided that he or she meets the conditions for the residence of high-skilled workers. The application for a residence permit shall be submitted not later than one month after the date of entry into Croatia.[648]

II. TCNs in the Framework of an Intra-Corporate Transfer

428. Workers who work for multinational corporations that have a branch office in Croatia may be sent from abroad for occupational or training purposes at the branch office, in the framework of an intra-corporate transfer as managers, specialists or trainee employees. In general, they can be granted a work permit within the annual quota, or outside the quota in the case of long-term mobility.

429. TCNs in the framework of an intra-corporate transfer will be granted a work (and residence) permit within the annual quota under the following conditions:

- the host entity and the undertaking established in Croatia belong to the same undertaking or group of undertakings;
- employment within the same undertaking or group of undertakings, at least nine months immediately preceding the date of the intra-corporate transfer in the case of managers and specialists, and at least six uninterrupted months in the case of trainee employees;
- a work contract and an assignment letter from the employer containing the following: details of the duration of the transfer and the location of the host entity or entities; evidence that the TCN is taking a position as a manager, specialist or trainee employee in the host entity or entities in Croatia; the remuneration as well as other terms and conditions of employment granted during the intra-corporate transfer; evidence that the TCN will be able to transfer back to an entity belonging to that undertaking or group of undertakings and established in a third country at the end of the intra-corporate transfer;
- provide evidence that the TCN has the professional qualifications and experience needed in the host entity to which he or she is to be transferred as manager or specialist or, in the case of a trainee employee, the university degree required;
- the remuneration is not less favourable than the remuneration granted to employed persons in Croatia in comparable positions, in accordance with applicable laws or collective agreements;
- the main purpose of establishing an entity in Croatia is not to facilitate the regulation of the stay of TCNs in the framework of an intra-corporate transfer;

647. Article 195, paras 1–2, Aliens Act.
648. Article 201, paras 1–2, Aliens Act.

– the maximum duration of the intra-corporate transfer is no longer than three years for managers and specialists, and one year for trainee employees.[649]

430. TCNs who hold a valid intra-corporate transferee permit issued by the first Member State are entitled to work in any other entity established in Croatia and belonging to the same undertaking or group of undertakings, for a period of up to 90 days in any 180 day period (short term mobility). In such a case, TCNs are not obliged to obtain a residence and work permit or work registration certificate.[650] However, if a TCN intends to work for more than 90 days, he or she can be issued a residence and work permit for long-term mobility outside the annual quota.[651]

431. Intra-corporate transferees are granted equal treatment as Croatia nationals as defined by relevant EU legislation.[652]

III. Posted Workers

432. The Aliens Act also regulates the work of posted workers, i.e., workers who were sent to Croatia by foreign companies in the framework of the temporary or occasional transnational provision of services. There are several situations when the worker can be posted to Croatia. Foreign employers can post a worker for their account and under their direction, under a contract concluded between the foreign employer making the posting and the service user for whom the services are intended operating in Croatia. Also, foreign employers can post workers to an establishment or a company owned by the same group. Finally, foreign employers can post the worker as a temporary employment agency to a user which was established or operating in Croatia. If the worker is posted in Croatia for a period of over three months, he or she has to regulate their temporary residence for work.[653] The length of the posting is calculated on the basis of a reference period of one year from the beginning of the posting. For such calculations, an account shall be taken of any previous periods for which the post has been filled by a posted worker.[654]

IV. Seasonal Workers

433. According to the Aliens Act, a seasonal worker is a TCN who retains his or her principal place of residence in a third country and stays legally and temporarily in Croatia to carry out an activity dependent on the passing of the seasons, under

649. Article 79a, para. 3, Aliens Act.
650. Article 79b, Aliens Act.
651. Article 79c, para. 1, Aliens Act.
652. Directive 2014/66/EU of the European Parliament and of the Council of 15 May 2014 on the conditions of entry and residence of third-country nationals in the framework of an intra-corporate transfer, OJ L 157, 27 May 2014, pp. 1–22.
653. Article 86, paras 1 and 4, Aliens Act.
654. Article 87, Aliens Act.

one or more fixed-term work contracts concluded directly with the employer established in Croatia.[655] The seasonal worker can work in Croatia based on the work (and residence) permit for work up to ninety days or six months, provided that he or she:

- has a travel document which is valid during the residence and work permit;
- has a valid work contract or a written confirmation of a concluded employment contract or binding job offer to work as a seasonal worker which contains the mandatory content of the employment contract;
- has health insurance and adequate accommodation;
- does not pose a threat to public order, national security and public health, and is not forbidden to stay in EEA or the RoC.[656]

434. The application for a seasonal work permit will be rejected under the following grounds: if the documentation provided is fraudulently acquired, restored or falsified, or if it is established that the seasonal worker will become a burden on the social welfare system, present a risk of illegal immigration, or does not intend to leave Croatia at the latest on the date of expiry of the permit. The application may be rejected if the seasonal worker has not complied with the obligations arising from a previous work and residence permit for seasonal work, or if, within twelve months immediately preceding the date of the application, the employer has abolished a full-time position in order to create the vacancy that the employer is trying to fill by employing the seasonal worker.[657]

435. A seasonal worker on the basis of a residence and work permit for seasonal work can work in Croatia for a maximum of six months per year, after which he or she must leave the RoC. Within six months per year, a seasonal worker may once extend the validity of the residence and work permit for seasonal work for the same or another employer.[658]

§3. Administrative Rules and Procedures

I. Application for Work Permit or Work Registration Certificate and Decision-Making

436. The competent body to grant work permits and work registration certificate is the police administration or police station based in the place of temporary residence of a TCN. Against decision, an appeal may be filed to the MoI's Commission.[659] Both an alien and his employer also can lodge the application for a

655. Article 2, para. 1, Aliens Act.
656. Article 75a, paras 1 and 3, Aliens Act.
657. Article 75a, paras 6 and 9, Aliens Act.
658. Article 75b, paras 1 and 2, Aliens Act.
659. Article 80, para. 1, Aliens Act.

residence and work permit. Apart from the general requirements for granting a temporary residence permit (*see* Part II, Chapter 2, §2), there are additional documents that must be submitted along with the application for residence and work permit. If submitting the application according to the annual quota, a TCN has to provide: an employment contract or a written certificate of the conclusion of an employment contract or other relevant proof of employment, proof of the acquired academic qualifications and the skills, proof of the registration of a company, branch office, representative office, trade, association or institution in Croatia.[660] If applying for the residence and work permit outside the annual quota, the applicant has to, in addition, submit an explanation of justification of employment of a TCN which contains information on the professional knowledge, qualifications and work experience, and the explanation why the working place cannot be filled by Croatian workers.[661] A TCN who has applied for a temporary residence permit for work under an employment contract concluded with the Croatian employer is not obliged to submit a proof of health insurance.[662] Depending upon the content of the work as the ground for issuing a residence and work permit, a TCN or employer have to provide additional documents.

437. TCNs who are high-skilled workers with the application for temporary residence permit have to enclose: a proof of education and an employment contract with the company registered in the RoC for the performance of a high-skilled job concluded for at least one year with a guaranteed salary of at least 1.5 times the average gross salary in RoC.[663] In addition, according to the implementing legislation, a TCN has to enclose an extract from the court register for a company, Central Craft Registry, Register of Associations and the Register of Foreign Trusts, which must not be older than six months.[664]

II. Refusal of the Application for Residence and Work Permit

438. A residence and work permit application can be rejected in the following situations:

- if the employer fails to comply with obligations concerning social security, workers' rights, working conditions and employment, and tax liability or collective agreement;
- if the employer is in the process of bankruptcy, or has been in the process, or does not perform an economic activity;
- if a TCN is in breach of the provisions of the Aliens Act relating to entry, stay or work;

660. Article 75, Aliens Act.
661. Article 77, para. 1, Aliens Act.
662. Article 54, para. 2, Aliens Act.
663. Article 191, paras 5 and 6, Aliens Act.
664. Article 4, para. 1, Ordinance on the stay and work of highly qualified third-country nationals in the Republic of Croatia (*Pravilnik o boravku i radu visokokvalificiranih državljana trećih država u Republici Hrvatskoj*), OG 120/2012, 81/2013, 38/2015.

- if a TCN or an employer has failed to pay a fine;
- if the employer is sanctioned for undeclared work or illegal employment;
- if the main purpose of establishing or acting on behalf of the employer is to facilitate the entry of TCNs.[665]

439. The application for the EU Blue Card will be refused if a TCN fails to meet the general conditions for approval of temporary residence permit, does not enclose proof of education and an employment contract, or whenever it is established that the documents enclosed have been fraudulently acquired, or falsified or tampered with. In addition, the issuing of the EU Blue Card may be refused if the employer is in breach of employment regulations, or if the TCN is in breach of the provisions of the Aliens Act relating to the entry, residence and work. The police administration or police station decides about the application for the EU Blue Card within ninety days of the submission of the application. An appeal against the decision of the police administration or police station may be filed to the Commission of the MoI.[666]

III. Extension of Residence and Work Permits

440. For the extension of the residence and work permits general rules for the extension of temporary residence will be applied (*see* Part II, Chapter 2, §2).

441. A TCN has to apply for the extension of the EU Blue Card to the police administration or police station based on the location of his or her temporary residence, at the latest thirty days before the expiration of the valid permit. An EU Blue Card holder who applied for the extension of the residence and work permit before its expiration may remain in the RoC until the decision concerning his application becomes enforceable.[667]

IV. Termination of Validity of Residence and Work Permit

442. According to the Aliens Act, the residence and work permit validity will be ceased under the following conditions:

- if general conditions for termination of temporary residence are met;
- on termination of the existence of conditions based on which it was issued;
- if a TCN performs jobs for which the residence and work permit was not issued;
- if a TCN works for an employer for whom the residence and work permit was not issued;

665. Article 81, Aliens Act.
666. Article 192, Aliens Act.
667. Article 194, Aliens Act.

– if a TCN or his employer do not respect regulations on employment, health and pension insurance and other regulations which regulate the activity.[668]

443. The residence and work permit issued to a TCN in the framework of an intra-corporate transfer can be annulled if the MoI or other state administration body determines that the legal entity was established with the main purpose of helping TCNs transferred within the company to acquire the residence in Croatia, or if it is established that the enclosed documentation is fraudulently obtained, restored or forged.[669]

444. In the case of the EU Blue Cardholder, the residence and work permit will be terminated if a TCN:

– fails to notify the police administration or police station of the change of employer;
– works for an employer for whom the EU Blue Card was not issued;
– performs jobs for which the EU Blue Card was not issued;
– performs other jobs for which he or she could not obtain the EU Blue Card;
– does not have any resources for supporting themselves and he or she applied as social welfare seeker;
– no longer meets the conditions on the basis of which the stay and work permit was issued;
– during the validity of the EU Blue Card, he or she was unemployed for more than three months without interruptions, or remained unemployed two or more times;
– is considered to be a threat to public order, national security or public health;
– is barred by the prohibition of entry and stay.[670]

445. If the employment contract or other relevant contract is terminated through no fault of a TCN, he or she could stay in Croatia until the expiration of the residence and work permit. The employer and a TCN must notify the police administration or police station about the termination of the employment contract or another relevant contract, or that the other conditions based on which the residence and work permit was issued cease to exist, within fifteen days of the occurrence of the circumstances concerned.[671]

668. Article 90, Aliens Act.
669. Article 79e, para. 1, Aliens Act.
670. Article 197, Aliens Act.
671. Article 91, Aliens Act.

Chapter 3. Sanctions Against Irregular Participation in the Labour Market

446. The Aliens Act regulates sanctions against irregular participation in the labour market. The Penal Code also envisages sanctions against employers for illicit work of aliens.

§1. Sanctions Against Employers

447. There are two types of sanctions against employers: penal and misdemeanour. According to the Penal Code, the employer who employs a person who is irregularly residing in the Croatia territory, excluding EU nationals, citizens and persons who enjoy the right of free movement in the EU, in working conditions characterised by exploitation or knowing that the person is a victim of trafficking in human beings, or that he or she is a minor or whoever over a long period or repeatedly employs such persons or simultaneously employs a high number of them shall be punished by imprisonment from six months to five years.[672] Misdemeanour offences are regulated by the Aliens Act.

448. According to the Aliens Act, the MoI is in charge of inspection supervision relating to the obligation to register the stay of aliens, while the other state administration bodies are in charge of inspection supervision concerning the work of aliens within their area of responsibility.[673] If the inspector established that an alien worked without obtaining a residence and work permit or a work registration certificate, they will prohibit the legal or natural person to perform the activity and to an alien to provide services for a foreign employer, in a duration of thirty days by a verbal on-the-spot decision to the minutes. This measure will be enforced by sealing of the business premises, machinery, equipment and other working equipment, or in some other appropriate manner, within five days from the date of the issuing of a verbal decision. However, the measure of prohibition of the performance of the activity will not be carried out, and the verbal decision shall be revoked, if the legal or natural person against whom the measure was issued submits proof within five days that it made the payment of HRK 30,000 (app. EUR 4,000) for each alien, in favour of the State Budget.[674] If during the inspection supervision it is established that an employer employs an alien staying illegally in the RoC, the inspector will notify the Tax Administration accordingly, which will identify the employer obligated to pay public contributions and the basis for calculating such public contributions, the period of work of the alien and the amount of the obligation (payment to the alien).[675]

---

672. Article 135, Penal Code.
673. Article 207, para. 1, Aliens Act.
674. Article 208, paras 1–3, Aliens Act.
675. Article 218, Aliens Act.

449. In cases where the inspectorate finds individual violations, the employer will be sanctioned for committing an offence and a sanction which depends on whether the perpetrator is a legal person or a natural person. In addition to the sanction for a legal person, there is always an additional sanction that can be imposed on the responsible person of a legal person. In the field of irregular participation in the labour market, the following acts are considered offences:

- concluding employment or with the alien without residence and work permit or a work registration certificate or using his or her work, and employing the alien on jobs contrary to those for which he or she was issued a stay and work permit or a work registration certificate, a fine for legal persons ranging from HRK 50,000 to HRK 100,000 (app. EUR 6,667 to EUR 13,334) for each alien; against the responsible person in the legal person a fine from HRK 10,000 to HRK 50,000 (app. EUR 13,334 to EUR 6,667); and for a natural person from HRK 10,000 to HRK 15,000 for each alien (app. EUR 13,334 to EUR 2,000);
- employing or using the services of an alien staying illegally in Croatia, a fine for legal persons ranging from HRK 70,000 to HRK 150,000 (app. EUR 9,334 to EUR 20,000) for each alien; against the responsible person in the legal person a fine from HRK 20,000 to HRK 70,000 (app. EUR 2,667 to EUR 9,334); for a natural person from HRK 10,000 to HRK 30,000 for each alien (app. EUR 13,334 to EUR 4,000);[676]
- employing the EU Blue Card holder on jobs contrary to those for which he or she was issued a stay and work permit, a fine for the legal person and the responsible person in the legal person raging from HRK 50,000 to HRK 100,000.00 (app. EUR 6,667 to EUR 13,334) for each person; and for a natural person from HRK 10,000 to HRK 15,000 for each alien (app. EUR 13,334 to EUR 2,000).[677]

For those offences, the protective measure of prohibition to perform the activity may be imposed.

450. There are other offences connected with participation in the labour market. The inspector can issue a fine in an amount from HRK 500 to HRK 3,000 (app. EUR 66 to EUR 400) against a natural person and against the responsible person in the legal person, and a fine in an amount from HRK 5,000 to HRK 7,000 (app. EUR 666 to EUR 934) against a legal person who failed to:

- notify the police administration or police station about the changes in accommodation of a seasonal worker;
- conclude a contract or does not have some other relevant working certificate with the alien whose services he or she is using;
- notify the police administration or police station that the grounds based on which the residence and work permit was issued no longer exist;

676. Article 226, paras 1–4, Aliens Act.
677. Article 227, para. 1, Aliens Act.

– notify the police administration or police station of the assignment of an employee to work outside the place of his or her temporary residence or permanent residence;[678]
– notify the police administration or police station of the termination of the criteria based on which the EU Blue Card was issued.[679]

451. The fines are also envisaged against employers who fail to adhere to the rules of employment of a posted worker.[680]

§2. SANCTIONS AGAINST WORKERS

452. According to the Aliens Act, the alien will be fined if he or she:

– failed to notify the police administration or police station that the grounds based on which the residence and work permit was issued no longer exist; a fine ranging from HRK 500 to HRK 5,000 (app. EUR 66 to EUR 666);[681]
– worked without a residence and work permit or work registration certificate, or did not work on those jobs for which he or she has been granted a residence and work permit or a work registration certificate and did not work solely for the employer who employed him or her; a fine ranging from HRK 7,000 to HRK 10,000 (app. EUR 934 to EUR 1,333).[682]

453. The holder of the EU Blue Card will be fined in the amount from HRK 500 to HRK 3,000 (app. EUR 66 to EUR 400) if he or she:

– failed to notify the police administration or police station of the termination of the employment contract or another contract, and of the conditions based on which the residence and work permit was issued;
– failed to apply for the extension of the EU Blue Card, within thirty days before the expiration of the deadline of the valid residence and work;
– failed to apply for the EU Blue Card, within eight days;
– failed to notify the police administration or police station of the change of employer.[683]

In addition, the EU Blue Cardholder will be fined from HRK 3,000 to HRK 7,000 (app. EUR 400 to EUR 934), if he or she did not work on those jobs for which he or she has been granted a residence and work permit and did not work solely for the employer who employed him or her.[684]

678. Article 220, paras 1 and 2, Aliens Act.
679. Article 221, paras 1 and 2, Aliens Act.
680. Article 228, Aliens Act.
681. Article 220, para. 3, Aliens Act.
682. Article 224, Aliens Act.
683. Article 221, para. 4, Aliens Act.
684. Article 223, Aliens Act.

454. Until the amendments of the Aliens Act in 2017, against the alien who worked without a residence and work permit, or worked on jobs for which he was not issued a residence and work permit or a work registration certificate, or for the additional employer, the protective measure of expulsion could be imposed solely, without imposing a fine. After changes in legislation in 2017, this measure does not exist anymore.

Chapter 4. Legal Remedies and Procedural Safeguards

455. Against the decision on rejection of an application for residence and work permit, an applicant can submit an appeal to the MoI's Commission.[685] Against a decision refusing the issuing of a residence and work permit if the annual quota is full, or if the annual quota for the extension, new employment or seasonal employment was not set, an applicant can initiate an administrative dispute.[686] In cases in which there is no appeal against the administrative decision (such as against the decision of the MoI's Commission), there is a possibility to initiate an administrative dispute before the administrative court. The claim to the administrative court will not postpone enforcement of the administrative decision. The court may decide that the claim will postpone the enforcement of decision if its enforcement would cause a claimant damage that could be difficult to repair, and the postponement is not contrary to the public interest.[687] Possibilities of extraordinary legal remedies, which are available for the parties after the judicial decision becomes final, are available in very limited circumstances.

456. The legal remedies and procedural safeguards apply as described in Part VI, Chapter 1, §3.

685. Article 81, Aliens Act.
686. Article 50, para. 3, Aliens Act.
687. Article 26, Administrative Disputes Act.

Part VIII. Access to Self-Employed Activities

Chapter 1. Overview of Applicable Legislation

457. Self-employment of aliens in Croatia is regulated by the same legal sources as the employment of aliens in general. Like access to the labour market, the self-employment of aliens is also regulated by the Aliens Act. The Aliens Act regulates the possibility of granting temporary residence and work permit to aliens based on self-employment activities.

458. Aliens can register their own business in Croatia as a craft (*obrt*) or as a company (*trgovačko društvo*). A craft can be free, associated or privileged. Domestic and foreign companies trade under the same conditions, and a foreign investor may establish or participate in the establishment of a company and acquire rights and/or obligations under the same conditions as any domestic investor. The procedure for establishing the company is regulated by the Company Act[688] and for crafts by the Crafts Act.[689]

688. Company Act (*Zakon o trgovačkim društvima*), OG 111/1993, 34/1999, 121/1999, 52/2000, 118/2003, 107/2007, 146/2008, 137/2009, 125/2011, 152/2011, 111/2012, 68/2013, 110/2015.
689. Crafts Act (*Zakon o obrtu*), OG 143/2013.

Chapter 2. Conditions for Entitlement to Work in the Country as a Self-Employed

§1. General Conditions

459. According to the Aliens Act, a TCN may found or co-found a company or a craft in Croatia. TCNs who are self-employed in a company they own or in a company in which they hold a share over 51% or own craft may be issued the residence and work permit outside the annual quota.[690] In addition, the work permit outside the annual quota may be granted to a TCN who performs key activities in a company or holds an ownership share in that company of at least 51%, and the company benefits from incentives in accordance with a regulation on the award for incentives for investments or performs strategic investment projects in accordance with the regulation on Strategic Investment Projects of the RoC.[691]

460. The conditions for setting up the company in Croatia are the same for the Croatian nationals and aliens. The Company Act stipulates that foreign investors (under the condition of reciprocity) acquire the same rights and obligations and have the same position as domestic investors when incorporating a new legal entity or acquiring shares/stakes in an existing legal entity in Croatia. A foreign investor with headquarters or permanent residence in a non-WTO country must meet the condition of reciprocity.[692] The lowest amount of initial capital for establishing a joint-stock company (*dioničko društvo*) is HRK 200,000 (app. EUR 26,667), and the nominal value per share cannot be less than HRK 10 (app. EUR 1.34).[693] Minimum initial capital for establishing a limited liability company (*društvo s ograničenom odgovornošću*) is HRK 20,000 (app. EUR 2,667), while individual representation per investor cannot be less than HRK 200 (app. EUR 27).[694] Companies that have no more than three members and one Board member may be established through a simplified procedure as a simple limited liability company (*jednostavno društvo s ograničenom odgovornošću*). The minimum initial amount for the establishment of such companies is HRK 10 (app. EUR 1.34), while individual representation per investor cannot be less than HRK 1 (app. EUR 0.13).[695] The alien who founded the company in Croatia can decide to be employed or not in that company. In the first case, the alien has to obtain a residence and work permit.

461. The conditions for setting up the craft in Croatia are the same for Croatian nationals and aliens. According to the Crafts Act, the craft is an independent and continuous performance of approved economic activities by natural persons with the aim of achieving profit through production, turnover or providing services on the

690. Article 76, para. 1, Aliens Act.
691. Article 79, para. 1, Aliens Act.
692. Article 620, Company Act.
693. Articles 162 and 163, Company Act.
694. Articles 389 and 390, Company Act.
695. Articles 387, para. 2 and 390a, Company Act.

market.[696] There are three kinds of crafts: (1) free crafts which may be performed only with a trade licence while professional qualification or master craftsman's examination is not required; (2) associated crafts which may be performed with a trade licence, exam on professional qualification and appropriate secondary school qualification; and (3) privileged crafts which may be performed only with the authorisation of the competent body (obtaining of which is required for registration) issued by the competent ministry, depending on the type of crafts.[697] Apart from the special conditions (which depends on the type of crafts), the Crafts Act stipulates general conditions that need to be met in order to obtain approval for crafts. The general conditions that the owner has to fulfil are: to comply with special health conditions if prescribed by law; that a security measure prohibiting the performance of the activity was not imposed on him or her by a court judgment or a misdemeanour decision or a decision of the Court of Honour of the Croatian Chamber of Trades and Crafts; that he or she has the right to use the facilities if it is necessary to perform the craft activities.[698]

§2. Administrative Rules and Procedures

462. The residence and work permit for self-employed aliens can be issued under the following conditions:

- an alien invested at least HRK 200,000 in the establishment of a company or craft;
- at least three Croatian nationals are employed in the company;
- gross salary of the alien who is self-employed in a company is at least in the amount of an average gross salary paid in the RoC according to the official data from the Croatian Bureau of Statistics;
- the alien who is self-employed in a trade he owns has to provide proof of the amount obtained through self-employment activities is at least in the amount of an average monthly net salary paid in the RoC according to the official data from the Croatian Bureau of Statistics;
- the company or craft does not do business at a loss;
- an alien encloses proof of the settlement of tax obligations and contributions in Croatia.[699]

463. In order to be granted residence and work permit for self-employed activities, a TCN has to provide an employment contract or a written certificate of the conclusion of an employment contract or another relevant proof of employment and proof of the registration of a company, branch office, representative office, craft,

696. Article 2, para. 1, Crafts Act.
697. Article 6, Crafts Act.
698. Articles 8 and 9, Crafts Act.
699. Article 78, para. 3, Aliens Act.

association or institution in Croatia. TCNs who are self-employed in a craft they own are not required to enclose proof of employment to the application for the issuing of the residence and work permit.[700]

464. The residence and work permit on the grounds of self-employment is issued with a validity of one year and can be revoked and annulled under the same conditions as all other residence permits.

§3. Conditions for Special Categories of Self-Employment

465. A more lenient regime is provided in the case of EEA citizens and their family members, including EEA citizens who are family members of Croatian citizens. Those categories can be self-employed in Croatia without the work permit and will be granted a certificate of the registration of temporary residence for work if provided proof of self-employment.

466. After Croatia's accession to the EU on 1 July 2013, EEA nationals can freely provide services in Croatia. The Act on Regulated Professions and Recognition of Foreign Professional Qualifications[701] regulates the question of recognition of foreign professional qualifications in Croatia for establishment and free provision of services on a temporary and occasional basis in Croatia based on the foreign professional qualifications. The Act has been harmonised with the Directive 2005/36/EC,[702] which guarantees that persons who have acquired their professional qualifications in a Member State, both EEA nationals and TCNs, have access to the same profession and can pursue it in another Member State with the same rights as nationals. The Act stipulates that all those who want to provide services within a regulated profession[703] in Croatia and have acquired their professional qualification abroad must contact the competent authority (professional associations – chambers, or competent ministries) which grants access to that regulated profession and apply for the recognition of foreign professional qualifications.

467. Several categories of TCNs can work, therefore also be self-employed, without the work and residence permit. Those include TCNs with:

– permanent residence;

---

700. Article 77, Aliens Act.
701. Act on Regulated Professions and Recognition of Foreign Professional Qualifications (*Zakon o reguliranim profesijama i priznavanju inozemnih stručnih kvalifikacija*), OG 124/2009, 45/2011. The new Act has been published in OG 82/2015.
702. Directive 2005/36/EC of the European Parliament and of the Council of 7 Sep. 2005 on the recognition of professional qualifications, OJ L 255, 30 Sep 2005.
703. Regulated professions include health workers, veterinarians, lawyers, notaries, auditors, engineers, architects, tax consultants, tourism workers, etc. The full list of regulated professions adopted by the Government of RoC (in Croatian only) is available here: http://www.mrms.hr/wp-content/uploads/2019/01/Popis-reguliranih-profesija-u-Republici-Hrvatskoj_3.1.2019.pdf (accessed 10 Jan. 2019).

- granted asylum or subsidiary protection and asylum seekers under the conditions prescribed by the Act on International and Temporary Protection;
- temporary residence for family reunification or life partnership with a Croatian national, an alien on a permanent stay, an asylee and an alien who was granted subsidiary or temporary protection;
- temporary residence granted under humanitarian grounds;
- granted an autonomous stay;
- the status of a full-time pupil or student where they perform their work through authorised agents, without contracting employment;
- temporary residence for scientific research and family members of researchers;
- temporary residence for study for the regular student provided that he or she is self-employed for up to twenty hours per week.[704]

704. Article 73, para. 3, Aliens Act.

Chapter 3. Sanctions Against Illegal Exercise of Self-Employment

468. The Aliens Act does not prescribe any particular sanctions against an illegal exercise of self-employment. In general, the alien will be fined if he or she failed to notify the police administration or police station that the grounds based on which the residence and work permit was issued (which can be issued for self-employment) no longer exist, a fine ranging from HRK 500 to HRK 5,000 (app. EUR 66 to EUR 666);[705] or worked without a residence and work permit, or did not work on those jobs for which he or she has been granted a residence and work permit and did not work solely for the employer who employed him or her, a fine ranging from HRK 7,000 to HRK 10,000 (app. EUR 934 to EUR 1,333).[706]

705. Article 220, para. 3, Aliens Act.
706. Article 224, Aliens Act.

Chapter 4. Legal Remedies and Procedural Safeguards

469. There are no specific legal remedies and procedural safeguards relating to the legal status of self-employed aliens that are different for those regarding employment of aliens in general (*see* Part V and Part VII).

Selected Bibliography

Books and Articles

Bara, Mario; Lajić, Ivan, Prisilne, iznuđene i organizirane migracije u etnodemografskom oblikovanju Hrvatske: primjer Slavonije (Forced, Impelled and Organised Migration in the Ethno-Demographic Shaping of Croatia: The Example of Slavonia), 25 *Migracijske i etničke teme* 4, pp. 337–362, 2009.

Bayer, Vladimir, *Prestanak prava azila u Hrvatskoj* (Termination of Asylum Law in Croatia), Biblioteka Instituta za historiju države i prava na Pravnom fakultetu u Zagrebu, 1957.

Berković, Svjetlan, Azil u međunarodnom pravu (Asylum in International Law), PhD Dissertation, Pravni fakultet u Zagrebu, 1989.

Dimitrijević, Vojin, *Pravo utočišta na teritoriji strane države (teritorijalni azil)* (Right of Refuge in the Territory of a Foreign Country – Territorial Asylum), PhD Dissertation, Pravni fakultet u Beogradu, 1965.

Gelo, Jakov; Akrap, Anđelko; Čipin, Ivan, *Temeljne značajke demografskog razvoja Hrvatske (bilanca 20. stoljeća)* (Fundamental Characteristics of Demographic in Croatia), Ministarstvo obitelji, branitelja i međugeneracijske solidarnosti, 2005.

Giljević, Teo; Lalić Novak, Goranka, Coordination Instruments in Croatian Integration Policy: Classification, Evaluation, and Proposals for Improvements, 18 *Hrvatska i komparativna javna uprava*, 3, pp. 373–396, 2018.

Gregurović, Snježana.; Mlinarić, Dubravka, Challenges of Migration Policies in Croatia: Migration History, Trends and Prospects, *AEMI Journal,* 10, pp. 99–113, 2012.

Heršak, Emil, Panoptikum migracija – Hrvati, hrvatski prostor i Evropa (A Panopticum of Migration: Croats, the Croatian Area, Europe), 9 *Migracijske teme* 3–4, pp. 227–302, 1993.

Hidas, Peter I., Our Beloved Hungarians – Hungarian Refugees in Yugoslavia in Transit to Canada, 2001, http://www3.sympatico.ca/thidas/Hungarian-history/Yugoslavia.html (accessed 15 Oct. 2018).

Koprić, Ivan; Kovač, Polonca; Đulabić, Vedran; Džinić, Jasmina, *Legal Remedies in Administrative Procedures in Western Balkans*, Regional School of Public Administration, 2016.

Lalić Novak, Goranka; Giljević, Teo, Integration of 'New' Refugees in the Non-immigrant Countries along the Balkan Route of Migration – Overview of Legal

Framework and Practices. In: Dalibor Jílek & Pavel Pořízek (eds), Ročenka uprchlického a cizineckého práva 2017, Kancelář veřejného ochránce práv, 2018, pp. 453–470.

Lalić Novak, Goranka; Vukojičić Tomić, Tijana, Integracija stranaca i manjina u lokalnu zajednicu kao zadatak lokalne samouprave (Integration of Aliens and Minorities in Local Communities as the Role of the Local self-government). In: Ivan Koprić, Anamarija Musa & Teo Giljević (eds.) Građani, javna uprava, lokalna samouprava: jesu li mogući povjerenje, suradnja i potpora, Institut za javnu upravu, 2017, pp. 273–294.

Lalić Novak, Gpranka, Azil: pravni i institucionalni aspekti (Legal and Institutional aspect of Asylum), Pravni fakultet Sveučilišta u Zagrebu, 2016.

Lalić Novak, Goranka, Europeizacija hrvatskoga sustava azila: mehanizmi i instrumenti utjecaja Europske unije na javne politike i institucije (Europeanization of the Croatian Asylum System: Mechanisms and Instruments of European Union Influence on Public Policies and Institutions, 22 Društvena istraživanja, 2, pp. 237–255, 22, 2013).

Lalić, Goranka; Krešić, Mirela, Zaštita azilanata na hrvatskom području: od crkvenog azila do suvremenih tendencija (Protection of the asylum seekers in Croatia: from church asylum to contemporary tendencies). In: Zdravka Leutar (ed.), *Zbornik radova Međunarodne znanstvene konferencije Socijalni rad i borba protiv siromaštva i socijalne isključenosti – profesionalna usmjerenost zaštiti i promicanju ljudskih prava*, Zaklada 'Marija De Mattias', 2011.

Lukšić, Irena (ed.), *Ruski emigranti u Hrvatskoj između dva rata – rubovi,* memorija (Russian Emigrants in Croatia Between Two World wars), Hrvatsko filološko društvo, 2006.

Mežnarić, Silva, Expediency of statistics: War and Post-War Casualties in Croatia and Bosnia (1991–1999), 31 *Revija za sociologiju*, 3–4, pp. 211–218, 2000.

Mežnarić, Silva, *Osvajanje prostora – prekrivanje vremena: migracije umjesto* razvoja (Discovering Space, Overlapping Times: Migration instead of Development), Sociološko društvo Hrvatske, 1991.

Mlinarić, Dubravka; Bara, Mario; Gregurović, Snježana; Župarić-Iljić, Drago; Kuti, Simona, Croatian Migration History and the Challenges of Migrations Today, AEMI, January 2015, https://aemi.eu/croatian-migration-history-and-the-challenges-of-migrations-today/ (accessed 16 September 2018).

Nejašmić, Ivica, *Depopulacija u Hrvatskoj: Korijeni, stanje, izgledi* (Depopulation in Croatia: Roots, Condition, Prospects*)*, Globus, Zagreb, 1991.

Nejašmić, Ivica, Osnovne značajke unutarnje migracije stanovništva Hrvatske 1880–1981 (Basic Characteristics of Internal Population Migration in Croatia 1880–1981), 8 *Migracijske teme*, 2, pp. 141–166, 1992.

Pušeljić, Mato; Jelenski, Milivoj, Policijski sustavi – realizacija policijske funkcije kroz ustroj, 16 *Policija i sigurnost*, 1–2, pp. 1–19, 2007.

Roksandić, Drago, *Vojna Hrvatska – La Croatie Militaire*, Školska knjiga, Zagreb, 1988.

Škiljan, Filip, *Rusi u Hrvatskoj* (Russians in Croatia), Savez Rusa u Republici Hrvatskoj, 2014.

Staničić, Frane, *Policijsko upravno pravo* (Police Administrative Law), Narodne novine, Zagreb, 2015.

Vrbošić, Josip, Kategorije i brojčano stanje kolonista u Slavoniji i Baranji između dva svjetska rata (Categories and Numbers of Colonists in Slavonia and Baranja Between the Two World Wars), 6 *Društvena istraživanja*, 2–3, pp. 311–325, 1997.
Zlatković Winter, Jelena, Imigracije u Hrvatskoj: skica povijesnog toka (Immigration in Croatia – An Outline of Historical Development), 9 *Migracijske teme*, 3–4, pp. 303–325, 1993.
Župarić-Iljić, Drago, *Emigration from the Republic of Croatia after the Accession to the European Union*, Friedrich Ebert Stiftung, 2016, www.fes-croatia.org/file admin/user_upload/FES_ Iseljavanje_web.pdf (accessed 28 September 2018).

Reports and Other Documents

Croatian Law Centre, Health Care for Beneficiaries, AIDA report. http://www.asyl umineurope.org/reports/country/croatia/health-care-beneficiaries (accessed 12 September 2018).
Croatian Law Centre, The Croatian Asylum System in 2017 – National Report, http://www.hpc.hr/wp-content/uploads/2018/10/National-Report-2017-Asylum-S ystem.pdf (accessed 15 December 2018).
Eurostat, EU Member States Granted Protection to More Than Half a Million Asylum Seekers in 2017, 67/2018 – 19 April 2018, https://ec.europa.eu/eurostat/doc uments/2995521/8817675/3-19042018-AP-EN.pdf/748e8fae-2cfb-4e75-a388-f0 6f6ce8ff58 (accessed 28 September 2018).
Eurostat, Asylum in the EU Member States: 650,000 First-time Asylum Seekers Registered in 2017, 47/2018 – 20 March 2018, https://ec.europa.eu/eurostat/doc uments/2995521/8754388/3-20032018-AP-EN.pdf/50c2b5a5-3e6a-4732-82d0-1 caf244549e3 (accessed 28 September 2018).
Human Rights House Zagreb, Human Rights in Croatia: Overview of 2017, Zagreb, March 2018, http://www.kucaljudskihprava.hr/wp-content/uploads/2018/04/ KLJP_PregledStanja_ENGWeb.pdf (accessed 18 June 2018).
Human Rights Watch, Croatia: Asylum Seekers Forced Back to Serbia, 20 January 2017, http://bit.ly/2k9cLej (accessed 3 June 2018).
Ministry of Interior, List of Free Legal Aid Providers in the International Protection Approval Procedure – Administrative Court, https://mup.hr/public/documents/Ja vnost/Obrasci/Stranci/Lista%20pru%C5%BEatelja%20besplatne%20pravne%20 pomo%C4%87i%20u%20postupku%20odobrenja%20me%C4%91unarodne%20 za%C5%A1tite%20-%20Upravni%20sud.pdf (accessed 20 Aug. 2018).
Ministry of Interior, Survey of Basic Safety Indicators of 2017 the Republic of Croatia, January 2018. https://mup.hr/public/documents/Statistika/Statisti%C4% 8Dki%20pregled%20temeljnih%20sigurnosnih%20pokazatelja%20i%20rezultat a%20rada%20u%202017.%20godini.pdf (accessed 21 March 2018).
OXFAM, 'A Dangerous "Game": The Pushback of Migrants, Including Refugees, at Europe's Borders', April 2017, https://www.oxfam.org/en/research/dangerous -game-pushback-migrants-including-refugees-europes-borders (accessed 5 June 2018).
People's Ombudsman, Izvješće pučke pravobraniteljice za 2013. godinu, Zagreb, 31. ožujka 2014., https://www.ombudsman.hr/en/download/izvjesce-pucke-pravo braniteljice-za-2013-godinu/ (accessed 14 September 2018).

Report concerning the implementation of the Council of Europe Convention on Action against Trafficking in Human Beings by Croatia, GRETA (2015) 33, https://rm.coe.int/CoERMPublicCommonSearchServices/DisplayDCTMContent?documentId=0900001680630e7c (accessed 20 July 2018).
Save the Children, Refugee and Migrant Children Injured in Illegal Border Push-Backs Across Balkans, 24 January 2017, https://reliefweb.int/report/serbia/refugee-and-migrant-children-injured-illegal-border-push-backs-across-balkans (accessed 3 June 2018).
UNHCR, Fourth Progress Report on the Implementation of the Durable Solutions Process (Sarajevo Process) for Refugees from Croatia Displaced by the 91–95 conflict, Including Cessation of Refugee Status, June 2017, https://www.refworld.org/docid/5964cf5f4.html (accessed 22 September 2018).
UNHCR, Minority Return to Croatia – Study of an Open Process, 2011, ISBN: 978-953-95763-3-0, https://www.refworld.org/docid/553a08424.html (accessed 26 September 2018).
UNHCR, Submission by the United Nations High Commissioner for Refugees for the Office of the High Commissioner for Human Rights' Compilation Report – Universal Periodic Review: The Republic of Croatia, April 2010, https://www.refworld.org/docid/4bcd79502.html (accessed 22 September 2018).
US Department of the State, Trafficking in Persons Report 2018, https://www.state.gov/wp-content/uploads/2019/01/282798.pdf (accessed 20 July 2018).
Welcome Initiative and Are You Syrious?, A Report on Unlawful and Forced Expulsion of Refugees from the Republic of Croatia, 24 January 2017, http://welcome.cms.hr/wp-content/uploads/2017/01/Izvje%C5%A1taj-o-nezakonitim-i-nasilnim-protjerivanjima-izbjeglica-iz-RH-AYS-i-Inicijativa-Dobrodo%C5%A1li.pdf (accessed 1 June 2018); Second Report on Unlawful and Forced Expulsion of Refugees from the Republic of Croatia, 7 March 2017, http://welcome.cms.hr/wp-content/uploads/2017/03/DRUGI-IZVJE%C5%A0TAJ-O-NEZAKONITIM-I-NASILNIM-PROTJERIVANJIMA-IZBJEGLICA-IZ-REPUBLIKE-HRVATSKE.doc (accessed 1 June 2018); Report on the new wave of violence against refugees on Croatian borders, 29 May 2017, http://welcome.cms.hr/wp-content/uploads/2017/05/REPORT-ON-THE-NEW-WAVE-OF-VIOLENCE-AGAINST-REFUGEES-ON-CROATIAN-BORDERS.pdf (accessed 1 June 2018).
Welcome Initiative! and Center for Peace Studies, Are you Syrious?, and No-name Kitchen, Fourth Report on Illegal Pushbacks of Refugees from the Republic of Croatia in the period from June 2017 to February 2018, 28 February 2018, http://welcome.cms.hr/wp-content/uploads/2018/02/Fourth-Report-on-Illegal-Pushbacks_01032018.pdf (accessed 1 June 2018).
World Bank, Employment Protection Legislation and Labor Market Outcomes: Theory, Evidence and Lessons for Croatia, Policy Note, Zagreb (2011).

Table of Cases

Case Law

Soft Law

Table of Legislation

EU Legislation

Directive 2014/66/EU of the European Parliament and of the Council of 15 May 2014 on the conditions of entry and residence of third-country nationals in the framework of an intra-corporate transfer, OJ L 157, 27.5.2014, 431

Directive 2005/36/EC of the European Parliament and of the Council of 7 September 2005 on the recognition of professional qualifications, OJ L 255, 30.9.2005, 466

Regulation (EU) No. 604/2013 of the European Parliament and of the Council of 26 June 2013 establishing the criteria and mechanisms for determining the Member State responsible for examining an application for international protection lodged in one of the Member States by a third-country national or a stateless person (recast) OJ EC L 180/31, 29.6.2013, 227

Regulation (EU) 2016/399 of the European Parliament and of the Council of 9 March 2016 on a Union Code on the rules governing the movement of persons across borders (Schengen Borders Code), OJ L 77, 23.3.2016, 43

National Legislation

Act on Administrative Disputes (*Zakon o upravnim sporovima*), OG 20/2010, 143/2012, 152/2014, 94/2016, 29/2017, 32

Act on Employment of Aliens (*Zakon o zapošljavanju stranaca*), OG 19/1992, 33/1992, 89/1992, 26/1993, 52/1994, 412

Act on International and Temporary Protection (*Zakon o međunarodnoj i privremenoj zaštiti*), OG 70/2015, 127/2017, 28

Act on Labour Market (*Zakon o tržištu rada*), OG 118/2018, 127

Act on Mandatory Health Insurance and Health Care of Aliens in the Republic of Croatia (*Zakon o obveznom zdravstvenom osiguranju i zdravstvenoj zaštiti stranaca u Republici Hrvatskoj*), OG 80/2013, 15/2018, 128

Act on Movement and Stay of Aliens (*Zakon o kretanju i boravku stranaca*), OG 53/1991, 22/1992, 26/1993, 29/1994, 21

Act on Pregnancy and Parenthood Support (*Zakon o rodiljnim i roditeljskim potporama*), OG 85/2008, 110/2008, 34/2011, 54/2013, 152/2014, 59/2017, 299

Act on Primary and Secondary Education (*Zakon o odgoju i obrazovanju u osnovnoj i srednjoj školi*), OG 87/2008, 86/2009, 92/2010, 105/2010, 90/2011, 5/2012, 16/2012, 86/2012, 126/2012, 94/2013, 152/2014, 07/2017, 68/2018, 125, 453

Table of Legislation

Index

The numbers here refer to paragraph numbers.

Index

Index

Index

www.ingramcontent.com/pod-product-compliance
Ingram Content Group UK Ltd.
Pitfield, Milton Keynes, MK11 3LW, UK
UKHW020141290926
15471UKWH00004B/632